THE SUN ALSO SETS

TIMES BOOKS

RANDOM HOUSE

THE SUN
ALSO
SETS

THE LIMITS TO JAPAN'S ECONOMIC POWER

BILL EMMOTT

Grateful acknowledgment is made to the following for permission to reprint previously
published material:
Doubleday: Excerpts from *An Introduction to Haiku* by Harold G. Henderson.
Copyright © 1958 by Harold G. Henderson. Reprinted by permission of Doubleday,
a division of Bantam, Doubleday, Dell Publishing Group, Inc.
Little, Brown and Company: Excerpts from *Verses from 1929 On* by Ogden Nash.
Copyright 1935 by Ogden Nash. Reprinted by permission of Little, Brown and
Company.

Library of Congress Cataloging-in-Publication Data

Emmott, Bill.
    The sun also sets: the limits to Japan's economic power / Bill
Emmott.
        p.   cm.
    Includes index.
    ISBN 0-8129-1816-9
    1. Japan—Foreign economic relations.   2. Japan—Foreign
relations—1945–   3. Japan—Politics and government—1945–
I. Title.
HF1601.E49 1989
330.952—dc20   89-4477

Design by Robert Bull Design

Manufactured in the United States of America

9 8 7 6 5 4 3 2

FOR MY MOTHER AND MY LATE FATHER

PREFACE

"Money can't buy you friends," wrote the British comedian Spike Milligan, "but it can get you a better class of enemy." It also brings power, which is why, as Japan has become richer, it has also become more influential in world affairs. As Japan's wealth has grown, Japanese and Japan-watchers alike have quite naturally begun to wonder when and how Japan will begin to flex its muscles. Will it buy up the world? Will it dominate financial markets? Will it take on more international responsibilities? Will it become a superpower? How long will its strength last? How will wealth change Japan? Will it take over leadership from a declining America? Will it, above all, become a military force once again?

This book is, at its most ambitious, an attempt to answer these questions. It seeks to show where Japan is heading and how it is changing, in economic, financial, social, and political affairs. It is thus not intended as a snapshot of Japan, nor as a static description of how Japan works and why. There are already plenty of books that do that more effectively and with far greater expertise than this author could achieve. Instead, *The Sun Also Sets* is offered as an analysis of an ever-changing subject, an attempt to show the direction in which Japan is moving as well as to measure its speed.

Such an effort is fraught with dangers since it implies, at least in part, an exercise in prediction. As Sam Goldwyn warned, "Never prophesy, especially about the future." In its humbler moments, however, the book is also an attempt to show how to think about Japanese power. To that end, it seeks to identify those factors that will determine how powerful Japan will become, how long its strength will last, and

in what sort of circumstances Japan's potential power might be un-
leashed in military or political form. Then, anyone who agrees with
Sidney Webb that "economists are generally right in their predictions
but generally a good deal out in their dates," can come up with their
own timetable for Japan.

These tasks cannot be achieved by viewing Japan in glorious
isolation. National power and influence, whether political or economic,
are always relative to those of other countries, not absolute. In plain
language, the book's questions must not just be about Japan but rather
must also be about the United States and, to a lesser extent, about
Europe. Crucially, the book must concern itself with such issues as
whether America is a spent force and how its power and influence
compare with those of Japan. Some of that is attempted *en passant* in
chapters principally concerning Japan, in particular in Part Three. But
also the final chapter is almost entirely devoted to the United States.

That chapter is not offered as a rigorous and definitive study of
America's past and future, since such a task would require not only a
book of its own but also an author more expert on and immersed in
matters American than is this writer. Nevertheless, the chapter is offered as an essay on the state of America in the late 1980s, as it appears
to an outsider seated in London who is employed to write and think
about finance and business and who previously spent several years
immersed in matters Japanese. The chapter seeks to place America in
the context of Japan's strength, as well as to place Japan in the context
of America's.

Like America, this author is now a net debtor, although fortunately in terms of gratitude for help and advice rather than trillions of
dollars. At the top of my list of creditors must stand *The Economist*,
and in particular Andrew Knight, its editor until 1986, for having given
me the chance to learn about Japan as the paper's Tokyo correspondent.
Rupert Pennant-Rea, Andrew's successor and an earlier co-author of
mine, then generously offered a sabbatical in 1988, without which this
book would never have appeared. And Vince McCullough made it
possible for me actually to accept that time off by standing in (and
eventually succeeding me) as financial editor.

The list of those who helped through interviews, either know-
ingly for this book or unknowingly during my time as Tokyo correspon-

PREFACE

dent, is far too long for this space. Thanks are due to all of them. Special thanks must, however, go to Kiichi Kawamura, Toru Nagatsuka, and Junichi Yano of the Foreign Press Center for help in setting up interviews during a lengthy return visit to Tokyo in mid-1988. That visit was also made easier by help from Geoffrey Tudor and Martin Sillwood of Japan Air Lines, for which many thanks. Particularly heavy debts for advice, assistance, and nourishment during that visit are owed to Paul Maidment, Lisa Martineau, Taeko Kawamura, and Akio Mikuni.

Whatever the book's deficiencies, they would undoubtedly have been far worse had not the patient and ever-supportive Gordon Lee read the entire manuscript in several drafts, providing suggestions and criticisms galore, as well as boundless enthusiasm. Chapters were also read by Clive Crook and Steve Reilly, both of whom pointed out errors and were responsible for many improvements. Hiroko Asami, my former assistant at *The Economist* in Tokyo, helped with some of the research and Ritsu Suzuki with some of the trickier interpretation. Some of the ideas in the book were also contained in an essay entitled "The Limits to Japanese Power" that I submitted to the 1988 American Express Bank Review competition held in memory of Robert Marjolin. I am grateful, therefore, to AMEX not only for awarding me the first prize but also for tolerating the fact that my essay was, in effect, an early draft of chapter 11.

To my editors, Jonathan Segal and Ruth Fecych in New York and Nicholas Brealey in London, thanks are due not only for their interest and enthusiasm but also for their ideas in evolving the book's structure and content. Dasha Shenkman, my literary agent, helped to turn the book from a vague and abstract notion into a concrete, publishable project as well as providing constant encouragement. Delightful and secluded cottages in which to write were provided by Charles Ware and Helena Harding, as well as by John and Hilary Andrews. While credit is due to all of these and more, blame for any errors, omissions, or infelicities in the book remain, of course, entirely my own.

Bill Emmott
London, January 1989

CONTENTS

CONTENTS

PART

ONE

力

POWER AND PARANOIA

パラノイア

CHAPTER ONE

円

THE JAPANESE CHALLENGE

Prosperity is the surest breeder of insolence I know.
—MARK TWAIN

FOUR DECADES AGO, Japan was written off as a contender for political and economic power; two decades ago, it was no more than a voice offstage; now it is a leading player in virtually every arena of international endeavor. Its companies are impossible to ignore, at home or abroad; so, still, are its exports; so, increasingly, is the capital it is sending overseas in truckloads; and so, at last, are beginning to be its politicians and diplomats. The Japanese are no longer coming. They have arrived.

Contrary to what was once a common assumption, Japan's growing influence on the world is by no means limited to strictly economic affairs. The country that for centuries deliberately isolated itself is now reaching out and, one way or another, is affecting everybody's lives. Japanese fashions, for instance, draw whistles in Paris; amid the fads and fancies typical of haute couture, the Japanese have had their moments as trendsetters. Names such as Kenzo, Comme des Garçons, Issey Miyake, and Rei Kawakubo can be seen on clothes or shops in all the world's major capitals. After buying a Japanese outfit, you can have a healthy Japanese lunch to ensure that when you get home you will still be the same size as the garment. New York, Los Angeles, and, increasingly, London are packed with sushi bars and other Japanese restaurants, and not merely for the tens of thousands of expatriate Japanese who live in those cities.

All over Asia, Japanese department stores are coming to dominate retailing. Japanese banks can be seen everywhere all around the world, on street corners, in financial districts, in league tables, and on "tombstone" advertisements in newspapers and magazines. Japanese honeymooners dominate the Pacific islands. Groups of camera-toting Japanese tourists have taken the place in traveling stereotypes that was once occupied by tartan-trousered Americans. Teenagers in Hong Kong, Seoul, and Singapore listen to Japanese pop music on their Sony Walkmans (or, more likely, on locally made copies). Asian youth looking for the latest in style and popular culture no longer look merely to America but also to Japan.

By the same token, Japan is becoming, superficially at least, more international in character. Tokyo, in particular, has become agreeably cosmopolitan in appearance. There and in other big Japanese cities even the most traditional neighborhood feels incomplete without a French restaurant next to the noodle shop, a European-style bakery opposite the rice merchant. It is hard to eat badly in Tokyo, in whichever cuisine you choose. Ten years ago, that would not have been so, nor would the choice have been terribly wide. But Japan's ever-growing affluence and its taste for the new and exotic (although only mildly spiced, if you please) have lured foods, arts, and styles from everywhere.

Even modern architecture in Tokyo is more imaginative and attractive than much of what appears in London and is on a par with the best new structures in Manhattan, despite the fact that older Tokyo buildings are mostly hideous. Prince Charles would probably agree that, unlike in London, modern architecture is generally improving Tokyo rather than destroying it. Want to attend a Mick Jagger concert, look at impressionist art, or see the latest Hollywood movie? Come to Tokyo.

FROM SKEPTICISM TO TERROR

Just as Japan has changed, so has the outside world's attitude to this Asian upstart. Views of Japan have turned rapidly from a sort of skeptical admiration into awe.

In the not-so-distant past, Japan's economic progress was often described (by some Japanese, as well as by Westerners) as being impressive but surely too fragile to last. One argument along these lines was that Japan's economy is vulnerable because it is dependent on imports for its supply of raw materials. Interrupt that supply, or raise prices sharply, and Japan will be crippled. Another theory held that Japan is like a bicycle: fine when it is moving fast, but when the pedaling stops it will topple over. Most recently, it was assumed that Japan's strength depended crucially on a currency that was artificially undervalued. If market prices were to prevail, ran the argument, Japan would surely be put in its place.

The 1970s and 1980s destroyed, one after another, these notions of Japan's fragility. First, President Richard Nixon abruptly devalued the dollar against the yen. Then the price of oil rose by ten times inside six years. What happens? While the rest of the industrial world suffered in post-oil-shock stagflation, Japan became the world's most efficient user of energy and cut its imports of other raw materials from 3 percent of gross national product (GNP) in the 1960s to 1.6 percent by 1984. It recovered from a severe but brief period of inflation in 1974–75 to resume its lead of the world's growth rankings.

Between February 1985 and February 1988 the value of the yen more than doubled against that of the dollar. For a while, the economy seemed to be slipping into a recession. Even Japanese pundits warned of a coming *endaka fukyo,* or high-yen slump. Yet suddenly Japan's domestic demand boomed and, far from collapsing, the economy grew at its fastest rate in six years. Unemployment rose a bit, but then fell back again. Not even the world stock market crash of October 1987 could derail Japan, even though Westerners had queued up to predict that Japan's financial markets would plunge first and farthest. With this sort of record, it is little wonder that, through many Western eyes, Japan has become akin to an economic Superman, able, apparently, to achieve anything once he has popped into a telephone booth to remove his disguise.

In foreign policy, by contrast, Japan has more often been under- than overestimated. It has long been common to sneer at Japan's low profile and apparent insignificance: meager military spending, a "free ride" on American defense, a mealy-mouthed foreign policy, almost comically evasive prime ministers. Attitudes have changed since the early 1960s, when France's President Charles de Gaulle referred to a visiting Japanese prime minister as "a transistor salesman," but not by much. There is still, in fact, some truth to the sneer. But compare Japan's behavior in 1988 to that typical even a decade earlier, and things will look rather different.

For instance, anyone would have been called mad who, in the mid-1970s, predicted that a Japanese foreign minister would visit Israel and demand that his hosts withdraw from the West Bank and Gaza; or that a Japanese prime minister would arrive at a World Economic Summit (in Toronto) and announce plans to double Japan's overseas aid within five years as well as proposals to ease the Third World debt problem; or that Japan's defense agency would be buying and installing some of the world's most advanced weapons and radar systems. All of these happened during 1988. Ignore, for the moment, the more common and justifiably unfavorable static comparison of Japan's political profile and foreign policy with those of others. Look instead at the dynamics; the change in Japan's profile begins to appear impressive.

The underestimation of Japan's political position has, nevertheless, done little to calm attitudes to its economy. So remorseless has been Japan's economic rise that other countries now cower before actual and potential Japanese competition in virtually any area that Japanese firms might choose to enter. Think of a business in which Westerners have, so far, remained dominant—aerospace, biotechnology, supercomputers, luxury cars, design, retail financial services, computer software, and many more—and you will find someone, somewhere, who is forecasting a Japanese takeover of that market. Most likely, too, they will be lobbying for protective measures against such an event.

In addition, the awe inspired by Japan is now heavily laden with fear. The Japanese investments and loans that have flowed abroad since 1983 ought, in theory, to lessen such worries, since they spread finance, jobs, wealth, and technology more widely and evenly than does domestic Japanese production. On the contrary, this has prompted recipients to fear even more for the future. Japanese buying power (and actual buying) has grown so rapidly in the past five years that many American and European writers and pundits are wondering aloud what will be the consequences of being owned by Japan. Thanks to its trade and budget deficits, America has become the world's largest net debtor; thanks to its surpluses, Japan has become America's, and the world's, largest net creditor.

If that state of affairs persists for long, it is unlikely to remain happy and harmonious. As John Maynard Keynes wrote in his "Economic Consequences of the Peace" in 1919, "A debtor nation does not love its creditor."

Keynes was then referring to the likely feelings of a defeated Germany toward Great Britain and the United States. Thirty years previously, the same could have been said of America's feelings toward its chief creditor, Great Britain. In a most intelligent and perceptive paper in September 1987, David Hale, chief economist at Kemper Financial Services in Chicago, compared Japan's likely position in 1988 with the position of Britain as the financial bogeyman of American politics during the presidential election of 1896. In the 1880s and 1890s, Britain was far and away America's biggest creditor, with a portfolio of American investments equal to 20 percent of America's GNP (far bigger, proportionately, than Japan's current portfolio). The Democratic party platform in 1896 described the dollar's link to the pound as "a form of financial servitude." Hale cites an influential American monogram of the period, Coin's Financial School by William Harvey, that argued that the continuation of present policies would end

In England owning us body and soul. She is making a peaceable conquest of the United States. What she failed to do with shot and shell in the 18th century, she is doing with the gold standard in the 19th century.

It is not hard to find similar words being used for Japan in the late twentieth century. Having failed, it might be said, to beat the United States after Pearl Harbor in 1941, Japan is now making a peaceable conquest. Several books have already made similar assertions, including Marvin Wolf's rather hysterical The Japanese Conspiracy (how Japan is plotting to take over Western industry) and Russell Braddon's calmer The Other Hundred Years War (a former prisoner of war about Japan's long-term struggle to get on terms with the West). On present trends, it may be feared, Japan will soon own America body and soul.

JAPAN UNLIMITED, AMERICA ENFEEBLED?

This sense that Japan is buying up the world is beginning to alter expectations about Japan's political importance and role. The country's resilience, economic invincibility, and buying power have become so convincing that it is now common to read and hear forecasts that Japan could ultimately achieve some sort of supremacy in world affairs, despite all its present frailties and reluctance. At first it would merely take more "responsibilities" and share America's burdens. But that is only the beginning. Later it would take more power and would eventually rearm. The view is, in short, that extrapolating from present trends Japan is bound eventually to take over from America as the front-runner for the non-Communist world. Some clairvoyants see Japan taking the lead in partnership with China as a formidable Asian duo; more see Japan taking it alone, since China's economic development remains at such an early and uncertain stage.

In 1985, for instance, Kenjiro Hayashi, an economist at Nomura Research Institute, wrote of "Passing the Torch of World Leadership." In early 1986, Professor Ezra Vogel, a Harvard sociologist and author of a celebrated work in praise of the land of the rising sun, *Japan as Number One,* discussed the possibility of a "Pax Nipponica" in an article in *Foreign Affairs.* Although his conclusion was skeptical, he evidently took the idea seriously enough to examine it. Norman Macrae, then deputy editor of *The Economist,* wrote anonymously in October 1987 of "The Post-Hirohito Century" and about what Japan was going to do with all its money. Every risen economic power, he asserted, seeks eventually to mold its era. And in early 1988 a prominent American fund manager, George Soros, went further by writing, in an afterword to his book *The Alchemy of Finance,* that

The historic significance of the stock market crash lies in the fact that it marks the transfer of economic and financial power from the United States to Japan.

Japan, it is thus argued, is not only impressively successful; it is also on the verge of greatness and power. A recent proponent of this idea is Daniel Burstein, an American journalist and author of *Yen: Japan's New Financial Empire and Its Threat to America.* This sort of view about Japan's irresistible rise and where it is heading is not only derived from the country's strength in absolute terms, however. More important still is Japan's strength relative to that of the United States, a nation that, in the view of some prominent folk, is in decline. Take the book *Trading Places: How We Allowed Japan to Take the Lead* by Clyde Prestowitz, formerly a negotiator with Japan in the U.S. Department of Commerce. His first chapter is entitled "The End of the American Century."

The idea that the United States is a nation in decline is not new. Americans have long been all too aware of the slippage of their country's power since its zenith in 1945 and of the exposure of their mighty country's limitations. Deadlock in Vietnam, the helicopters leaving the embassy in Saigon in 1975, was the most public and demoralizing confirmation of this. President Jimmy Carter's failed attempt to rescue American hostages in Iran in 1979 only added to the misery. These failures, however, were largely seen as such by reference to Americans' postwar self-image as omnipotent global policemen, as a country with a mission, and as the world's most powerful military and political power. Such setbacks were a blow chiefly to the "can-do" spirit, the optimism of America. There was no particular need to make a comparison with any single rival. America may have been less than Americans thought it was, but it was still number one. Nobody else could do better.

The chief rival, then, as now, was of course the Soviet Union. That rivalry was seen primarily in military, strategic, and ideological terms, rather than economic ones. There was no likelihood or fear of Russia catching up with America's economy, even if it did manage to put men into space and to develop advanced weapons. During the 1970s, however, America and its European allies came to feel that the Soviet Union was gaining ground in military and strategic matters, building a more powerful armory, encroaching into parts of the world previously left largely to America (such as the Pacific Ocean), building a base in Vietnam, and invading Afghanistan.

That background is why Ronald Reagan entered the American presidency in 1980 with plans sharply to increase defense spending. Yet it has been that policy that has most clearly exposed America's decline and its limitations. This is a painful paradox, for President Reagan's goal was the exact opposite: to reverse a perceived decline in the United States and to show Americans that their country remained great. In that light, the spending increase was an imperative for Reagan purely in military and strategic terms, with little reference to economics. But as successful as that strategic effort appears to have been in forcing the Soviet Union into concessions and serious talk about arms reduction, it in turn laid the groundwork for Americans' present economic dilemmas.

Put simply, the American economy could not afford to finance the military spending that President Reagan demanded of it, without big cuts in other parts of the public sector (chiefly Social Security), which Congress was not willing to accept. Awkwardly, the spending policy coincided with another scheme dear to President Reagan's heart: the cutting of taxes. The outcome was that tax revenues proved insufficient to pay the bills, and America's pool of savings proved too small to lend the federal government enough money to pay them. The money had to be borrowed from abroad. The readiest lender was Japan.

The gigantic budget and trade deficits that resulted from the Reagan spending and borrowing binge culminated in the collapse of the dollar that began in February 1985 and in the stock market crash of October 16–20, 1987. The deficits coincided with the rise of Japan's huge current-account surpluses and the arrival of more Japanese exports than ever before. This, it seems, set many Americans worrying anew about the extent of their country's economic and political decline even though, for the time being, their prosperity was not harmed. The worries were about the longer term. What other explanation can be found for the fact that the most surprising best-seller in the United States in 1988 was a work of nonfiction by a British historian at Yale? This was Paul Kennedy's *The Rise and Fall of the Great Powers*.

Despite being an extremely weighty piece of academic scholarship, this book appears to have struck a chord in an America that is concerned about whether it is in decline as a great power, about its transformation into a net debtor after seventy-odd years as a net creditor, and about the resounding crash of its stock market. The popularity of this and of a previous best-seller, Allan Bloom's *The Closing of the American Mind,* has been termed "The New Seriousness." A better epithet might be "The New Worrying." Fewer will have read either book than will have bought them; nevertheless, the act of purchase reveals that anxiety has become fashionable.

Another less surprising publishing success in 1988 was Martin and Susan Tolchin's *Buying Into America: How Foreign Money Is Changing the Face of Our Nation,* a more accessible and populist book about the wave of foreign investment in America in the mid-1980s. The chord that this has struck is similar to that cited earlier from Coin's Financial School in the 1890s: the worry that America, and control over American jobs and welfare, is being bought by foreigners. The sale of factories, firms, and buildings to foreigners is merely another way for America to finance its trade deficit and to import the capital it needs, but that is scant comfort to a nation long proud of the mighty dollar and more used to buying into other countries than being bought into itself.

There is a strong sense here of the closing of an era. Unlike when Saigon fell, however, this time there is a serious and rising power against which to measure America's decline. That power is Japan.

WHAT, JAPAN? A GREAT POWER?

This comparison is natural, given the fierce competition between American and Japanese firms in all of the world's major industries and services, but in another respect, it is surprising. Surely, a modern Charles de Gaulle might still say, Japan can never really become a great power. Officially, it rejects military methods and, in part due to the dropping of atom bombs on Hiroshima and Nagasaki, possesses no nuclear weapons. Japan spends only about 1 percent of its GNP on defense and only 0.3 percent on overseas aid. It has a successful economy but is unwilling to take on responsibilities commensurate with that economic strength. It hates to commit itself in foreign affairs. It is inward-looking. It does not have what it takes to be an international leader. Stop worrying, America.

A close read of Professor Kennedy's *Rise and Fall of the Great Powers* (and of other economic histories) suggests that although this is true, it could easily turn out to be a red herring. Many of the same skeptical and frustrated comments were made about the United States during its emergence as a top power in the first half of this century. Before the 1914 war, as Kennedy writes,

> the United States clung to a laissez-faire dislike of mass standing armies and avoided fixed military obligations to allies. Less than 1% of its GNP went to defense. Despite its imperialist activities in the period 1898–1914, therefore, it remained what the sociologist Herbert Spencer termed an "industrial" society rather than a "military" society.

In the 1920s,

> the American people decidedly rejected a leading role in world politics, with all the diplomatic and military engagements which such a posture would inevitably produce; provided American commercial interests were not deleteriously affected by the actions of other states, there was little cause to get involved in foreign events.

All of these sorts of phrases are heard with reference to Japan today. It only worries about its commercial interests. Even in economic affairs, Japan resists leadership: Its trade is largely denominated in dollars, and the yen is far from being an international reserve currency. Yet in the first two decades of this century, most of America's trade was also done in somebody else's currency (pounds sterling). And as late as 1939, according to Hillmann (quoted by Kennedy), "the United States' political influence in the world was in no respect commensurate with her extraordinary industrial strength."

To be fair, these isolated statements greatly simplify American history. In the nineteenth and early twentieth centuries, America was not wholly averse to overseas adventures: The seizure of much of Mexico, tussles in Central America, the taking of the Philippines, and even the dispatch in 1853 of Commodore Matthew Perry and his "black ships" to open up Japan are all counterexamples. Yet, although it took part in regional or local scraps, America was loath to participate in global affairs. Historians will debate why until the last breath leaves their bodies, but several of the proximate causes are clear. First, as an immigrant nation, America was poorly placed to take sides in clashes between the immigrants' various lands of origin. The result was, as British patriots never tire of pointing out, that the United States was a late entrant to both of this century's world wars.

A second difficulty was that, at least until the 1930s, America's states were a powerful force for parochialism and against federal instincts for an active foreign policy. They saw little reason or interest in worrying about foreign affairs when there was so much to worry about at home. A third factor after World War I was disillusionment even among those, such as Woodrow Wilson, who favored an international role. The Treaty of Versailles gave many prominent Americans the view that Europe was not a place worth bothering with. But in the end, the United States overcame these obstacles to an international presence. So, in its own particular ways and circumstances, could Japan.

THE EFFECT OF NUCLEAR WEAPONS

A more serious objection to Japan as a great power is that it does not have nuclear weapons. These days, the only real powers are those capable of delivering a nuclear strike, which is why countries with no apparent need for such weapons (including Britain and France) insist on having them. Japan has renounced the use of all weaponry except in self-defense, and of nuclear weapons in any circumstances. Officially, nuclear weapons are not even allowed on its soil or in its ports. This is, after all, the only country to have been the subject of a nuclear attack, and the experience of Hiroshima and Nagasaki has left a deep psychological and political scar. Rightly or wrongly, rationally or irrationally, that experience makes it hard to imagine that Japan could ever possess its own nuclear weapons. The domestic opposition to such a move would be horrendous. Therefore, it may be concluded, Japan cannot be a top power.

However, it is also possible to argue that nuclear weapons have a double-edged influence that, at the very least, provides a chance for Japan to be an extremely important second-rank power. The nub of the argument is that the existence of nuclear weapons actually makes it easier for non-nuclear nations to exert power and influence. Nuclear weapons imply a strong danger of "mutual assured destruction" in the event of their use in a conflict in which both sides possess them. Therefore, as long as America and Russia both possess weapons of sufficient quantity and technical quality to ensure mutual destruction, there will not be another major war. A stalemate is guaranteed. According to this view, other powers do not need to hold nuclear weapons or to have sizable conventional forces in order to gain influence. They can shelter under the superpower umbrella and exert themselves by other means. In the nuclear age, such means could be purely economic.

The truth lies somewhere between these extremes. The nuclear balance does reduce the need for non-nuclear countries to build their defenses. But nuclear weapons are not the be-all and end-all even of military power. Of the hundreds of wars fought since 1945, none has been nuclear. Most have exclusively involved non-nuclear powers. Democracies have been remarkably reluctant to fight one another. Moreover, America's present weight in world affairs is not always and exclusively related to its nuclear arsenal. It is its potential in conventional war, either directly or as a supplier of cash and weapons, that makes it influential in the Middle East, for instance, or in Central America. Nicaragua knows that the United States would never drop an atom bomb on Managua; but the United States could send in troops and it does give supplies and money to the Contras. America's nuclear weapons did not dissuade the Vietcong from fighting U.S. troops in Vietnam, nor the North Koreans from battling on during the Korean War.

In that case, might Japan rearm in order to build a more powerful conventional force? As long as the United States continues to ensure a nuclear balance with the Soviet Union, Japan will surely have no reason even to consider becoming a nuclear power. Its protection will be assured, and it will have nothing to gain from building a nuclear force capable of threatening America or Russia. Not only would the force be unusable (and hence wasted; never a favored habit in Japan), the act of building it could endanger Japan's relations with the United States and its freedom of economic action.

But this does not mean that Japan will have no reason to turn to conventional military weapons. Japan can feel confident, perhaps, that it will not be threatened by a nuclear power—Russia, China, Europe—as long as it is protected by the American deterrent. But that assurance does not extend to local conflicts between non-nuclear powers. It is not hard to think of plausible (if hypothetical) examples of cases where Japan's growing interests abroad could be threatened.

Japan would be unlikely to seek out a military role in such conflicts. But what if America becomes too weak or, just as likely, too unwilling to play its present part as a regional policeman in Asia? What if, in those circumstances, a crisis erupts, say, a conflict between North and South Korea or a Communist insurgency in the Philippines or a Vietnamese invasion of Thailand? Would Japan stand by and watch? It would be tempted to stand aloof, but its interests might be threatened. In the case of Korea, the conflict would be right on its doorstep, not to mention the fact that 600,000 of Japan's residents are of Korean origin, divided in allegiance between North and South.

A conflict is unlikely, and it is also unlikely that America would ignore it. But if, for whatever reason (a severe recession, a change in political attitudes), America did leave a power vacuum, Japan would surely step in to fill it. It would not stand by and watch the Korean Peninsula turn hostile. Its conventional forces are perfectly adequate to cope with such an emergency. It was just such a power vacuum that brought America into this century's two world wars: Britain's inability to keep the peace in Europe, not to mention Asia. Out of the vacuum emerged American supremacy. In theory, the same could happen for Japan.

THE POWER GAME

The historical backgrounds and circumstances of Japan and the United States are different. Nevertheless, the point remains that Japan's candidacy as a great power cannot lightly be dismissed merely because the country does not yet display the trappings of leadership. Superpowers develop and emerge over decades, not overnight. Japan today is in a position similar to that of America in the 1920s. Twenty-five years later, America stood supreme. It is not at all inconceivable that Japan could be in a similar position twenty-five years from today.

Will it be? In fact, this is not quite the best question to ask, at least not yet. One of the most important, though scarcely noticed, lessons from Paul Kennedy's sweep of five centuries of history is that the nineteenth century and the twentieth century since 1945 have been exceptions rather than rules in world history. These were periods during which there was either one dominant superpower (nineteenth-century Britain) or just two (postwar America and Russia, of which America has been the pre-eminent force). Such dominance was extraordinary, not ordinary.

After its victory at Waterloo, in 1815, Britain's technological advantage sent its economy hurtling forward. Kennedy cites estimates that by 1860 Britain produced half the world's iron, coal, and lignite; consumed half the world's raw cotton; and had about 40–45 percent of the world's capacity in modern industries. Presumably as a result of this lead, its years of pre-eminence were fairly peaceful. No other country could or did challenge Britain's naval mastery; by and large, its only opposition was from poorly equipped natives in far-flung parts of the world. Until 1900, Britain could afford to keep its defense spending low.

Since World War II the United States has not had that luxury. But between 1945 and 1950, it did have the sort of economic lead enjoyed by Britain at its peak. In 1950, America's GNP was nearly six times that of Britain, three times that of the Soviet Union, and ten times that of Japan. Its GNP per capita was double Britain's, more than three times Russia's, and nearly seven times Japan's. This measure is artificial, however, because the period was immediately after a war during which Europe and Japan had been devastated and from which only America had become richer. Everyone emerged owing millions of dollars to the United States. Yet even after Europe and Japan had recovered, America still enjoyed a huge lead. Even now it represents one fifth of world output.

The point is that it is misleading to infer from the British and American periods of dominance that the world must now look for the next dominant power or even a dominant peacekeeper. Many pundits looking at Japan have sought parallels with the rises of Britain and America. This is neither necessary nor sensible. Apart from the American and British periods of hegemony, since 1500 there has always been a large number of fairly equally balanced powers rather than any particular dominance; although many dreamed of or sought hegemony in those times, none achieved it. After Pax Britannica and Pax Americana, there is no reason necessarily to expect a Pax Nipponica or indeed a Pax anything else. One might emerge, but it would be more in line with history to expect a balanced, multipolar world.

It would be extraordinary if there were now a "Japanese century" because it would imply that Japan will take on the sort of lead in the world economy enjoyed in the past by Britain and America. For all Japan's proven strengths and virtues, to expect it to build a truly dominant position requires heroic assumptions: America devastated by recession; Europe a sclerotic wreck; Japan's Asian neighbors, notably China, cooperating in the long term as quasi colonies providing markets and cheap bases for production. Nothing can be ruled out, but such an extreme possibility is hardly worth planning for. To say that is not, however, to reject Japan's candidacy as a great power. The right question to ask concerns how much power and leadership Japan will take in a world less clearly dominated by the United States. The choice, certainly for the next quarter century and probably for longer, is between degrees of American leadership and dominance. It is not simply between America and Japan.

MONEY MAKES JAPAN GO ROUND

Japan is emphatically not a mere economic animal. Even so, any examination of its potential for power and leadership must focus on Japan's economy. Economic strength is always the foundation of power, whether within a world that is multipolar or one that is bipolar. An examination of the power and position of Britain, France, or West Germany would also look primarily at the country's economy. Yet it would not be so exclusively an economic judgment as is the case with Japan. These three European powers have political roles and weights that are, arguably, larger than those justified purely by their economic strengths. All have large armies; Britain and France have spheres of influence in various parts of the world; all are well represented in top posts in international organizations; all have a loud, fairly clear political voice. The reason is historical. Present circumstances reveal traces of former strengths, certainly those of Britain and France but also, to an extent, of West Germany.

That is not so for Japan because it is a newcomer, a parvenu. Like Germany, it lost its status in 1945; unlike West Germany, it had neither the creation of the European Economic Community nor a position on the cold war's front line to force it back into prominence. Japan's political role is still in an early stage of development. How and whether it develops in the future will depend on the country's economic strength relative to that of others and on Japan's economic exposure overseas. This is not offered as a general theory of political power, but rather as an analysis of Japan's particular circumstances as the 1980s draw to a close.

The test of Japan's strength is, moreover, not merely the size of its GNP or its rate of economic growth. The idea of Japan as a superpower is based primarily on the country's huge exports of capital and on its sudden emergence as the world's largest net creditor. Its net exports of long-term capital reached $65 billion in 1985 and $137 billion in 1987; that 1987 figure is roughly equivalent to the entire GNP of Sweden or Switzerland. In short, Japan has piles of spare money.

Does this really equal power? To the historically minded, the country's capital exports sound a strong echo of the rise of Great Britain and of the United States. Britain was exporting capital in large quantities roughly after 1815, and it dominated world politics for the following century. America began exporting capital after World War I and until now has been the world's clear leader. After all, a surplus of capital produces the ability to support a large military force for a long period of time. But this point should not be exaggerated. Plenty of big powers did not export capital, or not much of it; France and Germany before World War I are two examples. The Soviet Union, moreover, is an importer of capital, yet undeniably is a superpower. In a multipolar world, some powers will be capital exporters and some importers. There is no necessary link between capital exports and great power status.

Nevertheless, Japan's capital exports are important in its own particular case. Bit by bit, they are giving the country three essential ingredients of international power: the means with which to exert it; some obligations to take a higher profile; and increasingly, motives for using and demanding power. At other times, other powers have obtained these ingredients from sources other than exports of capital. But capital is Japan's present source.

At the same time, Japan's surpluses of trade and capital are the most significant counterparts of America's deficits. They offer indications of the relative economic positions of the two great economies that flank the Pacific Ocean. More than likely, a sustained Japanese surplus of capital will imply a sustained American deficit on both its trade and capital accounts. It will imply an America increasingly in debt to Japan and to the rest of the world, and increasingly unable or unwilling to finance its military ambitions or obligations. It will be a measure of America's relative decline.

For Japan, capital is providing leverage. The more that Japan invests abroad, gives in development aid, or hands out as bank loans, the more the recipients become beholden to Japan and the more that Japan or Japanese institutions can demand in return. The leverage thus derived does depend, however, on the circumstances of the time and of the recipients; after all, the billions lent by American banks to Brazil have not noticeably provided America with much leverage over Latin America's largest economy. That said, America's ability (or inability) to provide fresh money does provide some leverage; if more cash is needed, Brazil has an incentive to kowtow, to some extent, to those from whom it wishes to borrow.

This is an important distinction. In the exertion of power, flows of capital must matter more than the stocks outstanding. It is the availability of future aid, loans, or investments that provides leverage to the provider and imposes dependence on the recipient. Stocks of capital can be sequestered, nationalized, or devalued; flows cannot. This is one reason why Japan's influence over America is likely to grow for as long as America depends on Japanese money to finance its budget and trade deficits. The link is indirect but real. If America wants Japanese institutions to buy more Treasury bonds, then it has a strong incentive to follow an economic policy approved by those lenders and not to take measures that damage those lenders' interests. America's options become narrower, just as Japan's options become wider.

Some sorts of capital export provide more obvious opportunities and pressures for leadership than others. The clearest example is in the provision of capital and loans to multilateral agencies, such as the World Bank, the International Monetary Fund (IMF), and the Asian Development Bank. For these institutions, shares in the provision of capital are supposed to be related directly to voting power. Since 1945, the United States has had a strong influence over both the World Bank and the IMF, not only because they are based in Washington, D.C., but also because America has provided the largest chunk of their money. That influence is slipping. The more that Japan provides, the more power it expects to have over the agencies' policies.

The motive for taking on power and leadership is just as important as the means. The more money Japan has tied up abroad, the more incentive it has to act to protect that capital and the flow of business or commerce that it implies. In the Iran-Iraq war, Japan's position was complicated by the fact that it had a large commercial exposure in both countries, so it preferred to sit on the fence. If it had been exposed only in one country, its posture might have been different. Loosely, the more investment Japan makes abroad, the more likely it is that Japanese citizens will live abroad and be vulnerable to aggressive acts. As in the case of its loans to the World Bank, the more money Japan ships directly to developing countries, the more likely it is to demand a say over how the money is spent or how investments are affected by legislation, for example. The influence may be implicit rather than explicit, just as with Japan's influence in America, but that will make it no less real.

More Japanese firms will be able to affect local politics by their threats of divestiture or by their donations to local politicians. As ITT drew controversy in Latin America, so could Japan's growing multinationals wherever they have big investments. When the United States makes overseas aid, it generally gets involved politically as well, perhaps to ensure the money is spent effectively, or to use it to assist some foreign policy goal, or, even less reputably, to ensure that it is spent in a way that benefits American firms or citizens. The same, increasingly, is becoming true of Japan.

As long as Japan has this surplus of money, it will continue gradually to find new ways in which to exploit it and to exert power.

It will gradually see beyond the narrow horizons of its parochial affairs. As long as it is thus blessed, Japan will also stand poised to become a military power if that were ever to be necessary. The longer the surplus lasts, the more likely it is that the United States will remain in debt and will become reluctant to continue to offer regional security to Asia. Such a regional vacuum is one part of the recipe needed to lure Japan out of its military and political shell. The other is a crisis. In that case, Japan has what it takes to become a significant power in a multipolar world. If the surplus disappears, if America's economy recovers its stability, if the vacuum never appears, then the world will not really be multipolar. America will still be the dominant power.

JAPAN'S MONEY TREE

This leads to one all-important question: How long will Japan's surplus last? To answer that requires a general idea of where the capital surplus has come from. Even in Japan, money does not grow on trees. A country generates a surplus when it saves more than it invests, broadly defined. If it has more money than it wishes to spend at home, then the money has to go abroad. Many of the stereotypes about Japan fit in with this: Japanese are workaholics who save lots of money and refuse to consume; their government spends very little; their industry is fearsomely efficient and has such a strong cash flow that it no longer borrows much.

Turned into more technical jargon, this means that Japan has a high personal savings rate, a relatively low propensity to consume, a small government deficit (deficits are dis-saving), and declining corporate borrowing. So it has a surplus on the current account of its balance of payments and is exporting capital. If you are an American or a European and you take the growth in Japan's capital exports since 1982 and extrapolate it through the 1990s, you will become very frightened indeed. At recent rates of capital-export growth, Japan by 1999 will have a capital surplus big enough to buy the equivalent of several European countries. That will surely make it very powerful; Europe and America by comparison will be wimps.

Or will they? The answer depends on whether or not it is right to extrapolate recent surpluses into the next decade. Are the 1980s part of a long-term trend or a passing phase? The shorter the phase, the less likely it is that Japan will take on significant amounts of power. Economic prospects in Europe and, especially, in America matter for this too. But the most important questions are about Japan. Is it always going to be a nation of savers, of producers, of workaholics, of the young, of the financially undemanding? Is it, in other words, stuck in the fast lane?

驚き

CHANGE AND SURPRISE

変化

CHAPTER TWO

門

A NATION OF CONSUMERS

*With the scent of plums
on the mountain road—suddenly,
sunrise comes!*

—BASHŌ (1644–1691)

FOR ALL the stacks of articles, piles of books, and miles of film written and made about it, Japan still attracts myths like a magnet. Some are held fondly within Japanese hearts and minds. Japan is unique (not much of a claim, but the myth is taken to imply that Japan is somehow special). The Japanese are a homogeneous race (they mix Mongoloid and aboriginal origins with more recent blends of Korean, Chinese, and Southeast Asian peoples; the emperor may well be descended from a Korean, but nobody is supposed to say so). Japan alone has four seasons. Japanese brains operate in a way different from everybody else's. And so on. Japan's myths about itself are generally either the product of its centuries-long isolation or outgrowths of nationalist ideas created deliberately by the country's Meiji-era modernizers and prewar militarists. Such myths would be comical if they weren't so infuriating. What is worse, "Japan is different," or *Nihonjinron,* as the syndrome is known in Japanese, is often used in business, trade, and other negotiations to try to put opponents on the defensive. When the myths are not too daft, this ploy succeeds.

Equally ingrained and unhelpful, however, are the myths believed by Americans and Europeans about Japan and the Japanese. These foreign myths usually derive partly from the fact that, in proportion to the country's size, importance, and social and political diversity, relatively little information about Japan has been absorbed in America or Europe. The little that is known becomes a set of clichés, and even these may be concerned only with the small part of the country that is exposed to foreigners and to foreign trade. The myths also derive from a related point: that, too often, Japan is viewed as a static place, not as the dynamic society that it actually is. Facts about Japan that may have been true ten, twenty, thirty, or more years ago are believed still to be true now. Or they are true now and assumed to be a permanent state of affairs.

The sillier *myth*understandings include, for instance, the idea that Japanese cities are so terribly polluted that pedestrians wear face masks. They were polluted twenty years ago but have now been cleaned up; the masks, then and now, are worn to avoid the passing on of colds and flu, not to keep out fumes.

"On Tokyo's underground trains, men in white gloves have to cram in the passengers." Actually this only happens at two or three especially busy interchanges, where it is probably the photographers who make the platforms so crowded. Most trains are no worse (or better) than rush-hour trains in London or New York.

"Japanese are workaholics who prefer to save rather than to consume and who seldom get the time to have fun." Well, factory workers are efficient and do work hard, but that is not necessarily true of office workers, who now make up the largest part of the labor force. If these *sararimen,* as they are called, do work long hours, it is often because they are keen on overtime pay or because of a mixture of peer pressure and inertia. They spend ten hours doing what others manage to do in seven or eight. Many is the office that has an opened bottle of Suntory whiskey on the shelf or the annual high school baseball tournament showing on the television.

And yes, the average Japanese household saves 18 percent of its disposable income, which is more than in Britain or the United States. But that is less than in Italy and far less than in Taiwan, and that figure is also falling. In 1975, the rate was 23 percent. An 18 percent savings rate also means that 82 percent of each household's income is consumed.

A NATION OF CONSUMERS

Take a trip to Akihabara, Tokyo's electronics district, or Harajuku, with its fashion boutiques, or the crowded ski resorts of the Japan Alps, and just watch them spend it. Japan is the ultimate consumer society.

And don't they have fun? Walk down any street of a Tokyo entertainment area, such as Roppongi, Shinjuku, or Ikebukuro, and watch the red-faced men, arm in arm, perhaps singing a tuneless ditty as they sway from bar to bar. And that is at 7:00 P.M. On this evidence, in "workaholics" perhaps "worka" should be replaced with "alco"? The main Tokyo subway company has had a long series of etiquette posters showing how to behave on the trains, usually employing some form of Japanese pun. In 1984, they had one that showed a *sarariman* superimposed on a motoring "No U-turn" sign, except with the "U" originating in front of his mouth. It was exhorting travelers not to vomit on the trains and platforms. So much for the polite, well-behaved Japanese.

Among the more sophisticated myths is the idea that all Japanese workers enjoy lifetime employment; in fact only a third the Japanese are usually thought of as working for big companies, part generally of huge industrial combines; "they are not entrepreneurial, because teamwork is what matters." Who, then, founded Matsushita, Sony, Honda, Seibu, Fanuc, and hundreds of others? They may be big combines now, but they were entrepreneurial once, and new entrepreneurs are springing up all the time. Individuals yearn for success and wealth in Japan just as they do in America, even if they go about it in a different way and perhaps treat the less successful with more respect.

"Japan is dependent on exports." In fact only the equivalent of 16.5 percent of its GNP was exported in 1987, compared with 21 percent in France, 32 percent in West Germany, 26 percent in Britain, and 57 percent in Holland. Japan's export share is big only compared with America's (11.4 percent). The more important point is simply that Japan exports more than is needed to pay for its imports; put another way, it imports too little. "Ah, yes, Japanese won't buy foreign goods." Then why do they buy gallons of Coca-Cola, cases full of Nescafé, thousands of Gucci handbags, vats of Unilever shampoo, scores of de Beers' diamonds? Why are they America's biggest market for farm products?

A TRADITION OF CHANGE

There is one foreign myth that is worse than all the rest. It is that Japan does not change or, expressed more mildly, that it is especially resistant to change. This mistake is understandable: To visitors Japan seems an alienating, rebuffing place, a place of insiders and outsiders, somewhere so huge and complex that it appears immovable, as if set in concrete. Nothing could be further from the truth. According to Edward Seiden-sticker, a learned Japanologist: "The relationship between change and tradition in Japan has always been complicated by the fact that change itself is a tradition." This does not simply mean renewal, such as the constant rebuilding of wooden houses. It means genuine change.

Just consider the sort of changes that have taken place in postwar Japan. The most notable has been an astonishingly rapid migration from the countryside into the cities. As recently as 1955, nearly 40 percent of the labor force was employed in agriculture; now only about 8 percent is, and many of those are part-timers. From the 1868 Meiji Restoration until 1940, the agricultural population was roughly steady at 14 million, a figure that rose to 18 million amid the postwar devastation. At the time of the 1970 census, there was a farm population of about 10 million, of which 7 million were full-timers. By 1985, the total was down to 4.9 million.

What this means is that thirty years ago those cities and conurbations that look such a permanent feature of Japanese life were a mere shadow of their present selves. Tokyo, in particular, is a far younger city than it seems to be when a visitor wanders around narrow, winding back streets, gazing into little old shops or nibbling a squid ball at a local festival. Communities that appear solid, traditional, and full of old obligations and loyalties may actually be only a generation old. Tokyo's ancient precursor, Edo, accounts for only a fraction of today's city. Professor Shunsuke Tsurumi of Kyoto University expressed this admirably in his short book, *A Cultural History of Postwar Japan*:

> In fact only a very small percentage of Tokyo's citizens are descendants of the old city, Edo, and most of the inhabitants of Tokyo have no connection with the local festivals today. The city is characterized by its uprootedness.

Much the same could be said of all Japan, which is one plausible explanation for the Japanese myths cited at the opening of this chapter: They provide the binding or the roots that are missing as Japan and the Japanese respond to constant turbulence and flux.

Ryohei Magota, a professor at Shitennoji Buddhist University, used to give a lecture that illustrated the changes in twentieth-century Japan by referring to the songs popular in each era. For instance, in the mid-1920s, Japan's economy was in a severe slump, and a song called "Rumpen Bushi" was very popular. The name signified a sort of tramp or hobo, whose refrain went something like this:

> Don't be depressed, even if you're without a penny. Even if you are rich, your hair still turns gray.

That is not exactly the striving, workaholic spirit that is normally associated with Japan. Jumping to the 1950s, when the youths of rural Japan were rushing to find jobs in the cities, songs tended to dwell upon the sorrows of leaving families and loved ones behind. One song called "A Farewell and a Cedar" concerned a man's sadness at working in Tokyo and leaving his girlfriend behind. Another, called "Hello the Moon," told of a man's sorrow at being left behind by a girl who moved to the capital. Jobs were still not terribly secure in the mid-1950s, and many young Japanese migrants found it hard to make ends meet. One song, in response, was called "Come Back":

> Mother, Father, and the rest of your family are all well. Come back, come back, to your hometown. Tokyo is not the only good place in this land.

That song is still popular, as is general sentimentality about the *furusato,* or hometown. At the *o-bon* festival in August, millions still return to old hometowns to pay their respects to their ancestors, even if they are second- or third-generation city-dwellers.

By the 1960s, songs had turned to working life. In 1961, a song called *"Suudara Bushi"* became very popular, telling as it did of an easygoing approach to life for office workers, or *sararimen:* going to the office every day and drinking heavily after work. Blue-collar workers were given some motivation by a song at about the same time called the "365-Step March," which went:

> swing your arms, raise your legs, one, two, three, go on walking without a rest.

Through the 1960s, as Japan's prosperity grew and grew, songs began to appear that exhorted people to try cities other than Tokyo, so heavy was the pressure on jobs and housing in the capital. At long last, attention began to swing toward the family and home life, as urban emigrants put down new roots. Verbs began to be invented to describe city living, including *mai-homu-suru,* to own your own home, or *mai-car-suru,* to own a car and drive around in it on weekends. Aspirations turned to the "three Cs": car, cooler (air conditioner), and color television. Popular songs in the late 1960s and early 1970s included the very domestic "Hello Baby" and "You." The latter included the lines:

> If I own a home, it will be a small one. But the windows would be open, and in the living room there would be a stove, red roses, and white pansies.

Although popular songs are no longer quite so preoccupied with social change as they once were, the Japanese are still fascinated by the movements they have lived through. NHK, the state broadcasting channel, runs long drama series, often early in the morning, that frequently dwell on the ordinary person's response to this century's buffeting. By far the most popular, a series called *Oshin,* ran in 1983–1984. Despite being broadcast at 8:00 A.M. every weekday for about a year (and repeated during working hours so that *sararimen* could see it in their offices), at its peak it was being watched by 58 million viewers. *Oshin* is the tale of a Japanese woman's struggles through life from the 1920s to the present day, a sob story featuring good Japanese virtues, such as endurance and stoicism, but also illustrating the changes Japanese have lived through in recent years. Even Prime Minister Nakasone claimed to have shed a tear or two watching it. In the end, *Oshin* becomes rich, owning a supermarket. She has her reward for suffering, but is nevertheless a little bemused about the values—or lack of them—prevalent in the new Japan.

A NATION OF CONSUMERS

This reflects a rosy view of the past of the sort found in many cultures. Urban Japanese have not simply uprooted themselves from the country and moved into town, lock, stock, barrel, values, customs, and all. Many things have changed. Many apparently deep-seated "values" are new. Supposedly old values were not quite what memories crack them up to be. For instance, absenteeism was rife in factories in the 1930s. Strikes abounded until the end of the 1950s.

As migration took place, many superficial things altered. For instance, rice is thought to be the staple of the Japanese diet and is seen as symbolic of Japanese culture: polished, pure, produced by teamwork. Then why is every Japanese eating 40 percent less of it each year than in the early 1960s? Tastes and habits have moved on. Affluent, urban Japanese eat more protein, more meat, more bread, more fat, more Western foods than they did—indeed they eat more than did their rural forebears.

This has made them taller. The average height of a twenty-year-old man increased from 5 feet 4.9 inches in 1965 to 5 feet 5.7 inches by 1979 and 5 feet 7.4 inches by 1985. That last is a full four inches taller than the average contemporary sixty-year-old. This even begins to change the body language that is important in all cultures and especially so in Japan. When McDonald's opened its first fast-food restaurant in Tokyo's Ginza in the early 1970s, cynics said it would never catch on; the Japanese favored good quality foods, not junk, and had an ingrained cultural rule against eating in the street. Wrong. McDonald's soon became Japan's biggest restaurant chain, pronounced *Makudonarudo* by millions of Japanese kids and assumed to be Japanese.

The Japanese household, too, differs from that of twenty or thirty years ago. It has fewer members; an average of 3.3 compared with nearly 5 in 1955. Nearly 15 percent of households consist of just a married couple, double the 1955 figure. More than 16 percent of Japanese households are now singles, twice the 1965 percentage. Previously, children were assumed to live with their parents until married, while elderly parents were assumed to live with their children. Both habits are becoming less prevalent. People are getting married later in their lives. In Tokyo, more than a third of all men aged thirty to thirty-five are now unmarried, compared with a quarter in 1975. The total number of reported abortions in 1985 was half the 1960 total; previously it was a common form of birth control for married couples. In 1960, there were 1.6 million live births and 1 million abortions. But while the overall annual total of abortions has halved, it has actually doubled among women under twenty.

EXPECT THE UNEXPECTED

It is not that everything in Japan changes, which it certainly does not. Nor would it be right to argue that everything is evolving in a Western direction, which it also is not. Simply, the point is that things in Japan do change, they change quickly, and they change radically. This is not always easy to detect while it is happening; even changes in politics or business are rarely associated with dramatic, headline-grabbing news or sudden announcements. That is one of the things that makes life especially difficult—interesting, if you are a masochist—for foreign journalists in Tokyo. Change happens incrementally and quietly. But that does not prevent it from being rapid and profound.

A good recent example was the sudden flowering of Tokyo as an international financial center. Ever since 1945, Japan's financial system had been regulated rigidly, with every institution kept in its proper place and the supply and cost of money kept firmly under government control. The system had begun to relax in the early 1970s but only, it seemed at the time, in minor respects. Tight control was thought to be a permanent state of affairs. Speculators were shunned. Foreign firms, especially, didn't have a snowball's chance in hell. The Reagan administration bashed itself against Japan's door but was greeted with the usual sucking of teeth and chanting of "Japan is different."

Yet by 1986 an Oriental Rip Van Winkle waking after just a three-year snooze would not have believed his eyes. The rise of Japan's capital exports after 1983, among other factors, produced new, free financial markets. Market-determined interest rates on a wide range of instruments. A huge market for yen bonds in Europe. The most heavily traded financial-futures contract in the world. Half a dozen foreign firms with seats on the Tokyo Stock Exchange. And much more to come.

A NATION OF CONSUMERS

Change can happen when it is most unexpected. The difficulty is in determining, in advance, why it will happen when it does and to what. Some things do not alter when they are expected to or wanted to. Nothing changes just for the sake of it, just out of logic, or just to fall in line with practices abroad. Usually, a powerful force must be pushing for change. Often, that force is money or a market, mixed with self-interest. Japan adapts quickly to new situations, if it is to its advantage to do so. Moreover, the Japanese have been caricatured, rather unfairly, as the only human ant race. Which way will the ants run next?

SUDDENLY, A CONSUMER BOOM

The Japanese, it has often been said, are producers and not consumers. More particularly, it is said that you can lead them to an import but you cannot make them buy. Although Japanese households consume more than 80 percent of their disposable income, until recently these prejudices still had some force, in the sense that from 1981 until 1985 economic growth was chiefly being driven by exports. Domestic demand—not just individual consumption but also government spending and domestic corporate investment—was at best flat, at worst falling. If only the Japanese could live a little, came the common criticism, domestic demand would rise and the trade surplus might be reduced.

But look how things changed. In 1987 and 1988, Japan experienced its greatest consumer boom ever, which produced its fastest rate of economic growth for more than a decade. That sudden movement also helped to expose and spotlight changes in consumption patterns that had been developing over ten years or more. And it showed that even imports can be popular.

Another old saw about Japanese society is that conspicuous consumption and the flaunting of wealth are frowned upon. Among the generation that lived through the war and postwar reconstruction, this was largely true. Company bosses boasted of how narrow was the gap between their pay and that of their firm's toilet cleaners, at least compared with pay scales in the United States. They also liked to moan that, like the rest of the population, they lived in small "rabbit hutch" housing. These claims were always somewhat exaggerated. You could tell the really expensive restaurants, geisha houses, Turkish baths, and brothels by the lines of sleek black limousines parked outside. And a trip to Kanazawa, the chic summer hill resort in northern Honshu (Japan's main island), was enough to show that plenty of businessmen and politicians had a yen or two to rub together. Nevertheless, compared with America or Britain, Japan did seem an egalitarian, discreet place.

No longer. In the space of three years, consumption came into the open. In the winter, city streets are full of women—and men—in fur coats. Japanese skiers want to wear not only the best gear but also the most expensive. Japan is the second largest market for cut diamonds in the world. The first few stretch limousines can now be seen in the narrow back streets of ritzy entertainment areas like Akasaka. While researching this book, I lived in a fairly ordinary neighborhood about an hour from central Tokyo. On the ten-minute walk to the local station stood a small, typically tasteless modern Japanese house with a built-in garage. The garage door could not be closed because its contents stuck out several feet: a gleaming white Rolls-Royce. Another house nearby had more parking space: this contained a Mercedes sports car, a Porsche, and a BMW. Welcome to discreet, austere Japan.

These changes, from consumer bust to boom and from discretion to boasting, arose from a mixture of some short- and some long-term factors. The most immediate causes were that income taxes were cut and wages began to rise. In 1986, everyone had worried that the rapid rise of the yen against the dollar was going to send Japan into a slump, so wage increases were moderate and people even started saving a bit more. Rainy days looked to be on the way. That year, economic growth slowed to un-Japanese levels of 1 to 2 percent. Unemployment was on the rise.

After a year of flinching, the realization that the blow was not going to come seemed to encourage people to start spending again. Wage settlements resumed their normal level of 4 to 10 percent a year compared with 1 percent consumer price inflation. Moreover, the government, reversing its previously austere fiscal policy, stoked the fires by injecting a further ¥6 trillion in spending on new public works. At the same time, people came to realize that the rise of the yen actually had benefits for the consumer. It made imports cheaper. The Bank of Tokyo reckons that in the roughly two and a half years between September 1985 and the end of March 1988 the rise of the yen added ¥24 trillion to domestic purchasing power. That is, depending on the exchange rate, $150 billion to $200 billion, or roughly the same as America's budget deficit.

Yet even this was not the biggest factor. The largest boost of all, and the main reason for the arrival of those stretch limousines and Rolls-Royces, has been a direct result of Japan's capital surplus: the country's booming property and stock markets. After rising steadily but unspectacularly for years, land and share prices took off in 1985 and 1986. Prices in Japan's six largest cities doubled inside two years. In Tokyo, they went through the roof, rising by 50 percent a year for three years, and by much more in some areas. Money was abundant, land was scarce. Share prices rocketed, too, rising by 50 percent in yen terms in 1987, despite the worldwide crash of Black Monday, October 19, 1987. Tokyo's two markets became linked; investors used their profits from land to trade in the stock market and vice versa, or borrowed on the security of their land or shares. (Chapters 5 and 6 will delve into the financial consequences and dangers of all this.)

The results for consumption were dramatic. While prices were rising, the main complaints to be heard were that young couples could no longer afford to buy a house, or that it cost several arms and legs to house a foreign executive in Tokyo, or that Tokyo share prices were absurdly high. Meanwhile, the people who were becoming extraordinarily rich kept ordinarily quiet about it. The paper value of private, residential land alone is estimated to have increased between 1985 and 1987 by ¥476 trillion. Share values rose in that period by ¥143 trillion. The total of those, ¥619 trillion, is twenty-five times greater than the increase in wages and salaries. It is also nearly double Japan's GNP. Anecdotes abound to bring these numbers alive. A favorite one is of the school janitor who worked every day for forty years for a pittance. When he retired, he sold his small central Tokyo house for $8 million and moved to the country.

This inflation in asset values produces only paper wealth, most of which cannot be spent in the shops. For a few people, the wealth is real, as it has arisen from property development or from land that is not a principal home. For the majority, though, such paper wealth has had a radical effect on feelings of well-being; they feel wealthier, so they spend more. This wealth effect is hard to quantify, but it is there. If your house is worth millions of dollars, it hardly seems extravagant to borrow, using it as collateral, to buy a BMW or even a Rolls-Royce. And the home-equity loan, a popular feature of 1980s America, has caught on in Japan, too. At the opposite end of the spectrum, many young couples now have no hope of buying their own home. So they might just as well spend their money on a fancy car or a foreign holiday.

A NEW BREED

This rise of the Japanese consumer has happened astonishingly quickly. Yet wage increases, tax cuts, the high yen, and even the wealth effect of property prices could all, in principle, prove as ephemeral as the cherry blossom. Behind this sudden boom, however, lie changes in consumption patterns that have been building up for a decade. Assuredly, these will not disappear overnight.

Chief among these changes is the arrival of a new breed of young Japanese. Today's twenty- to thirty-year-olds are the first generation of Japanese to have been brought up in affluence, to have been spoiled rotten by their parents, and to have learned most of the things they know about life from the television screen. Their attitudes to spending, to borrowing, to saving, to leisure, and to work are different from those of their parents. Most of all, they just wanna have fun. In Japan, they are known as *shinjinrui*, which can roughly be translated as "new humans."

It is easy to be skeptical about this supposedly new breed. In Japan, problems and changes are often anguished about long before they occur, if they ever do; previous targets of exaggerated worrying have included juvenile delinquency, divorce, drugs, urban crime, laziness at work, and many others. Anyone going on a Sunday to Yoyogi Park in Tokyo, an ordinary, rather dull public park that is now virtually a tourist spot, will see young Japanese dancing in the street and dressed to the nines as punks, rock-and-rollers, or whatever. At first it seems funny; after a while it seems a sad, slightly pathetic sight. For these are not rebels or innovators; they are conformists, dancing in groups with a leader blowing his or her whistle. Their clothes are squeaky clean. They return happily to work or school on Monday. Tokyo even has a bar and motorcycle club called "The Health Angels." Its members drink orange juice.

Moreover, it has long been true that university students have a high old time in the four years between leaving high school and getting a job. After all, due to the fact that universities are relaxed, almost dozy places where students do little work because their entrance exam largely determines their job prospects, it is the only four years during which they will be out of the rat race. At school, they were cramming desperately for exams. However, once they swap their jeans for a blue suit or a drab office uniform and become a *shakaijin,* or member of society, they will revert to normality. Today's youngsters are not even as rebellious as their 1960s counterparts were. When American kids were protesting about Vietnam, so Japanese kids were rioting on the campuses of Tokyo and Waseda universities. Yet now that these rioters are forty, they are the bedrock of Japanese industry: Like their elders, they work hard, drink hard, and then work hard again the next day.

The term *shinjinrui* was invented in 1985 by a weekly magazine called the *Asahi Journal,* or so claims its editor-in-chief, Tetsuya Chikushi. It began in an article headlined *"Shinjinrui no Kishutachi,"* or, roughly, standard-bearers of a new breed. It was apparently meant as a double pun based on the different sets of Japanese characters that can make up the same sound: *shinjin-rui,* or new faces, and *shinjinrui,* or new human race. No matter, for the word entered the language, an achievement that normally delights a journalist. Chikushi, however, has written that he is furious about the word's popularity, for he does not think the new race is any different from the old. He argues that it shares the same basic values of being hard-working, apolitical, materialistic, and preferring jobs in large, stable companies.

He is right, at least with regard to the most exaggerated claims for the new breed. There has not been, nor is there likely to be, a social revolution. Japanese industry is not about to fall apart because of lazy workers. Young Japanese are more like their thirty-five-year-old compatriots than they are like British football hooligans, or coke-sniffing

37

yuppies, or West German bearded "greens," or inhabitants of the Bronx. They offer no real threat.

One man in his mid-thirties, who worked in a Japanese company with a very close friend of mine, perhaps typifies his countrymen's conservatism. The man, who shall be called Watanabe to protect his identity, had been working so hard that his boss harangued him to take a vacation. Watanabe protested that the firm could not spare him even for a week, but eventually relented, saying he would spend a few days at home. Sure enough, his senior needed to ask him something on the second day he was out and telephoned his home. Watanabe's wife answered, saying, with some puzzlement, that her husband was at work and that she was terribly sorry if he was a little late. The boss decided he had better leave his question till later. When Watanabe returned the following week, his senior collared him, demanding to know what he had been up to. Eventually, Watanabe confessed that he had been too scared to tell his wife that he was on vacation, and in any case, didn't really know how to spend his time. So he had put on his suit each morning and had left for work at the usual time, spending the day in a succession of cinemas, saunas, and bars.

There is clearly a long way to go. Yet that does not mean there are no generational changes. After all, most of the Americans who marched with Jane Fonda or frolicked at Monterey and Woodstock are now in their late thirties and early forties. They have respectable jobs and suburban homes and may even have voted for Ronald Reagan in 1980 or 1984. But that does not mean they have become identical to their parents. They buy different things, vacation in different places and in different ways, are likelier to be in debt, are likelier to buy Japanese cars, and so on. They still smoke a surreptitious joint or two of marijuana even if they have given up cigarettes and jog twice a day.

LIVING FOR THE PRESENT

A similar sort of incremental change is taking place in Japan. New values and desires are seeping in through the younger generation in ways that are relevant for patterns of consumption and savings and that reflect other changes taking place in the Japanese economy.

Some of this can be measured in figures. For instance, a basic Japanese value used to be that it was bad to borrow. Better to balance your books; better still to save. In 1983, there were only 40 million credit cards outstanding in Japan, or one for every three Japanese. By 1987 that had grown to 110 million, or nearly one each; that is well below buy-now-pay-later America and Britain but is roughly in line with West Germany and is still growing. Consumers have begun to borrow. In that same period, the amount of consumer credit outstanding rose by a third, from just below ¥30 billion in 1983 to more than ¥40 billion in 1987. Not all of this is due to the new breed; indeed, some is probably being borrowed by adults in their thirties and forties who rioted at Waseda University in the 1960s. Either way, behavior is changing. According to the Association of the Japanese Credit Industry, 75 percent of eighteen- to twenty-nine-year-olds use some form of credit compared with around 50 percent of fifty- to fifty-nine-year-olds.

Evidence on the younger generation's propensity to save is sketchy; it is quite normal for young people anywhere to save a small share of their income and only really to start saving when they reach their thirties. Nevertheless, when in 1985 Hakuhodo Institute of Life and Living, a research affiliate of Japan's second largest advertising agency, surveyed 1,600 young men and women between the ages of eighteen and twenty-three, it asked them about saving. Hakuhodo found that the young folk did indeed save; 30 percent of them put money away each month. They were not saving for things like mortgage payments (being too young), and they "have the least number of financial worries of any generation of Japanese in history." Instead, they save to buy particular things, such as motorbikes, windsurfing boards, or clothes, or to pay for an overseas trip. Every summer weekend, snazzily dressed Tokyo youths can be seen climbing on trains bound for the seaside resort of Kamakura, clutching windsurfing boards that fill up the carriage. In winter, the same youths are seen wheeling ski-bags about the stations, ready for a weekend's skiing in the Japan Alps. Their clothes and equipment are expensive. They want the best.

These young adults are dedicated followers of fashion. They buy stacks of weekly magazines—*non.no, an.an, Big Tomorrow, Popeye, Men's Club, Say*—to keep up with trends in clothing, music, grooming, interior decoration, and food. That is true of men as well as women.

Big Tomorrow, which, with sales of more than 500,000 a month, is one of Japan's best-sellers, has been likened to a textbook for the simple-minded. Most of its articles offer how-to guidance on all the important things of modern life, from careers and clothes to asking out a girl from the office and making love to her.

Thus informed, young adults queue outside designer boutiques in Tokyo's Harajuku district for the privilege of spending five hundred or a thousand dollars on the latest clothes. Tokyo is the trendsetter, but the signs can be seen in other Japanese cities, too. Young Tokyoites emphatically do not all look the same, unlike previous generations at work or play. There are distinct groups. The Hakuhodo study, for instance, has ten sketches of "types" and their clothes, based on different magazines and different designer shops. Beards and mustaches have sprouted on youthful faces, while they are rarely seen on men over thirty. The young want to look different, not to blend into a crowd. If they have to blend in, they want to choose their crowd carefully.

The young are free of some of the social prejudices of older Japanese. A good example, cited in the Hakuhodo study, was the *shochu* boom of 1985–1986. *Shochu,* a clear alcoholic drink a bit like vodka, had been thought of as a lower-class hooch. Suddenly it caught on among young Japanese partly because it was cheap (taxes on it were lower than for whiskey or sake) but partly also because it mixed well in cocktails. Sales of whiskey and sake slumped. *Chu-hi,* a canned *shochu* cocktail, was a huge success advertised by John Travolta. At the same time, it was also fashionable to drink other cocktails such as screwdrivers in "café-bars." According to Dentsu, Japan's largest advertising agency, young Japanese don't necessarily drink a lot, as they want to play sports the next day. The new breed is nothing if not trendy.

None of this would sound remarkable if it were about young people in America or Sweden or Spain. It is only so because of the static, one-dimensional view typically held about the Japanese. Will it really last? In its extreme forms, the answer is certainly no, as in the case of America's Woodstock generation. But something will stick. The pressure for conformity in large Japanese firms and government ministries is intense. Yet glimmers of movement are found even there: more pastel suits, a more adventurous taste in ties.

A NATION OF CONSUMERS

JOBS FOR THE BOYS

The readiest sign of change is in young people's attitudes to jobs. Compared with their parents, they are more willing to change jobs, to take risks. Employment agencies, for permanent as well as for temporary staff, have been one of Japan's fastest-growing businesses in recent years. Magazines have sprung up advertising jobs, such as *Travail* or *Beruf*. Recruit, an employment agency established by an entrepreneur, Hiromasa Ezoe, had a turnover in 1987 of ¥420 billion. Its star fell in 1988, but this had nothing to do with the employment business; the firm became embroiled in a stock-trading scandal when it was found that Ezoe had sold below-the-offering-price shares in a real-estate subsidiary to politicians and top bureaucrats shortly before the subsidiary went public. Recruit may fade, but job-hopping goes merrily on.

This is not to say that nobody wants to work for big, established, lifetime-employment firms anymore. They do, and competition for jobs at Mitsubishi Corporation or NEC remains stiff. But, bit by bit, more young Japanese are anxious to work for smaller, more creative compa nies, often in computer software, design, or fashion. Japan's economy, like other rich ones, is swinging away from manufacturing and toward services, so this is in tune with the times.

Recruit surveys new science and arts graduates annually to see which firms they most want to join. In the mid-1980s, Suntory, the Osaka-based whiskey and beer maker, jumped to the top of the arts graduates' list. Its weird, arty advertisements were winning awards, and it gained a reputation for valuing creativity among its staff. That also made it popular among women. By March 1987, it had slipped a bit to twenty-fourth place, replaced at the top by Japan's and the world's largest company, Nippon Telegraph and Telephone (NTT). But even that reflected change. In 1984, NTT had been in thirty-second place for arts graduates and fifteenth for scientists.

Once the government began to sell its stock in NTT in 1987, the firm became fashionable. Top for arts graduates, it was fifth among scientists in that year, significantly one notch behind IBM Japan, the highest-placed foreign firm in either list. DEC Japan, the subsidiary of a smaller American computer maker, has climbed too, from fifty-fourth in 1984 to thirty-second in 1987. Even foreign securities firms are

41

becoming able to hire good graduates; not the very best from Tokyo University, but good students from reputable places like Keio and Waseda. The Tokyo branch of Barclays de Zoete Wedd, a British investment bank, for instance, interviewed 120 graduate applicants in 1988 and appointed 26 of them. One of those dropped out before starting work in order to become a rock musician.

All this will take time to penetrate the layers of Japanese conformity. The change will be marginal rather than fundamental, but it will be genuine. It will not suddenly make the Japanese more like Americans, but it will make them less like earlier Japanese. Young and youngish Japanese are becoming more flexible, more fashion conscious, more willing to borrow and to spend, more individualistic. They are more likely to live on their own, to travel, and to come up with new ideas for their companies. Unlike many of their parents and most of their grandparents, they were not born on a farm.

THE OLDEST BREED OF ALL

Japan has moved so recently from the countryside into the town that it has not yet shaken off its rural origins. Farmers are protected and subsidized more generously than anywhere else in the industrialized world. Even the cities feel rural in places. Take a train through the suburbs of Tokyo or Osaka and you will see rice paddies, factories, and blocks of apartments side by side. In Tokyo alone, there are 125,000 "farmers."

Part of the reason is sentiment related to the novelty of urban life. That is not surprising or unique; even Britons, who moved off the land fifty to one hundred years ago, still romanticize farming and listen eagerly to "The Archers," a daily radio soap opera about country life. Another part of the reason comes from hard-nosed politics: The ruling Liberal Democratic party (LDP) gets a disproportionate amount of its votes and money from farmers. Moreover, farmers live in thinly populated constituencies where a vote counts for more than it does in the big cities. That is not just true of the LDP, either; the largest opposition group, the Japan Socialist party, is also heavily dependent on rural votes, so it has no incentive to push for electoral reform. Only the

Communists and the upstart centrist groups are properly urban parties. Finally, agricultural support is part of the social-welfare system because many farmers are in their fifties, sixties, and seventies. Some even return to the farm from industry when they retire. The over-sixty-fives is the only age group in which the number of full-time farmers is increasing.

Protection was begun in the 1940s to help ease the difficulties caused by urban migration. Like most protection schemes anywhere in the world, Japan's has lasted for longer than was necessary. Vested interests have built up. Protection is given partly through direct subsidies but mainly through import controls, guaranteed prices, and government handling of food distribution. Government agencies pay producers between six and ten times the world price for rice and sell it to consumers at between four and eight times the world price (the ranges are wide because the world price has fluctuated, unlike the government's generosity). Imports of rice are banned except in emergencies.

As a result, Japan not only grows its rice expensively in small plots but also produces too much in most years, which the taxpayer has to store. Protection also extends to foods that Japan barely produces. Japan imports about 90 percent of its wheat, but all is bought by a government agency and sold at high prices to support the few domestic producers and to restrict competition between bread and rice. Similar systems apply to beef, sugar, and dairy products, none of them exactly traditional Japanese foods. Such is the power of the farm lobby.

Yet even this is changing. In July 1987, an announcement was made that marked a watershed in Japanese politics. Typically for Japanese drama, it was hard to tell at the time just how important it was. The news was that the government had persuaded farmers to accept an almost 6 percent cut in the price of rice. This did not bring rice prices down to California levels, perhaps, but it was the first cut in the producer price in the forty years since the farm-support system was introduced. Excuses were made: the high yen had lowered input costs, the government needed to balance its books, rude foreigners were demanding that Japan reduce its protection for farmers.

The real reason was that the farm lobby's power is on the wane. At long last, the LDP has begun to realize that it must transform itself into something resembling an urban party. All those *shinjin* strutting around in Harajuku have no interest in wading up to their knees in mud. The less they pay for rice, the more they can spend on clothes and, perhaps, the likelier they are to vote for the LDP. This pressure is gentle and has taken a long time to force a change. But now that the dam has broken, policies could shift surprisingly quickly. In July 1988, the government cut the price of rice by a further 4.6 percent. This was deemed to be generous to farmers compared with the previous year's cut. In future, the Ministry of Agriculture will use a new formula for rice support that would link the purchase price to production costs. The price of rice will continue to fall.

Other straws are in the wind. The government has begun to criticize the eight thousand *nokyo,* or agricultural cooperatives, that handle some food distribution as well as the fertilizer and farm machinery trades. Their central bank, Norin Chukin, is the world's largest institutional investor. A report by the government's Management and Coordination Agency in June 1988 said that the cooperatives charge exorbitant amounts for fertilizers and tractors and spend too much time trying to be investors and financial advisors rather than dealing with farming questions. Such criticism is unheard of; the report was apparently ordered by Prime Minister Takeshita. This is surprising because his constituency is a rural one and his family brews sake, which is made out of rice. Despite that, out of political interest and, at last, a growing consensus that lower food prices might boost the domestic economy, the farmers' days really are coming to a close. The era of the consumer has begun.

A WOMAN'S PLACE

The era of the Japanese woman has not begun, however, even though in most families the wife holds the purse strings and is the main decision-maker about consumption. Women remain condemned to second-rate jobs, second-rate pay, and third-rate treatment by men and by male employers. Equality of opportunity at work does not exist in

America or Europe either, but the situation is even worse in Japan. Roughly, Japan is at least fifteen years behind America and ten to fifteen years behind Britain. Even so, things are slowly altering in ways that could affect consumption and savings.

Participation in the labor force by women has increased substantially since the 1950s, a fact disguised in overall statistics because women in farming households have tended to stop working. No wonder; cultivating rice is back-breaking work. Thus, taking all households, 56.9 percent of women aged twenty to sixty-four were in the labor force in 1965, almost exactly the same percentage as in 1980. Yet taking nonagricultural households alone, the percentages rose in that period from 47.7 percent to 53.2 percent. At the same time, a smaller proportion of women were working in family businesses or were self-employed, while the percentage of the female population that was in paid employment rose from 17 percent in 1965 to 30 percent by 1980. Women had moved out of the farm or family business and into the factory.

A graph of female labor force participation by age group is shaped like an *M*. The percentage working rises sharply (the first upward stroke of the *M*) between the ages of fifteen and twenty-five and then declines until the age of thirty-five. The stereotypical Japanese woman still marries by the time she is twenty-five and quits her job to have children. After ages thirty to thirty-five, the percentage rises again to a peak somewhere around forty-five years old before declining gradually into retirement. But by no means all women quit when they get married. Peak participation between ages twenty and twenty-five is over 70 percent, which, in 1986, fell to 50 percent between ages thirty and thirty-four. So despite the stereotype, only about a fifth of women quit when they marry or become pregnant. Some of the remaining 50 percent probably change jobs, often moving from full- to part-time work. The returnees between thirty-five and forty-five generally move into jobs inferior to those they left, often part-time and menial.

The *M* shape is seen in other industrial countries, but Japan's pattern is the most pronounced. It is getting shallower, however, as gradually fewer women quit work on marriage. In 1975 the trough was just above 40 percent, so it has risen by 10 percentage points in a decade.

That may be small comfort to the top female Tokyo University graduates who work for large companies and still have to make tea, wear
unflattering uniforms, and receive less pay than men, but it is evidence
of a shift, however gradual.

Opinion polls suggest that women feel that things are improving, even from a lamentable starting point. A survey by the prime
minister's office taken in March 1987 asked four thousand men and
women whether or not they thought job opportunities had increased
for women. As might be expected, more men than women thought
they had increased, but both percentages were high: 89.2 percent for
men and 86.9 percent for women. Women aged twenty to twenty-
nine had the rosiest female view, with 90.5 percent thinking that
things had improved. Admittedly, that question included no point or
date for comparison, so the answer probably had to be yes. A further
question asked, more specifically, whether or not the position of
women in the respondents' companies had risen in the past ten years.
Again men were more optimistic, with 62.2 percent feeling that it
had, against 54.3 percent of women. Again the twenty to twenty-nine
age group was the rosiest among women, with 57.2 percent feeling
things had improved.

One factor makes it surprising that change has come so slowly,
but nevertheless does suggest that things will continue to improve.
That factor is that younger women are better educated than their
elders. The static M graph conceals a dynamic trend, as the twenty-
to twenty-nine-year-olds in the work force now have spent longer in
school and university than did those now resuming work between the
ages of thirty-five and forty. Japanese families have long favored education, but only recently have parents been able to afford to indulge their
ambitions. As in most cultures, if one child has to be relatively neglected, it will tend to be the girl. The result of educational improvement and affluence, however, ought to be that today's twenty- to
twenty-nine-year-old women expect more from their work, are less
likely to quit on marriage, and expect a better job when they return.
Although education should be a force for change, it has been slower
than might be expected. In a 1985 study, two eminent labor economists,
Haruo Shimada and Yoshio Higuchi, wrote that

historical developments . . . do not seem, in the first instance, to conform with the logical sequence of events anticipated by human capital theory. For example . . . increased higher education among women does not seem to have triggered conspicuous improvements in female wages or the greater participation of educated women.

This has been a case where the resistance to change has proved strong. There is no sign of a women's movement. In the early 1970s, there was a short-lived one known as the Pink Panthers because its members wore pink helmets during protest marches. Nothing came of it. In 1986, parliament passed an equal opportunity law, but without sanctions for enforcement.

Gradually, however, as in America a few women have begun to gain sufficiently senior jobs to act as role models for the young. The most prominent is Takako Doi, who was elected leader of the Japan Socialist party in 1986, the first woman to hold a top party post. Others creep up in the same sort of ways and industries that they have in America or Britain: in advertising, publishing, financial services, or running their own businesses.

One striking example of an entrepreneur is Chiyono Terada, who runs an extremely lively and innovative removals firm called Arto Hikoshi Center. In the mid-1970s, the Terada family was running a small trucking firm near Osaka, but it ran into losses. Terada suggested to her husband (the boss) that they have a go at home furniture moving. Although skeptical, he agreed, on condition that she run and own the new firm. By the mid-1980s her company was many times larger and more successful than his trucking firm, and Toshio Terada was working for his wife. Chiyono Terada, who is in her early forties and drives a very smart BMW, had two main ingredients for success, which may help eliminate a stereotype or two about supposedly dull and stolid Japanese firms.

One ingredient was heavy advertising, exploiting the chance fact that the telephone number the firm had in 1976 began with the numbers 0123. Arto Hikoshi found the number very memorable to users, and so purchased two hundred numbers all over Japan that ended with 0123. Wherever it has an office its phone number is the local exchange plus 0123. Television and radio advertisements carry a jingle that runs something like this: "zero, *ichi, ni, san;* Arto Hikoshi Center." *Ichi, ni, san* mean one, two, three. The firm has even begun to buy up 0123 numbers across America to help it become international. Chiyono Terada's second ingredient is to provide a premium service, with lots of new ideas attached. As well as the usual packing and loading, her firm can send along help to clean up at both ends of a move (called "apron service"), and is starting to offer house repair, decorating, and furniture sales. Terada also bought three double-decker buses that she converted into "dream saloons"; the furniture travels on the lower deck while the family sits in luxury on the top deck, sipping cocktails or taking a shower.

Along with such role models as Chiyono Terada, pop stars offer some symbolic encouragement. In the early 1980s, the most popular young woman singer in Japan was Momoe Yamaguchi. When she married, she followed convention by quitting her career almost over-night. Her successor to stardom was a young lady called Seiko Matsuda, whose wedding in June 1985 received the sort of treatment from the Japanese media that in Britain is reserved for royalty. The major networks broadcast the whole ceremony and celebrations, which lasted more than five hours. Afterward, Matsuda was expected to quit. Yet she continued working, even when she had had a child. Young Japanese women talk of her approvingly.

Two other forces could help speed things along. One is the consumer boom, as women are the biggest spenders. Companies are gearing more of their marketing to affluent women than ever before; gradually, they have realized that this also implies having women working for them so that they meet the buyers' needs, perhaps as designers, engineers, or advisors. Single women are a huge and rich market because they still tend to live with their parents and so have plenty of spare cash to throw around, on clothes or overseas trips.

Curiously, though, relative poverty could produce a second, stronger force. Young married couples who do not own a home or have no chance of inheriting one cannot afford to have the wife give up working. Given the way that land prices have risen since 1985, if they are to have any hope of ever owning a home, or even renting a reasonable one, they must both continue to work. The property boom has created two new classes in Japan: the new rich, who have property, and the new poor, who do not. As society becomes less equal, however, something particularly odd is happening: The new poor and the new rich alike are turning into pleasure seekers.

CHAPTER THREE

円

A NATION OF PLEASURE SEEKERS

Conspicuous consumption of valuable goods is a means
of reputability to the gentleman of leisure.
—THORSTEIN VEBLEN

AS JAPAN WENT from strength to strength in the 1970s and 1980s, Americans and Europeans found a neat way to deprive the country of some of its glory. The trick was to say that Japan's industrial success is all very well, but the Japanese do not really enjoy it. They make money and conquer markets, yes, but they miss out on that vital Western luxury: quality of life. All that working, living in rabbit hutches, traveling in crowded trains, saving all the time, not having any parks, and not taking any vacations. It must be awful.

Sir Roy Denman crystallized this attitude in 1979, when, as the European Economic Community's director-general for external relations, he wrote in an internal report that Japan was "a country of workaholics" who live in "what westerners would regard as little more than rabbit hutches." This was more than just a provocative joke. Then and subsequently, the notion has been used as an argument in favor of protectionism and against trying to increase European and American competitiveness. The idea is that there is something unfair about the way the Japanese work and live, and that this something contributes to the country's trade surpluses. If only they would save less, work less hard, take more vacations, and spend more on themselves, then the current-account imbalances would go away.

On the face of it, it should be hard to square this dim view of life in Japan with the fact that the world is swarming with Japanese individuals and firms buying assets and pleasure—luxuries, apartments, yachts, buildings, bonds, paintings, hotel rooms. In short, many Japanese are now stinking rich. But the Japan-is-awful school has plenty of replies. One is that this is proof that everything costs too much at home; another more conspiratorial view is that things are kept unreachable at home precisely to enable Japan to buy up the world.

What puzzles Westerners most is why ordinary Japanese do not make a fuss about how horrid their lives are. Why do they not campaign for more public-works spending, for lower food prices, for more hypermarkets, for a simpler distribution system? For example, in *The New York Times* of November 27, 1988, James Fallows wrote of "the Japanese public's astonishing apathy about the system of organized extortion that is Japan's consumer economy."

FEELING THE QUALITY

So why don't the Japanese listen when we tell them to stop being unfair? There is no adequate answer to this question, beyond the cop-out of "because they are different" or the conspiracy theory of "because they are not allowed to." But wait a moment. Another possibility might be that both the question and its premise are wrong. What if life in Japan isn't so bad after all?

The problem with testing this idea is that there is no accepted definition or measure of "quality of life." Quality is in the eye of the beholder. That said, there are statistics aplenty about individual aspects of life in Japan, that can be compared with life in similar countries, for instance the four other richest industrial economies in the non-Communist world (the United States, West Germany, France, and Great Britain, known with Japan as the Group of Five, or G5).

Start with the bad news. Japan's amenities are relatively poor. In 1984, only 33 percent of the population lived in houses connected to a main sewer, compared with 91 percent in West Germany and 72 percent in the United States. This is not quite so bad as it sounds, for the other 67 percent of Japanese had a septic tank or some sort of mechanized daily collection of waste. This may sound sordid but in practice is not enough to trigger campaigns for more sewer systems. The country is not exactly noted for its typhoid or cholera, even though only 94 percent of Japanese houses were connected to running water supplies in 1983, compared with 98 percent or 99 percent in other rich countries.

Everybody knows, thanks to Sir Roy Denman, that these ill-equipped houses are as small as rabbit hutches. Well, actually that depends on what you compare them with. In the mid-1980s, the average dwelling in Japan had floor space of 870.8 square feet, which was far below America's average of about 1,450 square feet. That should be no surprise: America is a big country, with only 10 people per square mile compared with 125 in crowded Japan. However, Sir Roy is a European, where housing is not quite so spacious. The average dwelling in France had 920.3 square feet, while the West German average was 1,010. Is a difference, on average, of between 50 and 160 square feet enough to turn an apartment into a rabbit hutch? Or are French and West Germans carrot nibblers, too?

One reason that the myth of cramped, low-quality Japanese housing has persisted is that Japan tends to compare itself to America and tends to be most written about by American journalists. Europeans, with their smaller houses and flats, ought to be less critical. But another reason is that pundits tend not to compare like with like. Typically, they compare their own upper-middle-class accommodation in London, Paris, or New York with the worst of Japanese housing: the company dormitories, or *danchi,* and perhaps the cramped blocks of public housing. Those, however, need to be compared not with Kensington or the Upper West Side but with the slums of Liverpool or the ghettos of New York or Detroit. An important if impressionistic point is that the range of housing standards in Japan is narrower than in other G5 countries. Whoever heard of a Japanese inner-city problem? There is good and bad, but there is not appalling.

Both good and bad, however, cost money. Property prices roughly doubled in the capital city in 1985–87. Housing costs reach into millions of dollars. However, the notion that this is a terrible thing does not quite square with the fact that more than 60 percent of Japanese own their homes (the rate is 53 percent in Tokyo), which is not far short of the level in Mrs. Thatcher's home-owning democracy of Britain, for example. What that means is that many Japanese are now very, very rich, at least on paper. Such rich folk are not at all displeased at the rise in property prices.

One of the oddities, at least to an economist, of the high price of property in Tokyo is that it took a very long time to dissuade people from moving to the capital. The combined cities of Tokyo and Yokohama have been growing by an average of 2.3 percent a year since 1960, reaching by 1985 a population of 18.8 million. That is one reason why prices have risen, although they may subside now that Tokyo's population has begun to fall slightly for the first time this decade. Even so, the capital, for individuals as well as for companies, is still attractive even if it is crowded. It is the center of fashion, of culture, of political contacts, and of information. In Japan, you are nobody unless you know about Tokyo.

A COSTLY PLACE

Still, it cannot be denied that houses are expensive in Japan, as are many other things. Japanese incomes do not go so far as other people's in terms of what can be bought with them. One attempt to measure such domestic purchasing power, by Union Bank of Switzerland, showed that although average net hourly earnings are highest in Tokyo among the five cities covered (Tokyo, Paris, Frankfurt, New York, and London), a New Yorker can buy twice as much with his money as a Tokyo resident can; a Parisian can buy 35 percent more.

Another more ambitious and rigorous attempt has been made by the Organization for Economic Cooperation and Development (OECD). It tried to adjust rich countries' GNP per capita to take account of the different price levels in each country and hence purchasing power. In 1987, Japan overtook America's GNP per capita for the first time, reaching $19,450. But after the OECD's adjustment for purchasing power, the figure fell to $13,000, compared with $18,200 in America. On this adjusted measure, Japan was neck and neck with France, ahead of Britain, but behind the United States and West Germany.

That calculation provides some indication that, while Japan's economy has surged ahead, its population's buying power has lagged a bit. It cannot, however, be taken as gospel. The trouble is that even a comparison as impartial as the OECD's cannot be culturally neutral. The officials had to try to find a basket of goods and services that is internationally comparable. But it is impossible to find a "correct" basket because some nationalities like to buy one lot of things, some another. The reason may partly be price, but may substantially reflect cultural differences. The sort of things that a New Yorker buys, or an expatriate banker buys in Tokyo, will not be the same as an ordinary office worker buys in Osaka. The comparison may be valid for American expatriates resident in different countries, but not for locals. Where one eats steak and French fries, another prefers fish and noodles; where one likes to go hunting or fishing, another likes to sit up to his neck in a hot-spring bath. Try as it may, the international basket cannot avoid being biased, one way or the other. It can be no more than an imperfect indicator.

LESS MEAN STREETS

Many Japanese like to walk their dogs, or even cats. Unfortunately, it is hard to do either. Tokyo has fewer parks than big cities elsewhere, just 43 square feet per head of population compared with 320 in London or 130 in Paris. London and Paris are particularly green examples, but Tokyo is nevertheless a rather ungreen place. That said, it is worth noting that Tokyo's forty-three square feet per head are safer to walk across at night (or by day, for that matter) than is New York's Central Park or Hyde Park in London. A New Yorker may have much more public green space than a resident of Tokyo does, but when walking in it the New Yorker is also at least 6 times more likely to be murdered, 25 times more likely to be raped, and 140 times more likely to be robbed.

It is not that there is no crime; it is that there is far less crime and it is deterred by tight community policing. A robber is three times more likely to be caught in Japan than in America.

Perhaps the low crime rate has something to do with job security and family stability. There are poor people, unemployed, and homeless in Japan (you can see them on benches at Tokyo's main station, reading comic books), but the Japanese remain only half as likely as Americans to be unemployed and are only a third as likely to get divorced. Many Japanese women would like the divorce rate to be higher, helped by better alimony laws and an easier job market. Still, for better or for worse, family life is more stable. And Japanese are half as likely to have a car as are Americans, but they are also about half as likely to die in a road accident.

Thus protected, the Japanese live longer than anyone else. In 1987, life expectancy at birth reached 75.6 years for men and 81.4 for women, the highest in the world. That compares with, for men, 71.3 in America, 71.8 in Britain, and 71.5 in West Germany. Diet has a great deal to do with this. Although Japanese are getting heavier, and McDonald's is Japan's largest restaurant chain, Japanese still eat far fewer fat and dairy products than do Americans or British. As a result, only 45 Japanese per 100,000 died of heart disease in 1985 compared with 230 in America and 243 in Britain. In that year the Japanese, despite clouds of smoke in Tokyo restaurants and bullet-train carriages, were half as likely to die of lung cancer than Americans or British.

Longer life may also be less painful; there is very little arthritis in Japan, a big cause of suffering in Western old age. But they have their own deathly specialties. Japanese are particularly prone to strokes and to stomach cancer, both probably related to diet. They are also prone to suicide, although not to the extent that Western myth would have it. In 1985, their suicide rate of 19.6 per 100,000 was below France's (21.3) and only slightly ahead of West Germany's (18.6).

THE JAPANESE VIEW

How can these numbers be added up? They cannot; it all depends on what weight is given to the various sorts of statistics. Do you value living space or security? Health or purchasing power? Annual vacation time or the knowledge that your desk will be there when you return? Family stability or the ability to reach for your lawyer? Community stores or a discount supermarket? There is no universal answer. What can be said, however, is that there is at least a case for arguing that life in Japan is not so bad after all.

This may explain why the Japanese do not seem to worry about whether their lives are lousy. Japanese seem happy to be Japanese and do not want to be anything else—indeed, they have a superiority complex about foreign cultures that extends into the lives of ordinary folk. Moreover, they are conscious of how their lives have changed and improved. For instance, it is well known that workers have to commute a long way into work every day; what is less well known is that, even in Tokyo, the average time spent commuting is decreasing, albeit slowly. Average Tokyo commuting time peaked at a hundred minutes in 1975 and was down to eighty-nine minutes by 1985, according to surveys. Most obviously, Japanese are paid steadily higher salaries in real (inflation-adjusted) terms every year and need to save steadily less for retirement, sickness, and education.

Certainly, some Japanese live in cramped conditions. Young bachelor *sararimen,* in particular, sometimes live in small single rooms in company housing blocks, presumably the origin of Denman's hutches. But this is seen as a normal part of life and has scarcely ever been questioned, even by *shinjinrui,* the new humans. Indeed, some of the less attractive features of Japan, such as commuting and cramped housing, tend to stir a sort of pride in Japanese hearts, reaching back to the old virtues of endurance and stoicism. When I was trying to rent an apartment in Tokyo and dared to comment that one place's rooms were a trifle small, the property agent responded by stiffening his back, sniffing noisily, and saying, not a little curtly, that a Japanese family would consider the apartment amply spacious. But neither is stoicism altogether unreasonable, for if a long train ride is the price to be paid for low unemployment, job security, rising earnings, and the ability to walk Tokyo's streets at night, then perhaps it is worth it.

ENTER THE RISING YEN

Nevertheless, while life is getting better for the average Japanese, it is gradually becoming recognized that some things have prevented life from being even better than it is. One of these is the poor development of infrastructure, such as sewers and parks. The government's desire to boost the domestic economy since 1986 has persuaded it to spend more on public works, which is helping slowly to improve matters a little, although much more remains to be done. Another block has been the protection given to farming, which, in turn, led to unnecessarily high food prices. That, as chapter 2 argued, is changing too. The greatest restraint, though, was something outside the control or understanding of the ordinary citizen: the exchange rate of the yen.

When it took ¥240–260 to buy one dollar, as it did between 1983 and 1985, the earnings of an average Japanese did not go terribly far, even if they were going further every year. Luxury goods, many of which are imported, remained prohibitively expensive. Having fun can be costly in crowded Japan, so the natural alternative would be to fly somewhere else to play golf, swim, climb mountains, or look at old buildings. But the exchange rate made it even more expensive to do these things abroad than at home. Things had improved in October 1978, when the dollar fell to ¥175, but that did not last long. From then until 1985, the dollar climbed against the yen. So while the Japanese were getting richer in yen terms, their currency was making them poorer in international terms.

The abrupt movement in exchange rates since 1985 has reversed this. Instead of neutralizing gains in domestic affluence, as it did in 1980–1985, the yen has greatly reinforced them. While the Japanese have been getting rich, the yen has made them very much richer still. It did this in four main ways. First, as mentioned in chapter 2, by lowering the yen price of imports, it increased Japanese purchasing power. All sorts of imported goods became cheaper. Price inflation, except for housing and land, virtually disappeared. This also helped produce influence number two: By sucking in imports, the rising yen began to force changes in the labyrinthine distribution system that had also helped to keep prices high. It gave local firms a powerful interest in changing the way they obtained their supplies of goods or components, breaking the hold of some traditional (and costly) distribution channels.

Influence number three from the high yen was that it made overseas travel far cheaper, so Japanese became better able to fly abroad to find their fun. That, in turn, led to number four: By sending Japanese overseas with their pockets full of strong yen to buy all the goodies and pleasures they might want, it made it harder or less credible for Westerners to accuse Japan of feeling poor or of missing out on its wealth. How can the Japanese be both poor folk and moneybags buying up the world?

A YEN FOR TRAVEL

To outsiders, the most apparent recent change in wealth and behavior has been that Japanese are more visible abroad. In historic European towns and cities, in many Asian and Australian resorts, on the West Coast of the United States, the largest single national group of tourists, certainly measured by purchasing power, is now the Japanese. Few Britons or Americans have ever heard of Rothenburg Ob der Tauber, a pretty medieval walled city in Bavaria, let alone thought of visiting it. Go there, and it will seem as if there are more Japanese tourists than West German residents; walking in groups, taking photographs of each other, giggling, stuffing their suitcases full of souvenirs. Take another example: In 1988, Moscow's international airport opened a proper duty-free shop for the first time. All prices were in rubles with one exception: liquor prices were also marked in yen. Who cares about the dollar these days?

Russia does have a special reason to pander to its eastern neighbors. Many of the flights between Japan and Europe pass through Moscow, so their passengers are a captive market if they need to disembark for an hour, especially as Japan allows people to lug in three liters of spirits, duty free, and as those spirits can cost perhaps four times as much in Tokyo's shops. The Soviet Union has only just cottoned to this easy source of income, so it has only recently allowed more than a handful of flights to cross its territory. This reluctance didn't matter much. Japan has only just cottoned to the potential, too.

Tokyo's international airport at Narita, forty miles away from the city, is a nuisance. Transport to and from the airport is poor and slow, adding a good two hours and a lot of aggravation to any international journey. That is despite the much-vaunted Japanese efficiency and the world-beating Shinkansen bullet trains that since 1964 have been plying other railway routes. Underneath the terminal building is an empty station, originally planned for bullet trains but never used because the special express-train lines have never been built.

Moreover, visitors arriving at the airport could be forgiven for thinking they are really in Moscow or some war-torn Third World country because Narita is ringed by heavily armed and protected riot police. The risk is not of hijack or murderous terrorism, but of being pelted by tomatoes or, at worst, by harmless homemade firecrackers. Ever since it was built in 1975, Narita airport has been plagued by demonstrations by local farmers and a rent-a-mob of radicals protesting the alleged loss of traditional land rights. This delayed the opening of the airport and is now delaying construction of a second runway.

The reason for all this is that Narita is an example of a rare Japanese species: an official screwup. What seems odd about it, at first sight, is that Japan's apparently all-powerful bureaucracy has never tackled head-on the transport and protest problems of the airport. The problems have simply been allowed to drift on, even though infrastructure is surely an important part of any modern economy. But at second sight, this is not odd at all. The bureaucrats didn't have a reason to tackle Narita, and they never do anything without a reason. Few Japanese traveled abroad. Japan was not a country that depended on a flow of people or on quick personal communications to other countries, unlike, for example, Britain, Holland, or even West Germany. Japan was at the end of the Earth and was quite happy to stay there as long as it was running deficits on the current account of its balance of payments. Overseas travel by residents is a drain on the current account, if it exceeds domestic travel by foreigners. The fewer people who traveled abroad, the less Japan had to export in order to balance its books. As recently as 1978, rules limited who could travel and how often. So why bother about making Narita easier to use?

But now things have turned upside down. Overseas travel has become A Good Thing as far as economic planners are concerned. The more Japanese who travel abroad, the larger will be Japan's deficit on tourism spending and the smaller the surplus on the current account of Japan's irksome balance of payments. Such travel will be facilitated if people can get to Narita quickly and if there are plenty of airports elsewhere in Japan. Anyway, the surge of overseas travel since 1985 is good for some business interests, which in turn tends to build pressure for bureaucratic action. If travelers fly in Japanese-owned planes, more income is generated for the airlines, which are, in effect, the clients of Ministry of Transport bureaucrats. Booming travel also helped make shares in Japan Air Lines (JAL) worth more, which came in handy when, in December 1987, the government sold its 34.5 percent stake in the flag carrier. Overseas tourism, at last, was deemed something worth encouraging.

In 1985–1988 it needed little encouragement, however. In those years, the growth of overseas travel surprised even the tourism professionals. Akira Osawa, JAL's marketing director, says that in 1986, when the high yen started to boost tourism, his department forecast that the boom would not last long. The department was wrong. In 1985, 4.9 million Japanese traveled overseas; in 1986, that rose to 5.5 million, a 12 percent increase; in 1987, the number jumped to 6.8 million, a 24 percent rise; and in 1988 it rose a further 25 percent to 8.5 million. Since Japan is costly, crowded, and a long way from America or Europe, many fewer foreigners visit Japan: only 2.2 million in 1987. The strong yen makes that unlikely to grow by much, if at all. Not only is Japan too crowded; it is also too expensive.

According to Osawa, the growth in trips abroad by Japanese is more than what could have been stimulated purely by the stronger yen. He feels that something psychological has changed, too, to give travel an even bigger boost. To understand why, start with some statistics. Of all Japanese overseas passengers in 1987, 78 percent were tourists and 22 percent were businesspeople. While the business traffic grew by a solid 16 percent, tourist numbers went up a remarkable 28 percent to 5.6 million. Of those tourists, 55 percent were male and 45 percent female. The female travel habit has been growing faster than the male, revealing the increasing spending power of women: In 1987, foreign tourism by females grew by 34 percent, while that by males grew 24 percent.

The psychological point, in Osawa's view, is that Japanese

women, in particular, do not want to miss the boat—or, rather, the plane. They have begun to travel in order to keep up with the Joneses. It has become fashionable. This seems to be especially true among those Japanese who do not own land and cannot afford to buy any, although it is true for others, too. Moreover, a JAL survey of overseas travel in late 1987 showed how overseas travel had jumped to the top of wish-lists. The survey asked two questions: If you had ¥500,000 available, what would you spend it on? And second, if you had ¥1 million? To the first question, three groups—elderly men, elderly women, and young women—put overseas travel at the top of the list. To the second question, almost all said their priority would be to invest the money. The exception was young women, who said they would rather travel abroad.

Young females in their twenties are the largest category of Japanese tourists, making up 1 million of the 1987 trippers. But the fastest-growing and most interesting type in that year was women in their thirties and forties. Travel by this age and sex rose by 39 percent. Most of these women traveled with female friends and went on fairly short trips, especially to Hong Kong. They have the free time as they quit work when they married; now they have the money, too, to go abroad on shopping and sightseeing trips.

No wonder, then, that the total amount of spending by Japanese tourists in Hong Kong doubled in 1987, even though their number entering the colony rose by only 42 percent. These women are spending like there is no tomorrow. After all, handbags, luggage, designer clothes, shoes, jewelry, alcohol, and many other items cost far less in Hong Kong than in Tokyo. The flight is not cheap (a minimum of ¥65,000 round trip in 1988), but that is small compared with the savings on shopping. These days, there is a constant queue outside the Louis Vuitton shop in Hong Kong's Central District. There is an intriguing commercial reason for this. In the past, a common ploy for ordinary Japanese on vacation was to fly to Hokkaido, Japan's northern island, and bring back enough salmon to recoup the fare by selling it to the neighbors. Osawa says that Japanese are now doing this for their Hong Kong trips, too, bringing back fashionable goodies to sell to their friends. The entrepreneurial spirit is alive and well and taking a package tour to Hong Kong.

A NATION OF PLEASURE SEEKERS

ROOM FOR IMPROVEMENT

For all these impressive rates of growth, Japanese tourism is still small by international standards. The 8.4 million travelers in 1988 only represented 7 percent of the population; the absolute number is large because there are a lot of Japanese. This percentage compares with the roughly 10 percent of Americans who travel abroad each year and the 40 percent of Britons. So there is still plenty of room for growth.

In 1986, the Ministry of Transport set a target of 10 million overseas trips a year by 1991. But if the 1987–88 rates of growth are maintained, that figure would be nearly 15 million. The country's deficit on tourism spending rose by a half between 1986 and 1987, to $8.6 billion. Some of that was caused by movement in the exchange rate. If the deficit were to expand by a steadier 25 percent a year, in line with the growth in tourism, by 1991 it would reach $21 billion. That would equal a fifth of the 1987 trade surplus, which would be no mean contribution to the easing of international imbalances.

It would also suggest a huge market abroad for the Japanese transport, tourist, and hotel industries, which are the natural choice of Japanese travelers. The 20 million or more Americans traveling abroad each year, plus the strong dollar, made it natural that the big international hotel chains of the 1960s and 1970s had names like Sheraton, Holiday Inn, and Hyatt. These hotels could easily be filled by travel agents and tour groups back home. In the late 1980s and 1990s, these are being joined by such names as Tokyu, Prince (the Seibu group), and Otani.

The forecast above of 15 million travelers by 1991 is based on simple extrapolation of the 1987–88 growth rates, which is a dangerous way to prophesy. To increase credibility, it is necessary to look at the underlying forces for and against overseas travel. First, those against. Apart from unforeseen shocks in the economy or currency markets, two obstacles could hinder the growth of Japanese travel. One is a shortage of airports, the other a shortage of holidays. Of these, the lack of airports is likely to be the larger snag.

Thanks to the government's past reluctance to encourage travel, Japan's international airports are few and relatively primitive. Flights in to and out of Japan in 1988 were already crammed: The average occupancy rate was 70 percent, with 75 percent for Japan Air Lines, which is very high for an industry that lives by selling space and that prefers to keep some seats empty in order to remain flexible about bookings and flying weights. Narita has only one runway, and that is operating close to capacity. Plans to build another have been held up by protest groups; at best, it will not be completed until 1991. Another solution would be to expand the use and facilities of Haneda, Tokyo's domestic airport that is on the edge of Tokyo Bay, only a short trip from the city. That would require some tricky negotiations to determine which airlines would be allowed its use and gain the advantage of closeness to Tokyo. Since Narita opened, only Taiwan's China Airlines has used Haneda for international scheduled flights, to keep it separate from its mainland Chinese rival.

Tokyo's airports are the largest problem because the Tokyo area has had the fastest growth in numbers of travelers. Once Narita reaches its capacity, there will still be room to encourage growth in other areas of the country, where airports are less crowded. Tokyo tends always to lead Japanese fashions, so it would not be surprising if the travel bug caught on later in other big cities. If demand outstrips supply at Narita, Tokyo residents can be diverted to other airports; airlines will then have an interest in routing charter flights, say, through Fukuoka, Osaka, or Sapporo, connecting to Tokyo's Haneda by domestic flights. Japan's largest travel project is the construction of a new international airport on reclaimed land in Osaka Bay, to serve the Kansai region, although it will not open until 1993, at the earliest. Improvements are also planned for the airports at Hiroshima and Kita Kyushu. The result of all this is that the capacity constraint could prove to be a drag on growth, but not an insuperable one.

The lack of holidays sounds, at first, to be an even more difficult problem to overcome. The average Japanese gets only fifteen days of paid vacation each year and still takes only ten days of that, or 60 percent, such is the pressure to stay at work. This ten days compares with nearly twenty days taken each year in the United States, twenty-three in Britain, and thirty in West Germany. Only 30 percent of Japanese workers get a full two-day weekend, compared with virtually everyone in other wealthy countries. Most firms still expect to be open for business on at least one Saturday a month, usually two.

These differences are mitigated by the fact that Japan has many more national holidays than other countries, eighteen a year compared with nine in America, eight in Britain, and ten in West Germany. But that may not be much comfort if on these days it feels as if all the other 120 million Japanese are trying to travel on the same plane, train, or road. With these sorts of social barriers, it sounds next to impossible for Japan to spend very much more on travel without a revolution. Japanese, especially young ones, are gradually taking more of their vacation entitlement and are being given more. Yet that alone is too slow to provide much of a fillip for overseas travel.

This need not matter, however. The growth in 1987 and 1988 instead came from two other sources: travel by nonworkers, such as married women; and from people vacationing abroad instead of in Japan. Despite the short holidays, the domestic travel market is so big that there remains a huge potential for switching to foreign destinations. In 1986, more than 50 million people made domestic trips, an average of three times each. In the future, this second source promises to be the most important.

One large part of the domestic travel business is the company trip. Workers go off together for long weekends, often two or three times a year. Either they pay for it out of a levy on their salaries or the company foots the bill. Much drink is drunk, many songs are sung, team spirit is reinforced, and any infelicities are instantly and conveniently forgotten. In recent years, these trips have gradually become more adventurous and varied, with more sports and sightseeing and a bit less of sitting naked together in hot-spring baths and of pouring drinks for one another. The big advantage of these trips, however, has remained the same: They are tax deductible.

In 1987, for the first time, the Ministry of Finance extended this tax concession to company trips overseas, but for trips of a maximum of three days. That limits the potential, but according to Japan Travel Bureau, the country's largest travel agent, a few firms have begun to switch to overseas tours. The idea could easily catch on. A three-day trip really means they can only go to Hong Kong or South Korea, but the cost is still not much different from a long-distance domestic tour, and the novelty value is much greater. There are hopes that the ministry will soon extend the concession to longer overseas trips.

The chances are that the travel bug will keep on growing. Japanese have long had a phobia about the outside world and the dangers or embarrassments that it holds. Yet once the word gets around that abroad is really quite easy, fun, and, most important of all, cheap and uncrowded, there will be no stopping the tourists. They are already becoming more discriminating about where they go (Hawaii remains top, but Hong Kong, Korea, and Australia are catching up), although not yet about how much they spend.

Japan Travel Bureau, for instance, offers six different "brands" of trips to Europe, only one of which is a cut-price package. It admits it does not encourage people to take the cheapest trips; they have to ask for the brochure rather than finding it on display. Another of the brands is specially geared to the elderly, more conservative, and nervous traveler, offering transport on Japan Air Lines, a Japanese-speaking tour guide, and Japanese food throughout.

As tourism grows, so it will evolve. There are already signs that more Japanese will be taking independent, more adventurous trips and a smaller proportion will go on conventional package tours. Japan Air Lines says it is changing its marketing accordingly and is trying to develop new destinations to meet demand, including a resort in Indonesia and another in Saipan—all part of what JAL calls its "Pan-Pacific resort strategy." Much of this is aimed at the fashionable, sun-seeking young, the sort that can be seen, every summer weekend, windsurfing or sailing at the crowded resort of Kamakura, an hour outside Tokyo. JAL's Akira Osawa has a neat slogan for what he thinks Japanese, especially the young, want when they travel abroad. He calls it "the six esses": sports, shopping, sightseeing, sanitation, safety, and, last but not least, sex.

A YEN FOR IMPORTS

As all these Japanese travel abroad to buy their pleasures, might they change their minds about foreign goods and services? Might they stop thinking that "foreign" is a synonym for shoddy or disloyal and start to buy more manufactured imports? The answer is yes, but not only or mainly because travel makes them realize that they are being overcharged in Japan. A fashion for imports is catching hold for the same reason as the travel boom, but it is not yet caused by it.

The idea that Japanese do not buy foreign goods is in any case partly a myth and partly a misunderstanding. It is a myth because even in 1985, when its trade surplus was heading for the sky, Japan bought $118 billion worth of imports, about the same as Britain did. A lot of Japan's imports were in the form of oil and other raw materials, while only 30 percent was in manufactured goods. But even that was worth $36 billion, which, it hardly needs saying, is not "no foreign goods." In addition, many foreign multinationals sell goods in Japan that they make locally. Examples include Nestlé, Unilever, IBM Japan, Coca-Cola, Philips, Procter & Gamble, Texas Instruments, 3M, and many more.

When Japanese consumers are told that something is foreign-made, they might well turn up their noses at it. Ask them a straight question, and the reply will mostly be that Japanese is better. They also feel more than a little patriotic about buying goods made in Japan. But usually they cannot tell the difference between foreign and Japanese when they scan the supermarket shelves, and they do not take the trouble to find out, just as British consumers do not know that Kellogg's cornflakes are American.

Take the Japanese market for disposable diapers. The products have Western babies pictured on the boxes and have names like Moonies, Pampers, Merries, and Mamypoko, all written in English. Which one is foreign? Procter & Gamble developed this market from nothing in the early 1980s with its Pampers. Previously, Japanese mothers tended to use diapers made from old kimonos, or they used rental services, where local firms took diapers away and washed them. Gradually, Procter & Gamble persuaded enough Japanese mothers to use disposables and was at first relaxed when rivals entered the market because that promised to popularize disposable diapers even more.

But between 1983 and 1986, Procter & Gamble was nearly driven out by its local rivals, notably a small newcomer called Unicharm. At that time, it would have been easy to conclude that consumers were rejecting the foreign product, now that there were made-in-Japan equivalents. This conclusion would also have been wrong. Unicharm's technology was better (that is, the diapers were more absorbent and less leaky), and so was its advertising. Japanese mothers were acting like any foreign mother would: They wanted the best for their babies. Beginning in 1986, Procter & Gamble fought back with new technology and more attractive advertising that was more in tune with the local cutesy style rather than following a hard-sell American style. One popular ad even featured a "talking" diaper. Procter & Gamble won the market back, its share rising from around 5 percent to 30 percent and beyond.

Is there really any phobia about foreign goods? Certainly not, if you count goods made in Japan by subsidiaries of foreign firms, as well as imports. Kenichi Ohmae, managing director of McKinsey & Company's Tokyo office, added up the published sales of American-owned firms in Japan in 1984 and compared them with the sales of Japanese-owned firms in the United States. He found that the 300 largest American-owned firms in Japan had locally produced sales of $43.9 billion; Japanese-owned firms in the United States had locally produced sales of $12.8 billion. Even when imports were added, the result was that the "product penetration" of American firms in Japan was virtually identical to that of Japanese firms in America, both around $70 billion. This means that Japanese in fact buy more "American" goods per capita of population than Americans buy of "Japanese" goods. Ohmae's figures were a bit rough and ready and may have included some raw materials sales, but the point remains: Japanese are not allergic to foreign goods. Japan has a trade surplus, but that is a different thing.

The common misunderstanding about foreign goods derives from a confusion in Western minds between the desires and attitudes of individual Japanese consumers and those of commercial firms. Consumers have no clear prejudice against foreign goods. They want goods to be well made, familiar, and safe and to be advertised in a Japanese way rather than in an American one. They are no more biased against imports than Americans were ten years ago or Britons were twenty years ago. This will change gradually. Commercial firms, however, are a tougher problem.

It is mostly true that Japanese firms are reluctant to use foreign suppliers if they can avoid it. They want supplies to be reliable, and they want some control over quality and design. They want to minimize their inventory in order to save money. All this is naturally easier with a factory just down the road whose managers speak Japanese than with one halfway around the world that might be subject to dock and railway strikes. Furthermore, existing suppliers do their best to tie customers in by purchasing shares in their firms, lending them money, or by some other form of mutual backscratching. It takes more than a slightly cheaper price offered by a fly-by-night American company to break such local relationships.

Changes since 1985 have shown, however, that those local relationships can be broken. They are broken by a price that is much cheaper, and that looks to be cheaper permanently. The doubling in the yen's value against the dollar between February 1985 and mid-1988 sent Japanese manufacturers and distributors scuttling abroad looking for new suppliers of parts, components, and finished goods. If they could manage it, they persuaded a Japanese supplier to build a parts factory abroad as that would make them more confident about quality control. But usually that couldn't be done or would take too long. Imports soared, especially of manufactured goods. In 1987, Japan imported $128 billion worth; that total was depressed as oil imports fell in value with the oil price, but about 45 percent was manufactures. In 1988, more than half Japan's imports were manufactures, up from a third just three years earlier.

The consumer market for imports has changed, too. First, just as in the industrial market, the high yen forced switches of supply, chiefly to Japan's Asian neighbors and particularly in medium-tech goods. For example, in 1987 imports took 52 percent of Japan's calculator market compared with 12.9 percent in 1980; and 56 percent of the market for electric fans compared with 21.6 percent in 1980. In 1987, by volume, imports took 40 percent of the camera market, 60 percent of portable radios, 70 percent of tennis rackets, 40 percent of golf clubs, and 40 percent of textiles. Imports of color televisions rose from 25,000 units in 1986 to 370,000 in 1987; those of video recorders rose from 15,000 units to 138,000. Many of these items will have been looked down upon as made in Korea or Taiwan and hence inferior, but still people bought more and more of them. They would not have done so if they had just been 5 percent or 10 percent cheaper than Japanese products; at 40 percent cheaper they were irresistible.

In turn, that has led to a second change: Japanese retailers are beginning to dodge Japan's costly and inefficient distribution system by buying abroad directly. In 1988, imports accounted for about 13 percent of supermarket sales, up from 8.7 percent in 1985. Nomura Research Institute added up the share of direct imports (as opposed to those through wholesalers) in the total imports of eighteen large supermarket and department store chains. In 1987, direct imports made up 28 percent of their food and beverage imports; 35 percent of their textiles; and 24 percent of furniture, interior goods, and home appliances. Daiei, the country's largest supermarket chain, has been the most active on direct imports. For instance, it is buying color televisions and playback-only videos made by Samsung of South Korea and selling them under its own brand. Jusco, the fourth largest chain, is also buying Samsung products but is selling them under the Korean firm's name. Other chains are following suit.

This is important, but it should not be exaggerated. Japan's complicated distribution system is being forced to change, but it is not collapsing overnight. There are still far too many layers of wholesalers and other intermediaries, and too many small retailers. In particular, the share of total retail sales accounted for by supermarkets is restrained by Japan's Large-Scale Retailing Law, which limits the number and size of new stores in order to protect corner shops. Although a government committee was asked in 1988 to study whether this law should be eased or abolished, opposition to its end is fierce. Like farmers, small shops are a well-organized and powerful lobby group. Nevertheless, in time, some of this wind of competition will blow the way of the small shops.

The third way in which consumers' tastes for imports have changed is related to the conspicuous consumption outlined in the previous chapter. The strong yen, plus booming stock and property markets, have made many Japanese feel rich. That has led them to buy more luxury goods. Many, although by no means all, of these goods are foreign because that is what connotes prestige and also helps express individuality. The most apparent beneficiary has been BMW, whose sporty saloon cars have become a symbol of new wealth. Out of 100,-000 imported cars registered in Japan in 1987, BMW sold about 21,000, all at very fancy prices and profit margins. Its top-priced model was selling in 1988 at ¥13.58 million, or a little over $100,000.

Imports are still only 3 percent of Japan's car market (compared with 10 percent of Europe's and 30 percent of America's), but that does not mean that they are not profitable, especially at the luxury end. Moreover, BMW's sales in Japan should not be compared to Toyota's domestic market share but rather with BMW's penetration of a comparable foreign market. BMW sold 34,000 cars in the United States in the first six months of 1988, or about 70,000 a year. The firm's American sales were then suffering from the fallen dollar, just as its Japanese sales were benefiting partly from the risen yen. If the American trend were to continue and sales in Japan were to keep on growing, then by 1990 or so the firm's Japanese sales would equal half of its American sales. That would be a respectable proportion, given that the Japanese car market is a third the size of America's.

Other firms have also benefited from the same luxury trend. Neither Dunhill, with its men's clothes and accessories, nor de Beers with its diamonds, nor Cartier with its jewels, nor Sonia Rykiel with its dresses has been heard to complain that the Japanese will not buy foreign goods. Nor have they complained that Japanese society is becoming less equal, because that is exactly why they are making so much money.

THE NEW RICH

To an extent, virtually all Japanese feel richer, compared with how they felt in earlier times and compared with foreigners now. They are at last wealthy enough and confident enough to start enjoying themselves, helped by their mighty yen. Sure enough, they are having a ball: traveling abroad, eating in posh restaurants, dressing up, riding horses, playing pool, skiing, and windsurfing. Some, however, are now richer than others. A new inequality has arrived in the country, where 90 percent of the population say they are middle class.

That oft-quoted statistic relates to people's perceptions about their class rather than to any objective measures of it. Nevertheless, ever since defeat and land reform destroyed Japan's prewar aristocracy, the country has had one of the most equal distributions of income and wealth in the world. This is still true for income. The country's Gini coefficient, which measures how far the actual distribution of income diverges from a perfectly equal one, was 0.2 in 1987, compared with 0.4 in both Britain and the United States. But wealth is a different story.

The sudden increases in the price of land and stock between 1986 and 1988 created a new, asset-rich class. Judgments vary as to how large the class is. Nomura Research Institute defines the new rich as those with net assets of over ¥1 billion, or $8 million, and adds in the few that enjoy earned income of more than ¥32 million a year, or $250,000. It reckons there are about 200,000 of these "super rich." Japan's Institute for Consumer Economy Research sets its definition lower, at ¥100 million (about $800,000) in property assets, and calculated in January 1987 that 6 percent of Japan's households qualified. George Fields, chairman of ASI Market Research in Tokyo, thinks that 1987's land price increases may well have raised that number to 10 percent. That may sound small, but it implies that 2.2 million households containing more than 7 million people are newly rich. Theirs may be only paper wealth, but like any asset it can be used to generate income. Property owners can, for instance, sell their land to a bank in return for an annuity. Or land can be redeveloped as an apartment block and the owner live in the penthouse while selling or letting out the rest.

A professor of sociology at Keio University, Toshiaki Izeki, prefers to divide the new rich into types, rather than defining them crudely by assets. This helps to flesh out the picture of this new social development. Izeki identifies four groups of new rich, although he virtually excludes those who merely own and sit on property. First, he identifies a small number mainly of elderly people who used to own land in central Tokyo and have sold it and moved to the suburbs to live off the profit.

Second, there is a larger group of young and middle-aged people whose parents own property that the offspring will inherit. Such offspring generally live in rented apartments and either work in the services sector or own their own businesses. Their income is not high, but so confident are they of their future wealth that they have expensive tastes and a very high propensity to consume.

Izeki's third collection of rich folk owns their own businesses, usually in services that have benefited since 1985 from the consumer boom: restaurants, video rental, interior design, real-estate agencies, tourism, and others. They often run several small businesses at once. Their income has grown especially rapidly of late; not only has the domestic economy been expanding, but these entrepreneurs' firms also often own small buildings that have risen dramatically in value. Moreover, the stock market's climb has made their stockholdings in their own businesses worth much more, even if the firms are unlisted.

Finally, Izeki's fourth group is of what Americans call DINKs: couples who have a double income and no kids. With an average joint income of ¥15 million ($115,000), they are often professionals working as copywriters, designers, or architects. They are not interested in property, nor, often, can they afford it. They have quite a strong propensity to consume, want to live abroad, and want to enjoy themselves. All in all, Professor Izeki thinks his four groups could make up about 5 percent of the adult population.

The exact figure or precise definition does not really matter: There are suddenly a lot of rich Japanese. To a businessman, these new rich alone are a temptingly large market. More important still, by leading a fancier and more visibly opulent life, the new rich are setting an example to the millions who have only moderate wealth. The effect of their riches is trickling down, affecting what people spend, what they buy, and what they aspire to. The old, austere homogeneity of Japanese life is breaking down. Moreover, some of the new rich are reminding people what entrepreneurship can bring: Take a few risks, save less, and you too can end up owning a business worth billions of yen and driving a Mercedes. Or three.

To an economist, this arrival of a new class is important because it implies not only a change in consumption habits but also a widening of the gap between rich and poor. Gradually, Japan's egalitarian, meritocratic society has become less equal and less based purely on merit because of the high cost of education: The more you pay even for a kindergarten, the more likely your child is to get into the right schools and hence the best jobs. Those unlucky enough to be struggling to pay for housing will scarcely be able to afford the best education for their children as well.

This class of new poor does not, by and large, include today's elderly because so many of those scrimped and saved to buy property and are therefore now hugely rich. But Japan is aging fast, and the proportion of those over sixty-five is expected to peak in 2020, when today's thirty-year-olds retire. For those thirty-year-olds now among the new poor, what will life be like in retirement?

CHAPTER FOUR

円

A NATION OF PENSIONERS

Now this year goes away,
I've kept it hidden from my parents
that my hair is gray.

      —ETSUJIN (1656–1739)

Now this year goes away:
I've no parents left, from whom
to hide the gray.

      —SEIFU (D. 1814)

MANY OF THE changes that are taking place in Japan, its society, and its consumer market have risen very quickly indeed. Yet the most profound change of all has hardly begun. Despite that, it has been talked about in Japan for so long that it invites a yawn every time it is mentioned. The yawn-provoker is the graying of Japan, the country's transformation from enjoying one of the world's youngest populations to enduring one of the world's oldest. So far, this has involved all talk and no action. Just about the only thing that has happened is that in 1985 the Japanese government chose a new upbeat name for the over-sixties: *jitsunen,* which can be translated as the age of fruition, or harvest. Once there are a lot of over-sixties about, it will not do to be rude about them.

    The relative youth of Japan's population was a big advantage in the 1960s and 1970s compared with Western industrial countries.

Only between 5 percent and 8 percent of the population was over sixty-five, which meant that employees had to pay almost no pension contributions or social security taxes to support the elderly. Labor costs were competitive because the average age of the work force was low, which helped hold down average wages. This was reinforced by the strict pay-by-seniority system used in most Japanese companies. Youth was by no means the only or the main force behind the country's rise to economic prominence, but it was a big help. It still is. By the mid-1980s, the proportion of Japanese over sixty-five remained only a little over 10 percent of its population, one and a half percentage points behind the share in America and a full seven points behind the oldest of the industrialized countries, West Germany. That continued advantage is why graying has so far prompted only talk.

Nevertheless, Japan is destined to turn gray; all the talk about it is a typical Japanese example of good forward planning. Even Japan cannot dodge this development, short of an immediate and large rise in the country's birthrate, which would reverse the trend of virtually the whole of the postwar period. The writ of the Japanese bureaucracy can run a long way in Japan, but not that far. Assuming that present trends continue, Japan's population is due to age remorselessly and rapidly: According to the Economic Planning Agency's forecasts, in 1990, 12 percent will be over sixty-five, 14 percent in 1995, 16.2 percent in 2000, 18 percent in 2005, and 23.5 percent by the peak in 2020. Japan's percentage is expected to overtake America's by 1990 or 1991, and may even pass West Germany's around 2010. The outcome will not match these projections precisely, since birth and death rates fluctuate in mysterious ways, but the magnitude of this development is clear.

Japan's demography has changed for three main reasons, not all of them fully predicted. The birthrate has fallen sharply, as Japanese have become more affluent and less worried about producing children to look after them in their old age. That follows the pattern of other industrializing countries. The second force was also a familiar one: The death rate fell as health care improved and affluence permitted better sanitation and diet. The surprising thing was how far the death rate fell and how much longer Japanese life expectancy became than other countries'. A male Japanese born in 1947 might reasonably have expected (had he then been able to understand such things) a lifespan of fifty years; his twin sister could have expected almost fifty-four years. Both would have been wrong. By 1986, when they were thirty-nine, they could have expected to live for another thirty-seven and forty-two years, respectively. A newly born male in that year could expect a lifespan of seventy-five years, a female of nearly eighty-one years.

The average lifespan is still getting longer, having overtaken that in the United States in 1982. So in future not only will more Japanese be over sixty, more will also be over seventy and over eighty. The most obvious explanation for Japan's lead in longevity is a relatively healthy diet: As mentioned in chapter 2, Japanese still eat far fewer dairy products, meat, sugar, and fats than do Americans, even though their consumption of all these foods has increased. On average, a Japanese took in 2,600 calories a day in 1985 compared with an American's 3,650. The arrival of Big Macs and pizzas has doubtless worsened the diet of young Japanese, but not by enough, on present evidence, to narrow the health gap. The Japanese diet has even improved in one respect in recent years: Less salt is being consumed, which is reducing the number of deaths caused by strokes.

The third reason for demographic change is the one that will make Japan age especially rapidly around the turn of the century. After the war, Japan had a baby boom that was even more marked than that in the United States, just as health-care facilities were being put back into service and infant mortality was plunging. Figures for today's population demonstrate this clearly. In 1986, Japan had 8.4 million people between the ages of forty-five and forty-nine, in other words who had been born between 1937 and 1941. But it had 11.3 million between the ages of thirty-five and thirty-nine, who had therefore been born between 1947 and 1951. About 7 million of those were born in just two years. In the thirty to thirty-four age group, by contrast, there were only 8.6 million. The thirty-five to thirty-nine-year-old baby boomers will turn sixty between 2007 and 2011, adding a surge of pensioners. Most of these 11 million will probably still be collecting their pensions by 2030.

That seems a long way off. Nevertheless, the postwar baby boom is already producing some noticeable labor pains. This generation may be saving for its retirement, but what it most wants now is promotion into good, managerial jobs. But there are too few to go around. When

Japanese industry was expanding fast and the managerial generation was smaller, people could expect regular, predictable promotion. Those that did not quite make the grade in big firms could be found jobs in new, smaller subsidiaries. Now there are too few senior jobs and too many people to fill them. This is producing blockages to promotion as well as generating a surplus of failed managers. The numbers of the so-called *madogiwazoku,* the window-gazing tribe, have swelled, probably beyond the number of windows beside which they can while away their time; so too have the businesses of "outplacement" agencies, firms that help others get rid of excess staff. This is not a huge problem, but it can be awkward.

HARVEST TIME

Sitting by the window and reading comics every day may not be much fun in your forties, but at least it is better than the old rural way of dealing with surplus people. The poorest families could not afford to look after their elderly parents, so when an old woman had been widowed she often asked her sons to carry her into the mountains to die. She did not want to be a burden on them.

Today's urban Japanese do not dispose of their elderly parents in this way, but they are still likelier to be responsible for them than not. In 1985, nearly 65 percent of people over sixty-five were living with their children and, most probably, their grandchildren. That proportion has been declining, but only slowly. The ties holding together such three-generation households are less formal than in the traditional *ie* family system, which was dominant for hundreds of years until World War II. The *ie,* or house, was an extended family bound together both socially and legally, and in which the eldest son inherited leadership. It was assumed that after marriage he would live in the same house as his father. A family lacking a son could import one as a son-in-law, who would move in, take the family name, and eventually inherit.

The strict *ie* has disappeared. When the civil code was revised after World War II, the house was stripped of its legal status, and the emphasis was switched to the individual. Formally, families then became nuclear; instead of a "family register" certifying membership of the whole, extended group, a new register was set up for each marriage. This legal change in part accepted the inevitable result of rapid urbanization, since it was no longer feasible to keep families together in theory when part had, in practice, migrated in search of a livelihood. It also reflected a more equal role for women, since the new code gave wives a right to inherit. The arrangement of marriages could now be less for the sake of the house and more for the sake of the bride and groom.

However, Japanese families retain some of the informal obligations of the *ie* and have not entered the age of the nuclear family to the extent of American or British households. More often than not, newlyweds do leave home to set up their own home and family. Around 61 percent of households were nuclear families in 1985, rising from 57 percent in 1970. But a bride still has strong obligations to help with her mother-in-law's housework, for instance, a throwback to the time when the bride would have formally become part of her husband's *ie*. Eventually, one or both of the parents is likely to move in with their adult children or else the children will move in with their parents. By 1985, 15 percent of households had three generations living together, compared with 19.2 percent in 1970. Among other things, this means that, although living to a riper old age than Americans or Britons, Japanese are less likely to spend time in retirement communities or nursing homes.

One factor that is helping to keep families together in Tokyo is the price of land. When many of today's elderly moved into the cities, they were able to buy houses in prime, central locations at what now seem ultra-cheap prices. The rate of home ownership among heads of households of sixty-five or over is 75 percent, well above the national figure of 60 percent. Given that house prices in most parts of Tokyo doubled or trebled in the three years to 1988 and that prices in other large cities rose by 50 percent to 80 percent, this means that many of those retiring today are extremely wealthy. It also means that they generally live in a better place than their children, who, when they left to get married, could probably only afford a house an hour or more from the city center. So it can be quite convenient for the children to move back in with their elderly parents and rather handy when they inherit the property.

Although families still extend further than in other countries, life for the Japanese elderly is gradually changing. Wealth from property is making some retired couples independent by choice, at least as long as both are alive. Retirement may be the couple's first chance to enjoy themselves properly, so they want to spend at least some of their hard-earned and hard-saved cash on themselves, traveling at home or abroad and even, in a small but growing number of cases, buying vacation homes overseas. An opinion poll taken by the Ministry of Health and Welfare in 1987 suggested that, provided they are in good health, 75 percent of the elderly would prefer to live apart from their children. Once one of the pair dies, however, the widow or widower is likely to invite the children to move in.

Whether as couples or singles, old people who do live with their children are beginning to flout the *ie* tradition of living with their son and daughter-in-law and preferring instead to live with their daughter, if they have one. After all, it is the woman in a household who tends to look after its elderly members, so it is as natural in Japan as in the West for a parent to choose a nurse with whom he or she feels comfortable. Indeed, Asahi Chemical is offering new homes for multigenerational families in two different styles, called Duo and Duet, depending on whether the parents will be living with their son and daughter-in-law or with their daughter and son-in-law. In the case of the son and daughter-in-law, the houses are built to give the generations more privacy from each other, on the assumption that they are less likely to get on together.

In 1987, Hakuhodo Institute of Life and Living surveyed nearly 2,000 Japanese "seniors," as Hakuhodo called the elderly. One question sought to find out what old people do with their leisure time during retirement and what they would like to do with it in the future. The list of what the elderly do now for fun was fairly predictable, topped with reading, going to hot springs, trips in Japan, gardening bonsai, and shopping. The list of what they would like to do was very similar, with one notable exception: Of those over sixty, 24.7 percent of men and 16.4 percent of women said they would like to travel overseas, a source of fun that was not even in the top twenty of things that they do now.

This suggests two things: Elderly Japanese are feeling more adventurous, and they are feeling well-off. According to the government's 1985 *Annual Report of Family Income and Expenditure,* the elderly do have pretty respectable incomes during their retirement, leaving aside their property wealth. Those still working full or part time had an average annual income of ¥5.3 million ($40,000 at 1988 exchange rates); those not working had an income of ¥3.7 million ($28,000).

AN UNCERTAIN AGE

More Japanese continue to work after the mandatory retirement age than in any other of the seven largest industrialized countries. In fact, Japanese women lead the world with their labor participation rate in the over-fifty-five age group. In 1984, 62 percent of Japanese men over fifty-five were still working, compared with 40.4 percent in America, 48.4 percent in Canada, and 32.4 percent in West Germany. Nearly 30 percent of Japanese women over fifty-five were at work, compared with 21.2 percent in the United States, 20.2 percent in Canada, and 12 percent in West Germany. A quarter of Japan's over sixty-fives were still working (41 percent for men, 15.5 percent for women).

On the face of it, this looks like pretty good evidence in support of a common view: that Japan's social security and pension system is so rudimentary that not only must the Japanese spend their lives scrimping and saving for retirement, but in order to make ends meet they must also continue working when they are old. However, this conclusion may be premature.

One reason that more old Japanese work than anywhere else is that more of Japan's elderly are farmers. In 1980, 35 percent of workers aged sixty-five or older were in primary industries, mainly farming, compared to 11 percent for the total population. This is the residue of Japan's recent shift from country to city; the elderly are the ones left behind, and farmers do not usually have a retirement age. Others will have returned to their family farms after retiring from factory or office work, mainly in order to preserve their subsidies and tax breaks. It is not stretching cynicism too far to suggest that, for many of these, farming means little more than having their own vegetable garden.

So, taking account of that, are pensions as rudimentary as the myth would have it? The first difficulty in assessing whether or not Japanese pensions are inadequate is to determine who is compared with whom. If you compare the pension that today's average forty-year-old will receive when he retires with that for an equivalent American or West German, assuming all rules stay as they are now, then the entitlements turn out to be roughly the same. But if you compare what a Japanese who is now sixty can expect compared with the entitlement of an American or German equivalent, then the Japanese will be slightly worse off.

The reason for this discrepancy is not that Japan's pension system is rudimentary, but that it is relatively immature. Its model recipient is a worker who has contributed to the state pension fund for forty years. This model would be as well-off, roughly, as equivalents abroad. But since the bulk of the system began only in 1961, everyone retiring now falls short of the model target, even though the system offers several sorts of entitlement. Since 1986, when the system had its latest major revision, every employee has been entitled to two layers of pension: first, a national pension from the government that aims to provide a basic fixed-rate benefit; second, a corporate pension related to earnings. Those without a corporate pension plan, mainly the self-employed and the farmers, receive their whole pension from the state. To complicate matters further, employees in the public sector have different systems, run by mutual aid associations, that pay their entire pension. Such public-sector pensions are a jot more generous than everybody else's.

Nomura Research Institute has attempted to compare pension benefits received by retired couples in 1985 in Japan, the United States, West Germany, Britain, and Sweden. The Japanese, if the husband had been in a corporate pension plan, received ¥116,234 a month, compared with $697 in America. Converting all the results into dollars at 1985 exchange rates, Nomura found that compared with Japanese figures the American figure was 40 percent higher, Germany's was 26 percent lower, Britain's was 29 percent lower, and Sweden's 32 percent lower. But since 1985 marked the dollar's post–1971 peak against the yen and European currencies, this is unduly favorable to the United States. A similar comparison in 1988 would have placed America lower than everybody else.

Exchange rate movements and differences in the cost of living make the comparison rather misleading. A better yardstick is to express the sum as a percentage of average wages in manufacturing. On that measure, Nomura found that Japan's couple was at 38.8 percent, America's at 43 percent, Germany's at 38.2 percent, Britain's at 42.9 percent, and Sweden's at 36.1 percent. Such differences are not sufficient to describe Japanese pensions as inadequate. Moreover, if the Japanese couple had been paying in for the full forty years, they would have been receiving about ¥180,000 a month and would have scored higher as a percentage of average wages. Pensioners everywhere receive some benefits in kind, such as free medical care, cheaper bus passes, and so on, which further complicate the comparison. Such benefits do seem to be less comprehensive in Japan, but they do exist. In particular, pensioners pay only 5 percent of their medical bills.

PENSIONS AND SAVINGS

The maturing of Japan's pension system has important implications for the country's personal savings rate. Until now one of the main reasons for a high savings rate has been the immaturity of pensions; as that changes, so will this motive for saving. The effect seems to suffer from a time lag: Perceptions that pensions are rudimentary continue to affect savings behavior long after the system has become adequate. Nevertheless, in time, perceptions change. Japan's personal savings rate has fallen, albeit slowly. This will continue as the system's model recipients approach retirement. But that is not the end of the story. The urge to save for retirement and to continue working has been kept alive by another feature of the pension system: its uncertainty.

This uncertainty exists because a large part of the corporate pension arrives in the form of a lump sum at retirement, calculated on the basis of years of service and earnings. The sum can be very substantial: In 1985, the average male retiree who had twenty or more years of service received ¥12 million, or more than $90,000 at 1988 exchange rates. The sum is larger for a college graduate and for those retiring from big companies. But regardless of its size, a lump sum takes no account of how long the recipient is going to live. It might stretch far enough; it might not. So this uncertainty provides a powerful incentive to save, just in case you live to be a hundred.

Before 1960, virtually all firms paid their pensions as lump sums. Gradually, more and more have shifted to a monthly pension plan or to a blend of a lump sum and regular payments. By 1985, 71.8 percent of firms employing 1,000 workers or more used a blended scheme, 10.1 percent used only a pension plan, and 18.1 percent made only lump-sum payments. Small firms with between thirty and ninety-nine workers were still more likely to use a lump sum: Nearly 60 percent did this, compared with 13.3 percent using a plan and 27.8 percent using a blend of the two. Half of all employers still pay off their retiring workers with a lump sum.

It ought, on the face of it, to be in workers' interests to lobby their employers to switch from lump sums to pension plans since it would give them greater security. That would also bring down Japan's personal savings rate. The trouble is that lump-sum payments retain some advantages. They are taxed at an even lower rate than are regular pensions, and not all pension plans are index-linked to protect them against inflation. At least a lump sum can be invested in the hope of matching price rises with interest payments and capital growth. And in any case, not all pension plans are paid for life. Some last only ten years, about half the average life expectancy after retirement.

INTO THE TWENTY-FIRST CENTURY

Put crudely, the main worry about the future aging of Japan's population is that it might sap the will to work. Now that there are nearly seven people of working age for every one person over sixty-five, the elderly do not seem too much of a burden. When, in 2010, there are only three people between fifteen and sixty-four for every one over sixty-five, might things be different? Might Japan slow under the weight? Indeed, might Japan go bust trying to pay all those pensions?

The answer to the second question is certainly no, although only because the Ministry of Health and Welfare and the Ministry of Finance are planning together to ensure that there will be enough money. In March 1988, the two ministries made a fresh projection of how social security and medical expenses are likely to grow in the next quarter century. In 1985, Japan's total social security costs, including medical expenses, accounted for 14 percent of GNP. By 2010, assuming that nominal GNP grows by 4 percent a year, the ministries figure that social costs will have risen to 29 percent of GNP. If the economy grows more rapidly, by 5.5 percent in nominal terms, they think social costs will still have grown to 26 percent of GNP in 2010. As early as 2000, social costs will rise to 21.5 percent or 23 percent of GNP, depending on the GNP growth assumed. This is not merely pensions. The ministries figure that by 2010 the elderly will account for a little more than 40 percent of total medical costs, compared with a quarter in 1985.

Is this terribly high? International comparisons are tricky for these figures because different countries include different items under the heading of total social costs (unemployment pay? education?). In 1986, the International Monetary Fund made a comparison using standardized definitions of social costs in the seven largest industrialized countries. According to the IMF, Japan's all-in total as a percentage of GNP came in lowest in 1980 at 15.4 percent, behind 17.67 percent in the United States, 22.9 percent in Britain, and 31.08 percent in West Germany, which was the highest of the seven. But by 2010, the IMF forecast that Japan's percentage would rise to 25.86 percent and to 27.16 percent by 2025. By then it would have overtaken the United States (19.44 percent), Canada (20.69 percent), and Britain (26.52 percent). But it would still be well below France (35.07 percent), Italy (34.66 percent), and West Germany (38.77 percent). Japan will lose its advantage but will not be the most heavily burdened.

The burden that matters most for the economy's health is the level of tax payments and social security contributions by people still working, for it is mostly they who pay the bill. In 1985, pension premiums (counting employees' and employers' contributions) accounted for 12.4 percent of average pretax wages, excluding bonuses. By 2010, the ministries think they will have risen to 23.4 percent. They have set a maximum level of 28.9 percent for 2025 and are adjusting entitlements so that this does not have to be breached. This figure has been chosen because it is in line with the burden in recent years on West German workers and is therefore assumed to be tolerable. Given West

Germany's economic sloth in the 1980s, that may not be a terribly good omen. But at least West Germany's economy has been stable and has avoided the worst privations of unemployment and social disorder.

Pension funds should be able to meet this target, on current projections, because they are now building up a large surplus and because the ministries took a clever precautionary measure in 1986: They cut the state pension entitlements to those born after April 2, 1927. This did not cause a riot because the victims had not yet reached retirement age, so the ministries could not be accused of taking bread from the mouths of pensioners. It was also possible because it did not actually cut benefits in money terms, forcing tomorrow's pensioners to receive less than today's; instead it limited the extra amount that future pensioners could expect to receive by virtue of their longer period of contributions. So it could be presented as a restraint rather than as an outright cut. By rights, the victims ought to have had a case for suing the government for breach of contract. But Japanese are a docile lot.

Docile or not, in the future those of working age will be coughing up more and more of their pay to social security premiums to support pensioners and other nonworking social security recipients. The flip side of an aging population is that fewer workers are available to share burdens of direct taxation and social security contributions. Some economists, including those at the Bank of Japan, think this will dissuade the workers from saving. If you are paying only 12 percent of your pretax income as social security contributions, there is plenty of scope for saving. But if you are losing 25 percent or so, plus health insurance, which could double from the current 8 percent of pretax income, your behavior could change radically. There is a lot less spare cash with which to save voluntarily.

That disincentive on savings of taxation and social contributions is very hard to predict. What can be said with more confidence is that Japan's personal savings rate will be depressed after 1995 directly by the aging of its population. Everywhere, old people tend to be dissavers: They use the reserves they built up while at work, whether in private deposits or as pension contributions. The greater the number of old people, the greater the drain on savings. Together with any depressing effect on workers' savings, this will combine to cut the rate of personal savings well below the present level of 16 percent of disposable income. What cannot be predicted with confidence is how far the rate will fall. The Bank of Japan thinks it could fall as low as 8 percent. Other forecasts that will be cited in chapter 11 show that it could fall even lower, perhaps to as little as 3–5 percent. That is roughly America's level now.

By itself, that need not slow Japan down. All that can be said for sure is that if household savings do fall a long way, then Japan is likely to return to a deficit on the current account of its balance of payments as it will need to import capital. Another effect of an aging population could, in theory, be to raise unit labor costs, making industry less competitive. Older workers have to be paid more, especially if pay is according to seniority rather than to merit. But in practice, Japanese industry is too smart and adaptable to allow this to happen.

Firms have already anticipated the aging of their work forces by striking a clever deal: They have persuaded their workers to accept lower wages in their fifties and sixties in return for being allowed to retire later. Beginning in the late 1970s, large firms adjusted their wage structures so that the highest wages are now earned at around the age of forty-five rather than just before the former retirement age of fifty-five. In return, that age has often been extended to sixty. Although not true for all firms, the top age for earnings is gradually retreating, while the retirement age advances. By 1986, only 26.7 percent of firms had a retirement age of fifty-five compared with 47.3 percent in 1975. More than half of all firms retire their workers at sixty compared with only a third in 1975. The larger the firm, the more likely the workers are to retire at sixty.

This move is not simply farsightedness. Hit after 1978 by the second oil shock and then after 1985 by the rise of the yen, firms had to look for immediate ways to cut costs. This adjustment of the seniority system saved money straightaway. Another method has been to move, as far as possible, toward using part-time workers who can be eliminated easily and who do not need to be paid according to seniority. Both these ploys will come in handy as the twenty-first century approaches. Compared with today, by 2000 more Japanese workers will be paid by merit than by age, more will be part time, and more will retire at sixty-five.

THE SILVER MARKET

When they do retire, they will be the first group of Japanese old-age pensioners to be taken seriously by marketing folk. With a tenth of the population now over sixty-five, a few firms are already pushing their products at these aging rich. Once a fifth or a quarter are that old, they will be a very important market indeed, whether for clothes, houses, travel, or financial services.

A good sign of their appeal is that the mighty bureaucrats in the Ministry of International Trade and Industry are turning their attention to the old. In 1986, they came up with what looked like a brilliant scheme to ease simultaneously the problems of an aging society and the current-account surplus: send old people to live abroad and spend their savings over there. Called (for no apparent reason) the "Silver Columbia Plan," the idea was to develop retirement villages for Japanese in warm, inexpensive places, such as Australia, Spain, or Brazil. But the plan collapsed amid a storm of protest. The proposed foreign recipients of all these elderly Japanese did not take kindly to the idea of lots of pensioners being dumped on them—or rather their newspapers wrote rude xenophobic stories about it. The Ministry bureaucrats say that foreigners misunderstood the plan, thinking that Japan intended to send its sick and infirm. In fact, it was only going to send the healthy. That does not entirely make sense, for even healthy old people get sick eventually.

In fact there is nothing unusual about people living abroad when they retire. The Spanish coast is packed with retired Britons, but Spain does not protest terribly loudly. Nor should it, since they come laden with cash, as would the Japanese. So far elderly Japanese have generally proved too meek and conservative to become permanent expatriates, but that could change. The only real flaw in the Ministry's plan is that it was drawn up by bureaucrats. It is surely up to individual Japanese to choose whether or not they move abroad. Even the Japanese are not quite so malleable as are the companies with which the Ministry is more used to dealing.

Nevertheless, the Ministry issued a revived and revised plan in May 1988 with a report on "Extended Leisure Stays Abroad." This is a more sensible piece of research along classic Ministry lines: It provides an astonishing range of information to be distributed mainly to private firms that might be interested in developing foreign communities for elderly Japanese. The Ministry cannot force firms to do so, but it can make sure that they understand the opportunities. For example, the report includes a wealth of data on such things as prices, living conditions, and immigration rules in more than a dozen countries as diverse as Uruguay, Portugal, and Australia. Montevideo apparently has five Japanese and Chinese restaurants, and golf is cheap, but there are no Japanese-speaking doctors or nurses. In Hawaii, by contrast, there are plenty of Japanese-speaking doctors as well as good golf, but there is also some anti-Japanese sentiment caused by trade friction, Japanese purchases of real estate, and (unspecified in the report) "sporadic poor behavior" by Japanese tourists.

Almost certainly, more elderly Japanese will move abroad to places that are warmer and cheaper. Following the Ministry report, an affiliated agency called the Leisure Development Center began work on feasibility studies of community development with a hundred foreign and domestic companies. If there is money to be made (and there surely must be), something will come of it. Daiwa Securities, the country's second largest securities firm, has already led the way by building a retirement community for its own employees just outside Melbourne. Compared with prices in Japan, the land will have been dirt cheap.

Apart from travel, there will be mainly two other ways in which money can be made from the elderly: looking after their health and managing their money. Japan already accounts for 14 percent of the world's pharmaceutical drug market, compared with 22 percent in the United States. The supply of these and other health-care products will boom and become available in new sorts of places. About 5 percent of America's elderly live in nursing homes, while less than 1 percent of Japan's do. According to Dentsu, Japan's largest advertising agency, only 10,000 to 15,000 Japanese live in retirement and nursing homes now, but there are at least ten projects proceeding on the assumption that the number will increase. For example, Shimizu, a construction firm, has affiliated with Beverly Enterprises of America to design and build retirement colonies. Such accommodation is only for the wealthy: In existing retirement homes, it costs a husband and wife around

¥40 million to buy a lifetime right of residence, plus ¥300,000 per month for food and other living expenses.

The largest silver market of all is in financial services. Japanese banks and brokers are desperate to break into the management of corporate pension funds, which is now the preserve of trust banks and life insurance firms. The funds' assets outstanding are expected to grow by 20 percent a year to at least ¥60 trillion by 1995. Beyond that, there is the business of investing, trading, and simply securing the hoards of cash that Japanese take with them into retirement. Never mind the twenty-first century. Japan is already a nation of investors.

CHAPTER FIVE

円

A NATION OF INVESTORS

A stockbroker is somebody who takes your money and invests it until it's all gone.

—WOODY ALLEN

AS RECENTLY AS 1980, Japan's financial markets were a bore, for Japanese and foreigners alike. They were long on exotic names and bewildering regulations and short on business volume, innovation, and the freely flowing cash that lubricates markets elsewhere. To Western bankers or traders, Tokyo was well outside the first rank of international financial centers, and the Japanese were not thought of as a ready source of money for pet deals or projects. Far from it.

Japan was a place where things were made, while the finance to build and run the factories was under government control. In Asia, freewheeling Hong Kong seemed a better bet for financiers than Tokyo, unless you wanted to buy some Sony shares. And even that was easier in New York. Predictions that things might soon be very different (and there were a few bold souls who did predict this) seemed either heroic or lunatic.

Ordinary Japanese shared such weary skepticism too, about the service they received from their banks, stockbrokers, and insurance companies. Commercial banks, it is true, sent around door-to-door salespeople called *gaikoin* to be friendly and to drum up deposits, especially at bonus time. But the reward for handing over your money was no greater than being given a free packet of tissues, virtually no interest and lousy service.

The Ministry of Finance had strict rules to prevent nonprice competition among banks, so no fancy gifts could be given to make up for the fact that all banks offered the same interest rates. The Ministry could even regulate the quality of toilet paper used in banks. For retail customers, banks made it far from easy to get at or use their money. Typically, you would wait ages for service only to be told, when you finally reached the counter, that you had filled in the wrong form. Just about the only fun was in making up false names for tax-free accounts at the post office savings bank, in order to beat official limits on how much you could keep in *maruyu* tax-exempt accounts.

Some of this is still true. Nevertheless, an astonishing transformation has taken place in an astonishingly short period of time. Suddenly, the Japanese have become the world's largest and richest group of investors and—horror of horrors—speculators. Japanese financial institutions lead the world in almost every category: seven of the ten largest commercial banks, ranked by assets; the two top underwriters of Eurobonds; the four largest investment banks; some of the largest insurance companies. They now command the same mixture of fear, admiration, and hate as do Japanese car or video manufacturers.

Cocktail parties given by Japanese brokers and bankers in London and New York used to be minor affairs; now they are attended by the high and mighty paying homage to their wealthy hosts and admiring politely the ¥1 million ice statue that invariably adorns Japanese receptions. The Tokyo stock market overtook New York during 1987 in terms of market capitalization and by mid-1988 was nearly 50 percent larger. Nippon Telegraph and Telephone, its largest listed firm, has at times been worth more than all West Germany's stock markets combined.

It is not simply size and prominence that have changed. Tokyo has rid itself of much of its old reputation as a tightly regulated place with dull, slow-moving, parochial markets. Within the space sometimes of months, often of only a very few years, new markets have sprung into vigorous life. By 1987, Japanese government bond futures had become the world's most heavily traded financial futures contract, even though it only began in October 1985. Tokyo's foreign-exchange market has overtaken New York in terms of daily volume and is second only to London; as recently as 1983, it was tiny, cramped by rules forbidding forward trading. Yen bonds are a major part of the Euro-bond market, having been virtually nonexistent in early 1984.

These and other new markets have deprived bureaucrats of much of their old control. After 1945, this was mainly exerted over the price of money (i.e., interest rates) and its allocation, but that power also gave officials access to virtually the whole of business and financial life, whether serious or trivial. The remaining powers of Japan's Ministry of Finance are still greater than are those of similar departments in Britain, America, or West Germany, but the trend is firmly set toward freedom and a more open system. As might be expected, officials are fighting a rearguard action and are hanging on to whatever rules and powers they can. But it is a losing battle.

Life has changed for the ordinary Japanese depositor and investor, too. Banks' interest rates are still fixed and identical for small deposits, but they are allowed to offer a lot of new bells and whistles, as well as selling government bonds and lots of new sorts of investment-related accounts. The consumer has more choice; so to help influence him, banks bombard the public with ads for their accounts, which tend now to have names in English like "Big," "Wide," "Besto," or "Jumbo besto." Such names don't sound odd to Japanese, for English is often used in advertisements or brand names as a means of grabbing attention. Only in Japan would a gas company (Tokyo Gas) have as a slogan "My Life, My Gas." Only in Japan would there be a brand of condom called "Roni Wrinkle." Whatever the language, the story is the same: more competition, more freedom, more choice.

This has coincided with what Japanese newspapers have called, worriedly, "money fever": a rush to invest, to speculate, and, of course, to make money. A spate of new magazines and tipsheets has appeared, telling the ordinary Japanese how to do it, as well as, in a few cases, attempting to relieve him of his yen. Stockbrokers' retail branches have been crowded with budding money-makers. Housewives have become experts on buying gold or investing in bond futures. The riches made from stock or real estate investments have helped to create a new spirit of conspicuous consumption, discussed in chapters 2 and 3. Television programs have even been known to hold phone-in auctions of foreign penthouses and French châteaux, so abundant is the cash and so eager are ordinary Japanese to spend it.

Cultural commentators have, however, begun to wag fingers or poke fun at this. A film director, Juzo Itami, has been an especially active finger-wagger. In 1988, he produced a film called, in English, *A Tax-Collecting Woman (Marusa-no-onna)* about a female tax inspector in Tokyo chasing tax evaders. The subject sounds unlikely, but it enabled Itami to examine the world of the mom-and-pop store, the *pachinko* (pinball) parlor, the love hotel proprietor, the gangster, and even the member of parliament. All were trying to evade taxes. All such naughty rich drove foreign cars.

VIVE LA DIFFERENCE

The difference in Japanese finance in recent years can be summed up in one word: money. The overwhelming force for the sudden change, although not the only one, has been the arrival of Japan's huge surplus of capital. A large part of that surplus has flooded overseas into foreign instruments, such as U.S. Treasury bonds, Eurodollar notes, or Hawaiian property, through the willing intermediaries of Japanese financial institutions. But much of it has stayed at home, to alter the shape of financial markets, firms, and relationships. Its impact has everywhere been important.

In some areas, however, it could even prove damaging. When a vast quantity of money is looking for things to buy and invest in, the result, unless there is a correspondingly large or expanding supply of investable assets, is that prices rise. Demand rises faster than the supply of things to buy. This is what has happened in the Tokyo property and stock markets.

In both markets, a speculative bubble has developed, where people and institutions buy land, buildings, or stock well beyond what they believe is these objects' basic value. They buy because they have faith that prices will continue to rise, because so much money is around that other people can be depended upon to buy, too. Japan has little or no inflation in consumer prices or wages, but it has had a phenomenal inflation in financial assets.

A NATION OF INVESTORS

Will the markets crash? Nobody can be sure, but it is likely that a calamity will eventually occur. It need not be next week or next month or even next year, but it will come, in one form or another. The authorities will do what they can to avoid a collapse, but their power is far more limited than before. A crash could have dire consequences both for Japan and for the world. (There will be much more on that in chapter 6.)

Before assessing the present risk of Tokyo's financial markets, however, it is necessary to understand how they got there and what has changed on the way. It is a complicated tale, for which readers may have to engage in what my colleague Nicholas Colchester has called "mental four-wheel drive."

THE ROUTE TO FREEDOM

The shape of Japan's modern financial system was established during the American occupation in 1945–1950, as was the case for many of the country's institutions. Before the war, finance had been a pretty permissive business, with banks allowed to offer a wide range of financial services, from ordinary banking to stockbroking, and with speculative markets in fields such as commodities. Financial activity was of secondary importance to the large *zaibatsu*, industrial groups that formed the core of the economy. But that did not prevent financial booms and busts from occasionally getting in the way. Like America, Japan suffered from collapsing firms, scandals, and unstable markets. So under postwar American guidance and, in some cases, following an American blueprint, its new financial system became highly controlled.

Under Article 65 of a new postwar securities and exchange law, banking and stockbroking were separated just as they were in America's Glass-Steagall Act of 1933. Furthermore, banking was segmented into a number of safe and profitable niches: long-term loans to industry by "long-term credit banks," short-term finance and retail banking by "city banks," trust and custodial services by "trust banks," local retail and corporate banking by "regional banks," and foreign exchange by the Bank of Tokyo. The overall aim was to make finance the servant of industry, rather than the reverse.

The system's spirit, moreover, was crucially different from that in the United States: In America, by and large, firms and markets could do something unless they were specifically prohibited from doing it; in Japan, financial firms could do only those things that they were specifically permitted to do. In virtually every case, innovations had to wait for official approval.

Interest rates for deposits, whether by ordinary folk or by large corporations, were determined by the authorities, who also guided lending rates. Short-term money markets scarcely existed, nor was there much of a market for government bonds, as the government took care to avoid getting into debt. Speculative markets, such as those in futures, were either banned or shackled. In the 1950s and 1960s, Japan generally suffered deficits on its overseas current account and had to import capital, so foreign-exchange controls were maintained and capital flows were regulated. This apparatus enabled the Bank of Japan to run its monetary policy principally by determining the amount of credit available to the various sorts of banks. This type of direct influence on the supply of money, if it is possible, is far easier to operate than using interest rates, which is the chief method available in a free market.

By and large, all this worked. Free-market purists might allege that Japan would have grown even faster or become even stronger had it used free financial markets from the start, but there is no way to test this claim. The only available measure is Japan's economic "miracle" in the 1950s and 1960s. Tight financial control certainly did not prevent that from taking place. Probably it helped, by assuring the users of finance—industrial companies—of its stable, reliable supply, generally at low cost. In those cases where bureaucrats were managing the development of an industry, they had the power to ensure that cheap money would be on tap.

MONEY TALKS

Such a regimented system could not last indefinitely. Indeed, it may be argued that the system's very success in developing a strong economy guaranteed its demise by producing current-account surpluses and thus surpluses of capital. Crudely, when there is a surplus of cash, the holders of it begin to get choosier about where they want to put it and what returns they wish to earn; the force of the market begins to question the rules and compartments established by law.

Similarly, once capital is no longer scarce, borrowers become less beholden to lenders and start to look around for alternative sources of finance. The economy's success also meant that foreign investors and financial institutions wanted access to Japanese securities and sources of funds. Since Japanese banks wanted to expand overseas to serve their country's exporters, the government had an interest in keeping foreign authorities happy by allowing outsiders in.

These pressures made reform inevitable. But they did not determine its speed, timing, or extent. In all financial markets, vested interests in the status quo mean that pressure must usually become intense before change can be enforced. Laws lag behind events. Take the United States, for instance. It took rapid inflation in the late 1970s and early 1980s finally to get rid of America's Regulation Q, the ceiling on bank deposit rates, because it created a huge gap between free-market interest rates and the regulated rates offered by banks. That gap gave competing financial firms an opportunity to offer quasi-deposits based on money-market rates (so-called money-market funds); it gave individuals sufficient incentive to shift their money out of federally insured deposits into these new instruments; and it made it hard for regulators or legislators to oppose reform, since inflation was devaluing the savings of millions of ordinary people. America still has its Glass-Steagall Act, however, as well as federal interstate banking laws that are only now being eroded by court decisions and state laws. Vested interests have obstructed faster progress.

Except for a very brief period in 1974–75, Japan did not face such an inflationary pressure. There has long been a slow, general push for reform from the middle-aging of Japan, the demographic trend discussed in chapter 4. The over-forties are the most diligent savers in Japan as in most countries; by 1990, nearly half the population will be over forty, compared with 35 percent in 1975. Reared on low, fixed-interest savings accounts, these supersavers are becoming more worried about how much they earn from their savings and hence more interested in circumventing artificially low interest rates. Given the chance, they would move their money around and indeed have, whenever the chance has arisen. But on its own, this push has proved too weak or diffuse to force change. Japan still has its version of Regulation Q.

The earliest signs of reform came in 1970–72, when for the first time Japan seemed to be building up a large and durable current-account surplus. The government relaxed restrictions on the outflow of capital and began to talk about a more liberal approach at home. Foreign institutions were permitted to issue bonds in Japan to tap local capital, the first coming in December 1970 from the Asian Development-ment Bank. In 1972, Japanese residents were allowed to buy foreign securities. But such freedom proved to be short-lived. The 1973 oil shock sent Japan sharply back into deficit, so restrictions were tightened again.

Nevertheless, it was the oil-price rise that started the ball of liberalization rolling, albeit indirectly. Slower growth and efforts to spend a bit more on social security sent the government budget into a big deficit after 1975. This deficit was further expanded in a bid to stimulate the economy using fiscal policy. The widening deficit necessitated a rapid increase in the issue of government bonds, which meant that officials had an interest in finding buyers for them and, most important, in making them a more attractive investment. The most important reform in this area came in 1977, when financial institutions were allowed to sell government bonds before they matured. Previously, they had simply bought and hung on to them or had sold them to the Bank of Japan. As long as the banks did not have many bonds in their portfolio, they did not mind this lack of liquidity. But once the supply of bonds rose, the banks would have rebelled against holding them had it not been for rule changes.

One change led to another, as tends to be the case in financial markets. Governments cannot easily contain change or prevent snow-balling effects. Once a large secondary market in long-term securities (government bonds) had developed, investing institutions also wanted a larger and freer short-term money market in order to diversify their holdings and to ensure that they could raise money quickly. So the Bank of Japan eased its control of interest rates in the call money (very short-term cash) and bill discount markets, and allowed banks to issue yen certificates of deposit. On the back of the government bond market grew a market for *gensaki*, similar to bond repurchase agreements or repos in the United States. This market had existed since 1949 but had remained tiny. For a *gensaki* deal, an institutional holder of a government bond sells it to another institution, with an agreement that it will buy the bond back on a specified future date, always less than one year.

This market thus allows institutions to borrow short-term money against their long-term bond holdings. More important still, they can invest that money in other short-term securities if the interest rates available are higher, or vice versa. Such arbitrage opportunities forced interest rates to move freely in associated markets; if the Bank of Japan tried to hold rates in one market artificially low, institutions could (and did) simply move their money elsewhere.

Having adjusted to the oil shock, Japan was soon rebuilding current-account surpluses. So in 1980 a revised Foreign Exchange and Foreign Trade Law suspended most foreign-exchange controls, allowing capital to flow freely in and out of Japan. To put that into international perspective, it should be noted that even Britain did not rid itself of exchange controls until 1979. In Britain's case, however, a free financial market had developed despite exchange controls, although the controls had made it distorted. Similarly, Japan's removal of exchange controls could not, of itself, ensure a free and open market, but it made one more likely to develop. It meant that big institutions could invest abroad if they did not like the opportunities at home. It also meant that Japanese interest rates could no longer be insulated from international influences. It even meant, eventually, that Japanese companies would be able to borrow by issuing bonds abroad that would eventually be bought by Japanese investors, circumventing domestic controls.

Before all that happened, the government was still working out the ramifications of its borrowing binge of the 1970s. The largest buyers of government bonds, the commercial banks, demanded the right to sell them to as wide a range of customers as possible. In 1981, the banking act and the securities and exchange laws were revised to allow banks to sell bonds to the public and to deal in them, which they began to do in 1984. This enraged the securities firms, which, having had a monopoly on all bond trading, argued that this should extend to government bonds. As a quid pro quo, therefore, they were allowed to develop funds based on medium-term government bonds for sale in small units to the public rather like savings accounts. These funds became Japan's equivalent of America's money-market funds, investment-linked instruments that competed with ordinary bank deposits. As a result, by 1984 the barrier between banking and brokering, laid down in Article 65, was being eroded from both sides: Banks were trading in an important securities market; stockbrokers were competing for personal deposits.

FOREIGN PRESSURE

Until 1983, these reforms and developments were occurring steadily but without generating much publicity or international attention. Meanwhile, headlines were being grabbed by two other things: America's growing trade deficit, especially with Japan; and the gravity-defying strength of the dollar against all currencies, but particularly the yen. At this time, the Reagan administration was committed to a free-market ideology that said it should not interfere with the dollar's value. This had a surprising effect on the development of Japan's financial system.

American policy in the foreign-exchange markets was one of "benign neglect"; to those who criticized the dollar's strength, President Reagan and the then Secretary of the Treasury Donald Regan were inclined to say either that it was proof of foreigners' confidence in the U.S. economy or, in an extraordinary feat of logic, that the problem was that other currencies were too weak, not that the dollar was too strong. American industry, however, knew an uncompetitive exchange rate when it saw one and lobbied for something to be done. One firm at the head of the lobby was Caterpillar Tractor, which was fast losing markets in earth-moving equipment to Komatsu, a Japanese firm. Caterpillar and others revived an old allegation that Japan deliberately keeps the yen weak in order to boost its exports. Ergo, if the yen would only get stronger, America would not have its trade deficit.

If there were any truth to the allegation of yen-rigging, Japan's only means had to be its remaining controls on interest rates, markets, and the international use of the yen. That judgment was supported by the administration's free-market ideology, so in November 1983 the U.S. Treasury launched an attack against Japanese financial regulation, arguing that the country had to give itself a free and open market in order for the yen to find its true value internationally. This was where changes were deemed necessary in order to rectify the trade imbalance—rather than in American economic policy.

A secondary target of this attack was to gain better access to Japan's financial markets for foreign banks and securities dealers. Foreign commercial banks had rushed to Japan in the 1960s and 1970s in order to lend money to the growing economy. They were prevented from offering direct competition to local firms by, for instance, restrictions on the number of branches they could open, which forced them to raise yen from the money markets rather than from cheap deposits. But they were made profitable by being given an exclusive right to make foreign-currency loans to Japanese industry, known as "impact" loans because of their favorable impact on Japan's balance of payments. That right disappeared in 1980, when exchange controls were suspended, and Japanese banks swamped the impact market. This left foreign banks not only with a tiny share of the loans market—by 1983 the 103 foreign bank branches in Japan had less than 3.5 percent of loans and 1 percent of deposits—but also an increasingly unprofitable one.

Foreigners wanted new sources of profit. Despite being expert managers of money in London or New York, they, like Japanese city banks, were barred in Japan from trust banking and from managing pension funds. Investment banks and securities subsidiaries of foreign commercial banks wanted to deal in and underwrite Japanese securities. Only a handful had licenses for this and none had a seat on the Tokyo stock exchange. (This is less outrageous than it sounds: No foreign firm was then a member of the London stock exchange either.) To an extent, they wanted doors to be opened to them alone, but largely they wanted open markets to be allowed to develop in which they felt they might do well. Their foreign-exchange trading skills, for instance, were barely exploitable in Tokyo's stunted currency market.

So the U.S. Treasury rode into battle on the side of free markets, the dollar, and foreign firms, and against Japan's Ministry of Finance. Occasionally, talks between American and Japanese officials became fraught: "I keep hearing words but I don't see action," fumed Regan after one particularly unconstructive meeting. Nevertheless, after six months of intense negotiations, a truce was called. In May 1984, the two sides signed what subsequently became known as the yen-dollar agreement, in which Japan spelled out a program for financial reform.

This deal was hailed as a breakthrough for the American side in opening up the Japanese market. Naturally, American officials had to please the public back home. Indeed, Japan's most specific commitments were to improve access for overseas firms, notably to permit foreign banks to deal in government bonds and to enter the trust banking business. It also agreed to set up a market for bankers' acceptances (short-term IOUs) and to remove controls on foreign-exchange trading, which might thus liberate the yen. It also laid down a vague plan for the future liberalization of bank deposit interest rates.

What turned out to be the most important element was also the one that attracted the most skepticism: easier rules for Japanese and foreign companies to issue yen bonds in the Euromarkets. This was important to the Americans' purpose since it promised to widen the range of yen instruments available to international investors, thus in theory making the yen a more attractive currency. But the Ministry of Finance's insistence on retaining a withholding tax on nonresident earnings from these bonds appeared to ensure that the market would remain unattractive. The Japanese, it seemed, had done it again: made concessions on paper that in reality would mean little or nothing.

This interpretation proved to be wrong, but for a significant reason. It is usually bad policy to accept the official interpretation of any deal with Japan; the Japanese are perfectly happy to allow foreigners to make claims in public that do not correspond with what is actually going to happen. Foreign pressure was a red herring amid Japan's independent transformation into a nation of investors and financiers.

Apart from the improved access for overseas firms, the Ministry of Finance did not make reforms simply because a foreign government had asked it to. It made reforms because pressure was building up in the Japanese market itself, in the form of the capital surplus. It also made reforms because it realized that Japan's financial system was fit more for the economy of the 1950s than for that of the 1980s. Cash no longer had to be channeled because it was no longer scarce. For the 1980s, what had to be ensured was that industry's cost of capital was the lowest possible, and as a result, a new industry grew in Japan: the financial services sector. This realization did not come in a flash of

brilliance; it seems to have dawned gradually on more and more top
officials at the Ministry.

Foreign pressure was useful in this exercise because it could be
exploited to circumvent domestic opposition to reform: It was an excuse
rather than a decisive force. It may have meant that some changes were
made earlier than they otherwise would have been, but even that is by
no means clear. The domestic imperative was so strong that, one way
or another, change would have occurred.

DAMS AND RIVERS

The results were rapid and dramatic. Huge new markets developed in
foreign exchange, bond futures, swaps, offshore banking, and Euroyen
bonds. Foreign firms rushed to set up shop in Tokyo; before 1983,
American investment banks as famous as Salomon Brothers, Morgan
Stanley, and Goldman Sachs had had no offices there. At best, they had
covered Japan from Hong Kong. Japanese banks and brokers moved
hell for leather into new businesses. Almost from a standing start,
Tokyo suddenly emerged as one of the world's three top-rank international financial centers, along with New York and London.

This does not mean, however, that the old system has been demol-
ished and a completely new, liberal one put into place. Far from it. The
forces opposing change have proved to be as strong in some areas as
those pushing for change. There are areas of progress and areas of
resistance. The pace of reform has often been spectacular, but it has not
been even. It is rather like a dam bursting or a river overflowing its
banks; nothing happens for a long time, but when the dam breaks or
the banks are overcome, water suddenly floods everywhere, and the
landscape is transformed almost instantly.

Water is a good image for money because capital, like water, finds
its own level by swiftly seeking out new opportunities. A financial
system is like an entire river system with many dams, many riverbanks,
and many channels. Money circulates through the complex system in
a constant flow. What has happened in Japan is that some dams have
burst, enforcing radical change. But some have managed to resist the
flow or have diverted it elsewhere.

The reason for this complexity lies less in the structure of finance than in the way in which power is distributed. The postwar financial establishment in Japan gave different privileges, rights, and obligations to the various sorts of institutions—securities houses, trust banks, long-term credit banks, city banks, life insurance firms, the postal savings bank, and so on. Reforms to the system inevitably involve depriving one set of institutions of some or all of its privileges or of forcing it to share them with others. If a new business is developing, institutions will battle for exclusive rights to it, usually by arguing that it somehow fits within the definition of its existing businesses. One way around this is to change the rules sufficiently slowly to permit all those affected to adjust to them. Another is not to make changes at all.

In theory, this difficulty ought to be resolved by the authorities, namely, the Ministry of Finance and, ultimately, the government. Unfortunately, Japan does not quite work like that. The Ministry is constructed to reflect the division of powers and interests among financial institutions. There is a banking bureau and a securities bureau, a tax bureau and an international bureau, and so on. Like the firms they regulate, these bureaus, and the subdivisions within them, compete for position and power. This is especially curious because the individual bureaucrats in these departments are not usually specialists; rather, they move among functions every two or three years. But when they are in a particular job, they see it as their duty to represent the firms under their charge. So if a logjam develops between city banks and securities houses about the rights to deal in a new financial instrument, more likely than not this will be reflected in a logjam inside the Ministry. There is no clear leadership, which is part of a wider problem about Japanese politics that will be discussed in chapter 10, on the country's reluctance to lead.

This reluctance should not be taken absolutely literally, as that would imply paralysis among the policymakers, which has by no means been the case. Conflicts have been resolved and reforms have been made not much differently from the way things evolve in other countries. Vested interests in the United States have, for instance, blocked and delayed the development of interstate retail banking; others have lobbied to prevent the rescinding of the 1933 Glass-Steagall Act that bars banks from dealing and underwriting in corporate securities. The City of London's "Big Bang" in October 1986 that broke open cartels and restrictive practices in stockbrokering took place only after a long and grueling battle. The difference in Japan is of degree, not kind; resistance has shaped, and will continue to shape, the way in which financial reforms evolve.

The policy logjam has been particularly strong and important in two areas: the deregulation of bank deposit rates; and reforms to the corporate bond market. These are worth giving especially close attention to because both have had—and will continue to have—a crucial effect on Tokyo's development as a financial center, although in interesting and different ways. In the first case, the effect has been greatly to slow the pace of change. In the second, change has been diverted to an offshore market.

DEPOSITS, POSTMEN, AND TAX EVADERS

The case of deposits has been tricky because not only has it involved divisions between businesses and between parts of the Ministry of Finance, but it has also involved another ministry altogether, the Ministry of Posts and Telecommunications. What is more, it has become bound up in international rows about Japan's high propensity to save as well as in domestic battles over tax reform.

Interest rates on deposits have been set by the Ministry of Finance and Bank of Japan ever since December 1947, when the Temporary Interest Rate Adjustment Law went into effect. This temporary law has proved to be extremely durable. The aim was to keep banks stable by preventing them from entering a price war in their basic business: collecting the public's money.

The complication is that the largest collector of deposits, the postal savings bank, has its interest rates set by a different authority: the Postal Ministry. The post office, which has been taking deposits since 1875, has 24,000 branches, roughly ten times as many as each of the large retail banks. As well as deposits and postage stamps, it may also sell insurance and remit earnings from stocks and bonds. Unlike the banks, however, it is not incorporated and so does not have to file proper accounts or make a profit every year. It is a government department.

Bankers think its competition is unfair. One top city banker described it in a press seminar a few years ago as "the cancer on the Japanese financial system."

That is not a nice way to refer to the largest taker of deposits in the world, but it is easy to see why a private sector banker would feel that way. Until April 1988, the post office had two clear advantages over the banks: The Postal Ministry generally set its interest rates a bit higher than those in the banks and with more generous terms, and interest on most of its deposits was exempt from tax. This second advantage was not unfair in theory, only in practice.

Under the tax rules, every individual was supposed to be able to earn tax-exempt interest on an ordinary savings account of up to ¥3 million, plus up to an additional ¥11 million in government bonds, savings for house purchase, and others. It did not matter on paper whether the money was in a bank or a post office. In reality, it did matter: Japanese tax officials were not given access to the post office records, so people could have unlimited amounts of tax-exempt savings in the post office by simply opening accounts in false names. As a result, the post office came to have more accounts than the total number of Japanese men, women, and children.

The combination of higher interest rates and tax evasion meant that the postal savings bank's share of personal deposits rose from 19 percent in 1972 to more than 30 percent by the mid-1980s. Up against a competitor of that size, city banks were naturally reluctant to accept deregulation. Others favored it, of course: Stockbrokers wanted part of the business; long-term credit banks, which are barred from taking ordinary deposits, wanted rates freed so that their city bank rivals would be less competitive in the loans market. But city banks dug their heels in. Regulated interest rates at least guaranteed them a profit margin, even if their market share was falling. These bankers, and their backers in the Ministry of Finance, argued that interest rates could not be freed until the postal bank had been stripped of its advantages: The tax exemption must go, and the postmen must be subject to commercial pressures similar to those bearing down on the banks. The Postal Ministry, naturally enough, was unwilling to cede its power.

There were further complications. Local post offices often provide a useful information network and some backing for Liberal Democratic party politicians during election campaigns, so the politicians supported their helpers. Most important of all, the postal savings bank lends virtually all of its money to the Ministry of Finance trust fund bureau at rates below those offered on government bonds. The funds are used for infrastructure projects. If deposit rates were to be freed, the postal bank would insist on ending this arrangement; it would want to be paid fair rates for its cash and to have more control over where it can invest its money. This would raise the government's borrowing costs. So that made at least one bureau of the Ministry of Finance loath to be nasty to the postmen.

By 1988, a full four years after the yen-dollar agreement, this blockage to reform had been only partly cleared. The entire government finally became convinced that Japan's savings surplus was causing problems and that tax incentives for savings not only were no longer needed but also were a menace. So within a general package of tax reforms, a deal was made with the post office to get rid of all tax-exempt accounts, known as *maruyu,* except for cases of hardship, such as for the disabled, those over sixty-five, and working single mothers. The system was scrapped on April 1, 1988, freeing about ¥300 trillion ($2.3 trillion) in tax-exempt deposits (of which nearly half was in the post office) to seek out new, more attractive homes. In return, the post office was allowed gradually to invest part of its money at market rates and where it chose, rather than exclusively at the trust fund bureau.

Yet even then the story was not over. Free-market interest rates have gradually been introduced for deposits and similar instruments, but by 1988 the minimum lot size for a market-determined instrument was still ¥10 million ($75,000). That is well above what the ordinary depositor can afford. The postal savings bank remains a government department. Its interest rates are still set by the Postal Ministry, to the fury of the Bank of Japan, which sets everybody else's rates. Japan's deposit markets are still far from free.

Why have other institutions, such as securities firms, not been strong enough to force change? Why hasn't the market itself—namely, ordinary investors and depositors—burst the dam? The answer to both questions is that they had distractions and compensations elsewhere, which diverted their attention. Securities firms were doing booming business, so they did not need access to the deposits market, nor did they want to expose their own profits to competition as a quid pro quo. And rising stock prices and property values gave many depositors and investors a source of income sufficient to compensate for meager rates on bank deposits.

CORPORATE BATTLEFIELD

Eventually, banks want to be allowed to be stockbrokers, and stockbrokers want to be allowed to be banks. But the richest pickings, and therefore the fiercest battles, have not been over personal finance. They have been in corporate finance.

The postwar system handed most of this business to the banks in the form of loans at interest rates guided by the Bank of Japan. The corporate bond market was made the domain of the securities firms, which, to prevent bonds from becoming too competitive with loans, were shackled by tight rules about collateral and the approval of issues. In the 1970s, when foreign institutions and companies were permitted to issue yen bonds in Japan (known as *samurai* issues), that market was also handed to securities firms. But ways were again found to prevent the market from overwhelming the banks' business of making loans to foreigners.

This balancing act began to collapse in the early 1980s, when more money became available and large companies needed less of it. As they became less dependent on borrowing, industrial firms could afford to shop around for less expensive rates because they no longer felt so worried about preserving long-term relationships with their bankers. Companies drifted away from the banks and toward the securities markets, where cheaper finance was available. But not, by and large, in Japan, where the shackling of domestic bonds kept them uncompetitive. The cheapest place to raise money was in the Euromarkets, based in London. The dam burst in 1983–1984. All of a sudden, the market for corporate finance had flowed abroad.

This ought to be a shock to anyone who believes that Japanese industry is tied by unbreakable ropes to its banking partners, as is the case in West Germany. Japan is far too flexible for that ever to have happened. Once it was in the industry's clear interest to break its ties, that is what happened, and banks had an interest in allowing firms to depart: After all, banks are often important stockholders, so they want their firms to be as competitive as possible.

Since then, Japanese companies have continued to borrow by issuing most of their bonds overseas. The apparent oddity is that this was happening just as Japan's capital surplus was growing larger and larger, which ought to have made domestic borrowing cheaper than that abroad. In reality, it is not odd at all because by and large these foreign issues were still aimed at Japanese cash. The bonds, whether straight or convertible, mostly ended up in Japanese hands because those hands held the most money and accepted the cheapest rates for Japanese firms' issues. International bond markets are curiously inefficient, as separate groups of investors have different perceptions of the creditworthiness of different nationalities of borrower. Japanese investors are the most familiar with Japanese firms, so they are the most likely to consider them creditworthy and thus to accept low coupon rates.

As industrial and trading firms grew less conservative and more confident about playing the money game, they found that they could often make better profits from financial deals than from manufacturing things. In the year to March 31, 1988, for instance, Toyota, Japan's largest car manufacturer, made ¥149 billion, more than $1 billion, from financial deals, or nearly 40 percent of its pretax profits. By 1988, it had a cash hoard of ¥1.7 trillion ($13.4 billion) but was still raising money in the offshore markets. The reason was that its convertible bonds could command tiny coupon rates (1–2 percent) and so the proceeds could be invested at a profit even in a safe instrument such as time deposits in a Japanese bank. This financial game was so new to Japan and Japanese industrial firms that it was given a name: *zaiteku,* or, roughly, financial engineering.

As this gained momentum, the big winners were Japan's four top securities firms. Why, then, didn't the losers—the various types of banks—throw a fit and demand compensation? Partly because they were under pressure to deregulate deposit rates but were not ready to acquiesce. Partly, also, because many small banks would not survive in a fully competitive system. The main reason, however, was that the Ministry of Finance allowed large banks to take a share of the profits from the flow of corporate business overseas. They were not permitted to underwrite corporate securities in Japan, but the Ministry of Finance allowed them to do so abroad, in any country where the host government permitted banks to do underwriting. So such banks as Industrial Bank of Japan, Fuji, and Sumitomo could set up securities subsidiaries in London and Zurich to battle for the offshore business.

Unfortunately, since 1975, when the Ministry first permitted banks to be brokers overseas, an important constraint has been placed on the banks. An informal deal called the Three Bureaus Agreement, among the Ministry divisions for banking, securities, and international finance, stipulated that banks could manage offshore issues as long as they were not the lead manager (main underwriter) for issues by Japanese companies. They could lead-manage issues by foreign firms or be a second-rank manager for Japanese issues, but they could not get the cream of the business.

This is a big frustration for Japanese banks, which have been lobbying for at least five years to end the Three Bureaus Agreement. The bureaus have not been able to find a way to abandon the rule. One reason is that complete freedom for banks abroad would make it harder to control them at home. Before Article 65 can be dropped and banks allowed into the corporate securities business, the Ministry must work out how to assist those banks and brokers that prove too weak or vulnerable to survive, as well as other jurisdictional problems. So it has suited bureaucrats to push the problem overseas, thereby releasing some of the pressure. Only when the United States abolishes the Glass-Steagall Act and thus isolates Japan in this regard will the Ministry feel obliged to tackle the problem at home.

Banks have had other compensations. They are better placed than securities firms to offer swaps, deals in which borrowers exchange one sort of liability for another. That business has in the past five years so ballooned that few Eurobond issues are made without some sort of swap involved. If one side of the swap is in yen, Japanese banks have an automatic advantage, since theirs is the largest and cheapest source of yen.

In finance, one thing can lead swiftly to another. A direct product of this business in currency swaps related to Euroyen issues has been the rise of a market in yen interest-rate swaps, known as yen-yen swaps. Barely existing in 1986, within eighteen months this had become after dollars the world's second largest swap market. In an interest-rate swap, firms exchange one sort of debt—say, a fixed-rate bond—for another, perhaps a floating-rate bond. That way, the firms can diversify their range of borrowings. In Japan, interest-rate swaps have mostly been between liabilities of different maturities, swapping a one-year debt for seven-year funds or vice versa. Very swiftly, this has eroded the barrier between Japan's three long-term credit banks and its twelve city banks; long-term banks were supposed to deal in long-term funds, city banks in short-term ones. Through swaps they can tread on one another's toes. Foreign banks, skilled at making and trading swaps abroad, have also done well in this market in Tokyo. Swaps generally go unrecorded by the authorities, but participants calculate the yen-yen swap market to be running at an annual rate of anywhere between $50 billion and $100 billion. By any standard, that is big business.

PRELIMINARY CONCLUSIONS

These developments may sound arcane and technical, but important lessons are to be drawn from them, and not only for the financial markets. The first lesson is that in Japan some of the pressure for change can be averted or shelved if the losers are also getting a slice of the profits or some form of compensation. This is a common principle in all aspects of Japanese life. Banks have accepted the loss of their large corporate borrowers because they have been able to grab a share of new markets. Securities firms—Nomura, Daiwa, Nikko, and Yamaichi—have made even greater profits than the banks, but that does not matter immediately. The dams have been maintained, for now.

This has given regulators the time to plan for change in a more stable, orderly way. In corporate finance, they have begun to do so, albeit reluctantly, by stripping away rules in the domestic corporate and *samurai* markets. They have allowed a handful of large firms to issue unsecured bonds and have cut the delay between registration of a new bond and its issuance from thirty days to fifteen. Steps are being taken to allow floating-rate issues and to develop an independent system of credit rating. The most important liberalization, made in the autumn of 1988, has been to allow shelf registrations. This system, used with spectacular effects in the United States since 1981, allows firms to register issues in advance and to leave them "on the shelf" until market conditions appear optimal. The issue can then be made in a matter of hours.

These changes should breathe new life into the domestic market and attract some of the Japanese issues back from abroad. It will never bring all of them back home, unless domestic rules become as flexible as those in the Euromarkets. American firms, for example, make lots of issues in the Euromarkets even though their domestic corporate bond market has been modernized and freed in the past ten years.

THAT CAPITAL SURPLUS

The second lesson, however, is a less comfortable one. It is that financial reform is very hard to control, even if you are a Japanese bureaucrat. The water flows this way and that, seeking a way around new rules or old. The bureaucrat has to respond to pressure; he cannot determine it. That is especially so when there is an abundance of water.

The phrase that continues to crop up is capital surplus, or, put another way, savings surplus. This abundance of money has been the main force behind deregulation. But it has also turned finance on its head. Until around 1980, international banks in Japan, crudely, brought money into the country and lent it. Domestic institutions, too, were mainly concerned with providing money to borrowers. That is no longer so, now that capital is flowing out of Japan rather than into it. Once that happened, the business coveted by all financial folk was the chance to manage Japanese money. That general term, "manage," covers a wide range of financial services: handling pooled investments, dealing in stocks and bonds, trading foreign currency, issuing and selling bonds to Japanese investors, and so on. The markets in this sort of money management have grown most vigorously.

One of the most active new markets spurred by the capital surplus in the mid-1980s was not even in yen. It was in U.S. Treasury bonds, which became the most favored overseas investment and trading vehicle for Japanese institutions. It developed extremely rapidly. In 1983,

Japanese investors bought and sold $33 billion worth of all foreign bonds, ending the year having made net purchases of $12.5 billion. By October 1985, Japanese investors were trading more than $60 billion of foreign bonds in that month alone, with net purchases of $5.6 billion. About 70 percent of the bonds were dollar bonds, most of them Treasuries. In 1983, virtually all of the deals were being carried out in New York. By the end of 1985, a large chunk—some said $1 billion a day—was being traded in Tokyo. Since then, Tokyo's share of trading has grown, even though the vast bulk of the market remains in New York.

This local market for dollar bonds in turn helped spur the foreign-exchange market in Tokyo. If you want to buy a Treasury bond, you must first turn your yen into dollars. In 1980, Tokyo's daily volume in the currency markets was only about $6 billion. Dealing was restrained by a rule that banned forward transactions by nonbanks unless genuine commercial transactions were involved. Known as the real-demand rule, it was dropped in July 1984 as part of the yen-dollar agreement. Banks could not deal directly with one another and instead had to go through licensed money brokers, who in turn were not permitted to deal across borders. One by one, during 1984 and 1985 these rules were also dropped. Trading volume soared, doubling in a matter of months. By 1988, daily volume for the whole market was approaching $60 billion, overtaking New York and reaching two-thirds of London's level.

In the shadow of these and other markets, the capital surplus has had a big impact on those firms that have custody over the money, chiefly life insurance companies and trust banks, who together have a monopoly of pension-fund management. The cash is also held by other institutions, such as Norinchukin, the farmers' central bank that is Japan's largest institutional investor, and, as discussed earlier, the post office. What these money managers had in common when the surplus flooded around them was ignorance. The habit of investing abroad had barely caught on. It is no exaggeration to say that few of the fund managers had even traveled beyond Hawaii, let alone bought any foreign securities. Even in the domestic market, their fund management experience had been shaped by domestic controls over dividend payouts and other things. There was little competition among funds. Nor, surprisingly enough in overregulated Japan, was there much protection for investors.

Fund managers have learned fast because they have had to. But in addition, efforts have been made to bring in and buy in expertise. A new Investment Advisory Law was passed in 1987 in order to regulate money managers but also included clauses deliberately welcoming to foreign firms. The government hopes that domestic firms will learn from the foreign firms, either through competition or tie-ups. More apparent than that have been investments in fund managers and investment banks overseas in order to gain training and experience for Japanese managers. That was why in March 1987 Nippon Life, the country's largest life insurer, bought 13 percent of Shearson Lehman in New York for $538 million. In November of that year, Yasuda Mutual Life bought 18 percent of Paine Webber for $300 million. In March 1988, Sumitomo Life bought a 15 percent stake in a small Scottish advisory firm, Ivory & Sime. All are buying brainpower, not control.

THE MADNESS OF CROWDS

It is easy to see why they are interested in expertise if you look at Japanese losses from overseas investments. They bought dollar bonds in huge quantities just as the dollar began to collapse against the yen. Until April 1987, this was compensated in part by capital gains in the American bond market, as interest rates there were falling and the dollar value of bonds was thus rising. Even so, the Ministry of Finance has calculated that in the three years to the end of March 1988 the life insurance industry's combined losses were well over ¥4 trillion, or $30 billion at 1988 exchange rates.

It ought to be evident from this that a capital surplus is not always a source of joy. The Ministry has helped the insurers by allowing them to spread the losses over a number of years. Policyholders do not feel all the pain because the insurers are allowed to pay dividends only out of their income from investments, not out of capital gains—or losses. The life insurers still have to worry about their balance sheets, however, even if these features avert an immediate disaster. Fortunately for them, losses on foreign securities in 1985–1987 were more than outweighed by gains in two other markets: the Tokyo stock market and Japanese real estate investments.

The world stock market crash in October 1987 must have alarmed Japanese institutions, for it threatened to collapse their investments once again. As it happened, Tokyo survived the crash with a smaller fall than other markets (20 percent versus 35–40 percent), and it recovered much more rapidly and strongly. But is that the end of the story? What if there is another crash? The capital surplus, that abundance of money, has washed around Tokyo's stock and real estate markets in a very uncontrolled and, indeed, uncontrollable way. Japan, that country of strict social mores, of superefficient bureaucrats, of consensus, of Japan Inc., has become a nation of speculators.

CHAPTER SIX

円

A NATION OF SPECULATORS

Soon to die,
Yet noisier than ever:
The autumn cicada.

—Shiki Masaoka (1867–1902)

IN 1841, Charles Mackay, a Scottish songwriter and historian, wrote a book about mob psychology called *Extraordinary Popular Delusions and the Madness of Crowds.* The book chronicled some of the financial manias of the seventeenth and eighteenth centuries in Europe, including the South Sea bubble, the Dutch tulip boom, the Mississippi scheme, and others. What these financial events had in common was that apparently intelligent people rushed to invest in schemes about which they had almost no information. For instance, they bought shares in the South Sea company in 1711 for two reasons: everybody else seemed to be doing so; the price kept on rising. In an atmosphere of blind bullishness, thousands of investors thought they had become rich. Suddenly the price collapsed. The South Sea company turned out to be a fraud. Thousands then knew they were poor.

If Charles Mackay were alive today, he would be collecting material on Japan, in case Tokyo's financial markets provide a new example of the madness of crowds. So far, all that can be said with certainty is that the city's stock and property markets have enjoyed a bewilderingly rapid rise that has prompted talk of a speculative bubble. There has been no financial collapse.

In any case, times have surely changed since 1711. Japan and its economy are certainly not a fraud, and plenty of information is available about Japanese investments. Investors, whether Japanese or foreign, are not just apparently intelligent, they are intelligent, and they know all about the South Sea bubble and other such pieces of financial history. Markets are supposed to learn from past mistakes. As information now flows more freely, quickly, and cheaply than ever before, markets ought to be more efficient than ever before. Financial theory holds that at any given moment in an efficient market a share price accurately reflects all information then available. So Japanese share prices cannot be far from such efficiency and accuracy.

Despite this, plenty of Western analysts began to argue in 1986 that the Tokyo stock and property markets had risen ridiculously high and that they must soon crash. Something must be wrong, ran the argument, when the shares of Nippon Telegraph and Telephone (the former state-owned telecommunications monopoly) are priced at three hundred times the firm's earnings per share and when the land in Tokyo occupied by the imperial palace and gardens is worth more than the state of California. It was not just the level of stock and land prices, but also the speed with which they rose in 1986 and 1987 that was thought to be a classic sign of a bubble. By early 1988, the ratio of the Tokyo stock market's value to Japan's GNP was nearly four times its level in 1983. At the end of 1985, equities in the main part of the Tokyo exchange were worth ¥183 trillion; by the end of 1987, they were worth ¥326 trillion, a rise of more than 40 percent. Private residential land rose in value during the same period from ¥742 trillion to ¥1,218 trillion.

Prices seemed to have lost all contact with reality. All the world's stock markets were rising rapidly, but the first to collapse, it was assumed, would be Japan. What goes crazily up was soon bound to come crashing down. Yet throughout 1987 and 1988, it was the foreign pundits who looked ridiculous. Even as their American and European clients were, on their advice, pulling money out of Japan, the Tokyo stock market was climbing higher and higher. The unluckiest tipster of all was George Soros, an American fund manager justifiably famous for his investment success. On October 14, 1987, he had an article published in the *Financial Times* that predicted that Japan's stock market was about to crash. That happened to be two days before Wall Street began to slide and just five ahead of Black Monday, October 19, when the New York market disintegrated. As it happened, Tokyo was dragged down by New York, but it fell by only two-thirds as much as the British or American markets. By April 1988, it had regained all its losses, even as London and New York were languishing well below their pre-crash peaks.

This does not, of itself, prove that the pundits were wrong. Just because Tokyo has not crashed yet does not necessarily mean that it never will or that there is no speculative bubble. The trouble is that in investment timing is everything. For a professional analyst, it is no good having foreseen a crash years or even months ahead of the actual event, since you or your clients will then miss out on the price rises that precede it. Even if the prediction proves correct, by the time it has occurred you will probably have long since lost your job or gone bust because clients have moved their cash to less gloomy hands. For this reason, by 1989 few voices were to be heard predicting an imminent disaster for Tokyo. The conventional wisdom had, it seemed, fallen back on an old favorite: Japan does not follow the same rules as everywhere else.

IS TOKYO DIFFERENT?

The links between stock markets and the real economy are everywhere mysterious. Yet real life did provide some good reasons for Japanese stock to rise more rapidly than that elsewhere in 1985–88 and to fall by less on and after Black Monday. In that period, Japan's GNP grew more than did America's, despite the high and rising yen. Falling oil prices helped Japan more than the United States, because Japan imports all its oil whereas America is a producer as well as an importer. Although exporters were hurt by the strong yen, importers and the many firms serving the domestic economy benefited from it and from government efforts to stimulate consumption. Profits grew lustily.

This economic background can certainly explain much of Tokyo's strength. In 1986–89, which economy would you have bet on performing better, America's or Japan's? That said, this explanation does not feel sufficient to explain all of Tokyo's strength. Nor does it explain the widening disparity between the price/earnings ratios (p/e) for Japanese stock and those in New York and London. Earnings were rising in Japanese companies, but their stock prices were rising more rapidly still.

The p/e ratio is the most common yardstick for stock prices in America and one of the most popular in Britain. It compares a firm's stock price to its earnings per share, that is, profits divided by the number of shares outstanding. The idea behind this is that a share buys a right to a slice of a company's stream of profits, paid to stockholders as dividends or reinvested for the future. If a share costs $10 and the earnings per share is $2, the p/e ratio is 5; crudely, it can be said that it would take five years for the firm's earnings to cover the share price.

There is no "correct" level for a p/e ratio, but the test is thought to be a good way to compare the stock prices of similar firms, sectors, or markets. If one oil firm has a p/e ratio of 10 and another of 5, something must justify the gap; if not, the ratios should converge as investors sell the dearer firm and buy the cheaper. As investment has become more international in recent years, this same process ought, in theory, to take place across borders. Ratios should converge.

This has been one of the main arguments warning about a crash in Tokyo stock prices. In 1987 and 1988, the Tokyo market's average p/e ratio was converging only with the sky, rising to 60 and beyond, while those for New York and London stayed in a range between 11 and 18. But Tokyo has not crashed. Why not? Because, say some, Tokyo does not work like other markets. This Japan-is-different school has two solutions to the riddle of Tokyo's strength: Japanese p/e ratios are not so crazy as they seem; p/e ratios are irrelevant for Japanese stock. Let's start with the first of these assumptions.

P/e ratios are tricky to compare across frontiers because accounting methods differ widely. Profits can be disguised in myriad ways. This is especially so in Japan, where high corporate taxes encourage firms to keep their reported profits as low as possible, either by guile or by exploiting tax loopholes that permit them to divert profits into various sorts of reserves. Furthermore, compared with methods used in the United States, the Japanese method of consolidating the earnings of subsidiaries into those of the parent firm tends to understate earnings per share. For these and other technical reasons, Paul Aron, until 1988 vice-chairman of Daiwa Securities in America, has estimated that Japanese p/e ratios ought to be divided by three to obtain a figure comparable to American ratios.

A different argument, also showing that Japanese p/es are not so high as they seem, is based in the fact that only a small proportion of shares can actually be traded. Firms commonly ensure, through placings and other methods, that their shares are in "safe" hands, which means hands that will not sell them or seek to make a takeover bid. Firms often buy their commercial clients' shares and vice versa. Gideon Franklin, an analyst at the Tokyo branch of UBS-Phillips & Drew, a stockbroker, estimated in March 1988 that 77 percent of the shares quoted on the Tokyo stock exchange are of this long-term, untradable sort. This figure may well be an exaggeration, since it includes virtually all the stockholdings of financial institutions and companies, even though these investors do actively trade part of their portfolios. But there is no reliable means of determining how much of the portfolio is stable and how much tradable. Some estimates put the stable figure as low as 50 percent.

Nevertheless, it does appear that a very large part is not available for sale, and Franklin's estimate is at least a useful guide. Outside investors have to chase a small amount of marketable, floating equity. Franklin sought to adjust share prices for this scarcity factor, producing what he called a free-market p/e ratio. On this basis, he calculated that the ratio for Tokyo at the end of 1987, 58.3, should really be restated as 13.9, not far out of line with the ratios in New York and London. The conclusion drawn from this and Aron's study is the same: Japanese shares are pretty cheap after all, so fill your pockets with them, preferably placing the orders through Daiwa Securities or UBS-Phillips & Drew.

There is nothing misleading about either of these studies, as far as it is possible to tell. But both suffer from the same flaw: They take a static view of the market rather than looking at its dynamics. Whether the average p/e ratio in Tokyo is a third or a quarter of what it appears to be does not matter very much compared with its direction and speed of movement. What investors want to know is why it rose by 30 percent in 1987, even on Franklin's measure, and whether it will continue to rise.

Put another way, if Tokyo's p/e in 1988 was on a par with that in New York, it must have been much lower than New York's two years ago. Why? Why has Tokyo risen more rapidly since? The tendency for companies to understate their earnings has not changed. According to Franklin, the cross-holding of shares has increased, but only slightly. Another explanation must be found for why Tokyo stock prices have risen so rapidly.

DROP THE YARDSTICK

The second Japan-is-different solution—that p/e ratios are irrelevant—turns out to be more helpful. The argument has two prongs. The first is the fact that the p/e measure does not offer the eternal and universal force that devotees claim for it. As stated earlier, there is no such thing as a "correct" value for a p/e ratio, nor for a share. A share is worth whatever someone else is willing to pay for it. That involves a great deal of guesswork, both about the company's future prospects and about what other investors might be guessing about it. The p/e ratio is simply one tool to help this guesswork; by no means is it the only tool.

Consider an example. If an oil firm's p/e ratio is 5 and other oil firms' ratios are around 10, then you might buy the cheaper share if you guessed that other investors would make the same move, assuming 10 would become a consensus figure. You know that other investors use the p/e ratio as a tool of analysis. As they buy, so the p/e would rise toward 10. Matters are not that simple because information flows so freely and quickly that the gap should never have widened in the first place. So in practice, investment in the cheaper share would usually involve a bet that the present ratio of 5 was based on a misunderstanding about the firm or that a disadvantage now holding the firm back was about to disappear. The bet is about hard future facts or, just as often, about the market's future feelings about a company.

In London and New York, then, the p/e ratio is no more than a guide, one unreliable way to try to read the market's mind. The second part of the p/es-don't-matter argument is a simple empirical observation: Hardly anybody uses these ratios in Japan. Investors, brokers, and analysts in Tokyo are not commonly heard to mention p/es for a company or for the market as a whole. This does not mean the Japanese are wrong, as the price/earnings ratio has no particular monopoly on the truth. What it does mean is that the p/e ratio is no use for mindreaders in Tokyo.

It is impossible to know for sure why Japanese do not use p/es because, as with the chicken and the egg, cause and effect cannot be separated: p/es are a poor clue because nobody else uses them; nobody uses them because they are a poor clue. One possible, but not conclusive, explanation is that Japanese stockholders do not seek dividends from their shares, but rather want to reap capital gains. For all intents and purposes, dividends are taxed while capital gains are not. P/e ratios may be linked in the Japanese mind to dividends rather than to gains. Or it may simply be a cultural or historical quirk. The existence of foreign investors in the Tokyo market has not spread the gospel of the p/e ratio because foreigners still account for such a small proportion of stock ownership, less than 5 percent in 1988.

In this respect, it seems that Tokyo is different, but only superficially. Fundamentally, the game of investment in Japan is the same as it is in any market: A Japanese buys a share if he thinks the price is going to rise. In making that bet, the investor is reading the market's mind. He thinks that, in future, there will be more buyers for that share, relative to sellers, than there are now. If p/e ratios are not used as a clue or analytical tool in making that guess, something else must be. Even in inscrutable Japan, such guesses do not come out of thin air.

HIDDEN ASSETS

What does convince investors in Japan to continue to buy shares? Certainly not the income from dividends, which in mid-1988 provided an average gross yield of only 0.46 percent. It would be far better to put your money in the bank than to rely on that.

Superficially, investors feel confident about brokers' sales talk, which (at least in living memory) has always been bullish and tends to dwell upon "themes." For these, salesmen pick out general trends, of varying degrees of probability, and find stocks that stand to benefit. Examples during 1985–88 included the expansion of China as a market, public works spending and the redevelopment of Tokyo Bay, the AIDS scourge, cancer cures, opto-electronics as the technology of the future, the expansion of domestic demand, or the redenomination of the yen. There is nothing remarkable or deceitful about these themes, for they are merely efforts to extrapolate which part of the economy is likely to fare better than others. Occasionally, the economy is itself a theme, linked to the general prospects for corporate profits.

One theme during this period is worth close examination. Known as "latent assets," or "hidden assets," it began to be peddled in late 1984 and really began to take hold in 1985–86. The idea was that Japanese corporate accounting methods greatly understate the true value of assets held in firms' balance sheets. Property and shareholdings, in particular, are generally valued at the original cost rather than at the market price. So the trick was to find companies that had a large amount of undervalued assets and to argue that these meant that the firm was worth far more than its present share price.

Nothing changed to make this any more apparent in 1984 than it had been in 1980 or 1975. In an efficient market, share prices should already reflect the value of the underlying assets. So for hidden assets to cause a fresh rise in share prices, some additional new information is required. In the West, hidden assets matter to shareholders only if there is a chance that they might be realized, either by the firm being taken over and the assets sold or by the arrival of new opportunities for the assets to be turned into cash or to earn income. So a new enthusiasm for takeovers or new financing methods for them could make prices rise.

But could that really happen in Japan? Although there was some talk of a return of hostile takeovers in 1985 (they were common in Japan in the late 1960s but nonexistent since then), cross-shareholdings made this unlikely. Two attempts—one by Minebea for a firm called Sankyo Seiki, the other by a group of foreign investors for Minebea—failed ingloriously.

Nonetheless, several other changes did make hidden assets appear more valuable. Chief among them occurred in 1985, when the government began to give serious consideration to changing the laws governing property development. Rules on the maximum height of buildings and in zones where development was barred or restricted appeared likely to be relaxed. If the rules were changed, some firms' assets might be brought out of the closet and sold or developed in new ways, thereby generating new income. This coincided with two other trends. The government began to talk about spending more on public works to stimulate the economy, such as the revival of a twenty-year-old plan to build a combined bridge and tunnel across Tokyo Bay. This and other schemes promised to promote property development wherever they took place.

The second trend was that Japan National Railways, the state railway network, moved closer to being turned into a private company. The Nakasone government drew up a plan to split the network into six firms that would then be sold. By 1986, Japan National Railways was losing $20 million a day and had vast debts, so it seemed likely that the firm would have to sell some of its assets to ease that debt burden and prepare for sale. As it was one of the country's largest property holders, owning some of the best land in Tokyo at its marshaling yards in Marunouchi, Shimbashi, and Shinagawa, that promised to have a big impact on the property market. An increase in supply might be expected to depress prices, but this was not a worry to investors because it also promised to make possible the development of adjoining land owned as hidden assets.

Analysts and investors therefore began to chase after firms that might own property that could benefit from these changes. In particular, shares of private railways, retailers, warehousing firms, and real estate companies boomed. The purest example of a beneficiary was Mitsubishi Estate, the real estate firm in the Mitsubishi group of companies. It or its predecessor companies have owned almost all the land in the banking area of Marunouchi (near Tokyo station and the imperial palace) since the 1890s, when the place was a swamp. These and other assets are valued in Mitsubishi's accounts at prices current in 1937 or just after the war. By 1985, no office buildings in Marunouchi had been sold for eight years. Rent controls meant that average rents were rising by only 7–8 percent a year. But changes in zoning and other rules promised to allow Mitsubishi to redevelop part of the area. Japan National Railways' difficulties opened an intriguing opportunity to convert the Marunouchi side of Tokyo station, a century-old brick building facing an unused open space, into a large office, shopping, and station complex.

CROWD PSYCHOLOGY AND CIRCULAR MARKETS

By 1988, property regulations had been reviewed, and sure enough, zones had been shifted from one level of restriction to another. In residential areas that barred buildings of more than thirty-three feet high, forty feet are now allowed. But progress is slow. The government had begun to spend more on public works in 1986 and 1987, although it remained unclear how long the projects would last. Japan National Railways had been split up (and renamed as merely Japan Railways) and had begun to sell land. Mitsubishi's Tokyo station project, however, had been blocked by conservationists. Nevertheless, enough change was under way to convince the stock market. Share prices try to anticipate events, not follow them.

Moreover, interest in hidden assets was reinforced by two other powerful forces: the surplus of money and the dramatic increase in property prices. The savings surplus in Japan meant, simply, that there was an enormous amount of money available to buy financial assets. An economist would define this as "excess liquidity," the difference between the money supply and nominal GNP, which rose from 1.5 percent of GNP in 1985 to 5 percent in 1986. Brokers call it "weight of money," and it is as common a market theme in Tokyo as it is elsewhere. For instance, in early 1987 First Boston, a New York investment bank, predicted that New York's Dow Jones Industrial Average would reach 3000 sometime during 1988 because so much cash was waiting to be invested. By October 19, 1987, the money did not feel quite so compellingly heavy.

Similar arguments have been heard frequently in Japan to justify past and future rises in stock prices. Weight of money has a general inflationary force: More money chasing an unchanged supply of anything will mean that prices will rise. But the argument suffers from a crucial logical flaw: It fails to distinguish between potential demand and effective demand. Japan's savings surplus does not have to be invested in equities; if equities are unattractive, the money is free to sit around in deposit accounts, government bonds, gold bullion, property, or wherever else it chooses.

This logical flaw does not, however, mean that the weight of money has no force in stocks or in other markets. What matters is whether investors believe the argument. The psychology of crowds is central here because confidence is the key ingredient of any rising ("bull") market. A share is a risky asset that is worth something only if the holder can sell it; the apparent presence of waves of cash "waiting" to splash into the market helps to assure the holder that, in extremis, he will be able to find a buyer. Japanese equities are only attractive insofar as they enjoy capital gains. Weight of money helps the process to become circular: Shares are attractive because their prices are rising; prices are rising because there is money around that finds shares attractive.

That is exactly the sort of confidence that drove the South Sea bubble in 1711, or John Law's Mississippi scheme in 1820. Fraud played a big role in both schemes, but so did self-fulfilling confidence. As money flooded in, it provided its own justification for investment. If prices had risen 10 percent last month and people were still queuing up to buy shares, what could be more sensible than to buy a few yourself? Those who were warning that the price had gone crazy were the real idiots, as they were missing out on the profits. Ignorance was a factor in both schemes, since it was almost impossible to test John Law's claim, for instance, that gold mines in Louisiana and Mississippi would provide rich profits for shareholders. But ignorance is important in all financial markets, where an investment is no more than a bet about the future.

The only hard information that can flow freely in an efficient market is information about the past, and not always the very recent past given the slowness of companies in producing accounts. Relying on such information about the future is rather like driving a car with the windshield blacked out: inadvisable. It can only be done with confidence if it has been successfully done for the past few years and if there are lots of other cars driving in the same direction.

In Japan, this self-fulfilling confidence became linked to other virtuous circles, which returns to the theme of hidden assets. Imagine that a company owns land in central Tokyo that is undervalued on its balance sheet. Every rise in the property market adds to the value of those assets, so the firm's stock rises accordingly. Furthermore, there is another sort of hidden asset, namely, corporate shareholdings valued at original purchase cost. Every increase in the stock market inflates the market value of those hidden assets. So in turn the company's own shares ought to be worth more.

Japanese banks add a further twist because the Ministry of Finance includes their large hidden reserves of shareholdings as part of capital when calculating banks' minimum capital requirements. In 1987, an international agreement on such capital rules for banks stipulated that Japanese banks could count 45 percent of the market value of their shareholdings as capital. Every time the Tokyo stock market rises, Japanese banks' capital rises, enabling them to make more loans and offer more financial services, boosting their profits.

Similar forces operate for companies. Unless a new opportunity arises, firms do not want to realize or to revalue their hidden assets, as that would make them liable for capital gains and property taxes. Individual investors are, in effect, exempt from capital gains tax because it is only levied if a person makes more than thirty transactions a year with one broker exceeding an annual total of 120,000 shares or if the person makes a trade of more than 120,000 shares in one company. These conditions make the tax very easy to avoid. This is not so for companies, which gives them a powerful incentive not to sell or to revalue the shares. They can, however, exploit the market value of shares or property assets in another way: by using the asset as collateral for a loan. Money borrowed on the security of land could be invested in a factory. Or it could be invested in the stock market. The shares thus bought can serve as collateral for another loan. Perhaps to buy property?

This circular process of self-fulfilling confidence is by and large what has driven Tokyo for the past few years, above and beyond the undoubted strength of its economy. Yet another factor reinforced the movement, especially after Black Monday. This is the notion that a crash is impossible because Japan Inc. (or, more accurately, the government and the financial establishment) will not allow one to happen.

Such a belief begins with the fact that four securities firms account for half the trading on the stock market, so they have a powerful influence over prices. The Ministry of Finance would call on investing institutions to support the market. The world stock market crash in October 1987 gave this belief new strength because the Ministry and the financial institutions did indeed support the market. That effort is given credit for the fact that Tokyo's Nikkei stock market index fell "only" 23 percent during the crash, against 30 percent to 40 percent in New York and London. This belief in Japan Inc.'s safety net gives prices a further upward push. For what could be better than buying a riskless asset?

PROPERTY AND STOCKS

This description of how and why stock prices in Tokyo rose so high so quickly could equally well have begun in the property market, for the two became inextricably linked. Climbing land prices helped fuel climbing stock prices, and vice versa. Just as with stock, the standard explanations for high land values in Tokyo are unconvincing. Yes, Japan has a shortage of habitable land. Yes, businesses and individuals were moving into the capital city; its population grew, on average, by 2.3 percent a year between 1960 and 1985.

But neither of these facts is new. The vacancy rate for offices in Tokyo in 1987 was 0.2 percent, well below that in either Manhattan or London. But that was a culmination of a decade-long gradual decline from 2 percent in 1975. Nothing changed radically enough to explain why average land prices rose by 24 percent in Greater Tokyo in 1986 and 65 percent in 1987, according to the National Land Agency's official survey. Although the boom started in Tokyo and was most marked there, it spread to other cities; in 1986, the average price of all land in Japan rose by 7.7 percent, followed by 21.7 percent in 1987. Land prices rose by 20 percent in Osaka in 1987.

Two new facts, however, could plausibly explain Tokyo's property boom. The first was Tokyo's sudden emergence as an international financial center. As discussed in chapter 5, this lured a queue of foreign banks and securities houses, all eager for office space. It happened too rapidly and unexpectedly for the market to digest and to calculate what foreign demand might amount to in the longer term. Fact number two is linked, again, to the arrival of excess liquidity after 1985. Commercial banks had lost many of their corporate customers to the securities markets, at home and abroad, and were keen to find new areas of lending. The Bank of Japan helped encourage this by lowering interest rates and easing monetary policy. The best new market was in property.

Bank loans outstanding to real estate firms nearly doubled between the beginning of 1984 and the end of 1987. Most of that rise came during 1986 and the first half of 1987; loans outstanding rose from ¥17 trillion in January 1986 to ¥27 trillion by July 1987, after which growth leveled out. These figures, which bring property loans up to 10 percent of the banks' total lending, considerably understate the banks' exposure to property, however. They have also lent to individuals to purchase homes, to industrial firms against the collateral of their property assets, and to industrial and other firms to purchase land for industrial purposes. This lending boosted the market directly but also indirectly helped it along by establishing the circular link between property and stock prices already discussed.

Conventional financial firms are regulated by the Ministry of Finance. Although it cannot control everything that a bank or broker can do, it can monitor them closely. That is not true of firms involved in the real estate business, either directly as developers or indirectly as financiers. These firms may get started with very little capital and may operate almost entirely by borrowing. For example, in 1986 a firm called Kohrin Sangyo was active in real estate and stock investment. Although it had equity of just ¥1.5 billion ($11 million), its assets totaled ¥85 billion, roughly half of which were in short-term holdings of securities and half in short-term holdings of real estate. A far larger and better known example is Orient Finance, a publicly listed firm under the wing of Japan's largest bank, Dai-Ichi Kangyo. In the year ended March 1987, its equity capital was ¥173 billion against total assets worth ¥4.85 trillion. Its total borrowings were ¥2.66 trillion, fifteen times its capital.

The point is that in the real estate market firms can build a huge pile of assets and debt on a very small base of capital. That has been true at various times in other countries, most notably Britain in the early 1970s when property development was financed by fringe companies known as secondary banks. This is not dangerous in itself, as long as prices continue to rise or stay high. In 1974, when the British real estate market turned, the secondary banks collapsed in the country's worst financial crisis since 1945. The Bank of England had to organize a rescue by conventional commercial banks. The same could happen in Japan.

CONSPIRACY THEORY

The case argued so far is that stock and property prices in Japan in 1986–1988 rose more rapidly than can be explained by underlying developments and that there emerged a speculative upward spiral, or bubble, linked to the country's surplus of capital. Before examining the consequences of this and the likelihood that this bubble might pop, it is worth considering another question: If the Japanese bureaucracy is so good at running the economy and so adept at heavy-handed regulation, why did the Ministry of Finance allow this bubble to inflate? Surely it can see how dangerous this could become?

There are two possible responses to this. One is that the question is based on a false premise: The ministries have less control over the economy than is ordinarily believed, the burst of excess liquidity after 1985 coming too rapidly for them to handle it. At the same time, after the Plaza Accord of September 1985, Japan was committed to a loose monetary policy in order to help depress the dollar and raise the yen's value. An international obligation had deprived Japan of its freedom to make domestic policy.

The second response, however, is less sympathetic: The stock and property booms were actually quite convenient for Japan in 1985–87, when the rising yen was giving exporters' profits their tightest squeeze for a decade. These firms were faced with the task of restructuring themselves in a very short space of time to take account of a yen doubling in value against the dollar. As their income plunged from manufacturing and selling, it was rather handy for many firms to make some money on the stock market and to have a cheap source of capital. Chapter 5 has already discussed this *zaiteku* as a consequence of Japanese firms' ability to raise money cheaply in the Euromarkets. Direct *zaiteku* investment in the stock and real estate markets provided, for some firms, the difference between declaring a profit or posting a loss.

In its 1986–87 fiscal year, Nissan, Japan's second largest maker of cars and trucks, would have reported a loss had it not been for profits on securities trading. In the year to March 1988, securities profits accounted for more than half the pretax profits of Matsushita Electric (58.8 percent), Nissan (65.3 percent), Japan Victor Company (93 percent), and Sharp (73 percent). It was 134 percent of pretax income at Sanyo and 1,962 percent at Isuzu—that is, profits on securities were nearly twenty times larger than profits on ordinary business.

In addition to providing this bridge over troubled waters, the stock and property booms helped support domestic consumption and thus the economy. Having pointed all this out, however, it still requires a big jump to arrive at a conspiracy theory, namely, that the Ministry of Finance engineered the whole thing in order to keep Japanese industry healthy and competitive. There is no evidence either way. All that can be said is that it is hard to imagine the Ministry being able to dream up and execute the idea, although it was probably pleased that it happened. As the boom got under way, the Ministry of Finance could have intervened to choke it back, but chose not to. The main reason was that a tighter monetary policy would have conflicted with Japan's internationally agreed policy for the exchange rate. During 1987, the Bank of Japan did try to persuade banks to cut back on their property lending, with some success. The growth of loans did reach a plateau late in the year.

YEARS OF LIVING DANGEROUSLY

Having argued that Japan in 1986–88 blew itself a speculative bubble in its stock and property markets, albeit a convenient one, it still remains to be said whether the bubble will pop violently and what might be the consequences if it does. There is no way to prove that a crash will happen nor, in particular, to say when it might occur. The surest thing that can be said is that in the past speculative bubbles have usually ended in a pop—or an explosion.

It is very unlikely that the Japanese government and financial establishment could support the market if a collapse were to begin. The Ministry of Finance could call in financial institutions and ask them to buy more, or not to sell. For a while, this would certainly work. The problem is, however, that these institutions cover only the "stable" portion of the market. The 25 to 50 percent of shares that are "floating" or freely traded are what has driven the market high, and these are largely in the hands of individuals and foreign investors. Japan Inc. cannot prevent individuals or foreigners from selling in panic. Four big securities firms dominate the stock market, but their grip is on the dealing and marketing of shares rather than on ownership itself. They have influence but not power. All they can do is encourage individuals not to sell. Although their persuasion carries much more weight than would that of Merrill Lynch in the United States, for example, in the extreme, it is still only persuasion.

It is more plausible that the authorities could act to slow a crash down, perhaps to ensure a soft rather than a hard landing. Already the Tokyo stock exchange has rules that place a limit on the amount that the market can fall or rise in one day, which would slow things down. But this sort of rule can only delay matters. In October 1987, Hong Kong closed its stock and futures exchanges for a week; once they reopened, the markets still crashed. The surest power of the Ministry of Finance is over banks' lending policies: It could persuade the banks not to withdraw their credit from securities and real estate firms and thus not to make a crash worse. Again, this is a delaying tactic. It might smooth things over. But it might not.

What could cause a crash? In theory, it ought to be the removal of one of the factors that has driven the rise. If everything is as unstable as this chapter has suggested, then the mere end to growth in, say, property prices or bank lending, or the arrival of a tight monetary policy (i.e., higher interest rates) could be enough to turn a virtuous upward spiral into a vicious downward one.

Yet by 1988, some of this had begun to happen, without prompting a crash. Land prices in Tokyo peaked in mid-1987 and began to fall during the autumn. According to the Japan Real Estate Research Institute, in the year to March 1988 commercial land prices in the capital fell by 4.4 percent and residential prices fell by 7.8 percent. Since they had been rising sharply in the first part of that year, these figures imply drops of 10 percent to 20 percent in the later months. By March 1988, prices for condominiums had fallen from their peak levels by around 10 percent in central Tokyo and by 30 percent in the city's outer commuter belt. For the real estate market, this was quite a dramatic turnaround, but it had little apparent effect on stock prices. Other influences—a strong economy, a continued flow of liquidity—supported the market. A few small property companies went bankrupt after banks refused new loans, but not enough to hurt the financial system.

Put simply, what is required for a crash in the stock market is for the crowd of investors to lose their confidence, their belief in ever-rising share prices. The difficulty is to say what might cause that. Probably it would have to be a combination of things. All that can be done is to assemble a list of candidates. Chief among them must be an economic reversal. After the October 1987 crash, Tokyo was buoyed by the most rapid growth in the Japanese economy for more than a decade. It is hard not to be confident when that is going on, corporate earnings are increasing, and the streets are blocked by BMWs and Rolls-Royces. If that were to change, confidence would take a knock. With hindsight, the 1987 crash began in the United States because rising interest rates there prompted fears that the American economy must soon go into recession. A year later, it still had not done so. If, when it comes, the recession were to be serious, it would damage Japan too.

A second candidate for causing a crash would be a significant drop in the "weight of money," the excess liquidity that enabled stock and property prices to rise. That means more than just a marginal change in the flow of cash since the market has endured such changes before without collapsing. It means a sure indication that the flow is going to stop for a sustained period. What could cause that? One possibility is a sharply tighter monetary policy, which might become necessary if price inflation appeared to be accelerating. Another would be a large and sustained increase in the demand for funds by the government or by companies for physical investment. In the longer term, a fall in Japan's overseas current-account surplus will also mean that fewer funds are available.

THE CONSEQUENCES

These might not happen for a long time, if ever. There might never be a crash. The markets might, to use one of the favored economic phrases of the 1980s, have a soft landing. Nonetheless, Japan is running a risk that its markets will crash.

If that were to happen, the effect would be magnified by the many and various connections among firms, financial institutions, and markets. If, for instance, stock prices fell, so would the capital of banks (45 percent of unrealized share gains are allowed as capital, remember) and thus the amount they are permitted to lend. The collateral for some of their loans would disappear, too, prompting them to call some in. As lending shrinks, clients go bankrupt and economic activity contracts. Insofar as industrial firms' stock prices have been based on their real estate assets and securities investments, their shares should fall fastest of all. Moreover, the beneficial effect of *zaiteku* on their profits could go into reverse.

In short, the impact of a collapse could be cataclysmic. So what? America had its Wall Street crash in 1929, yet sixteen years later it was the greatest superpower the world has ever seen, in both political and economic terms. Japan could, and almost certainly would, recover from a crash in its financial markets. It has shown before how adaptable its economy and institutions can be to new shocks. That is not a reason for complacency, however, or for accepting risks lightly. Also, a financial crash would interrupt what will anyway be a relatively short period of economic and financial preeminence until declining savings and an aging population hamper Japan in the late 1990s. More important, a Tokyo crash would make Japan's emergence as a great power still less probable. It would be unable to build a sufficient lead over its economic and political rivals. Unlike the United States, Japan's time for leadership, power, and influence promises to be fairly brief.

本国

HOME AND ABROAD

外国

PROLOGUE

Little sparrow! Take care!
Get out of the way!—Mr. Horse
is coming there!

—Issa (1762–1826)

THE RISE AND rise of Japan has prompted a paranoid reaction in the United States, Europe, and elsewhere. In the 1950s, 1960s, and 1970s, the metaphors used for Japan were an odd mixture: At first dismissed as a defeated nation, Japan became a flash in the pan, then a copycat, even a political minnow. All were wrong, or will prove to be: Japan was subdued but never beaten, it has astonishing staying power, it is innovative in all areas of business and life, it is becoming a political force to be reckoned with. But now the terms most commonly used to describe Japan have changed: "mammoth," "economic giant," "unstoppable machine," "financial empire." Behind these lies the assumption that Japan's economic rise is unstoppable and unremitting and that, in the long run, Japan must surely assume some form of leadership.

This may appear to be so from the outside, but a look inside Japan's economy and society suggests a different conclusion. The most surprising change in the late 1980s has been that, one by one, Japan's myths are being toppled. The nation of producers is becoming a nation of consumers, eager to accumulate material possessions, to buy foreign goods, and even to show off wealth in conspicuous displays. The nation of workaholics is becoming a nation of pleasure seekers, eager to travel abroad, to enjoy leisure, and to find whatever is best in life. The nation of healthy, education-mad youth is becoming a nation of healthy pensioners, as the baby-boom generation ages and the lifespan lengthens. The nation of squirrel-like savers, whose cash was controlled by the government, is becoming a nation of investors and, most astonishingly of all, a nation of speculators.

This toppling of myths is happening because Japan is, despite all that has been written and said to the contrary, a country that, just like any other, is affected by human nature and market forces. The Japanese are not a breed apart: They respond to low prices by buying more imports; they respond to affluence by buying expensive things; they respond to financial freedom by seeking out good deals or a quick killing; they respond to better and more secure pensions by saving less of their incomes. Just like other surplus countries before them, Japan's surpluses of capital, trade, and, in effect, power will not last forever. The changes already evident since the yen began to rise in early 1985 will see to that. More consumption, more overseas travel, more imports, lower savings, higher government spending, more financial gambling: these trends spell the eventual end of Japan's surpluses. The rising sun, as chapter 11 will argue, also sets.

That sunset will not come quickly, however. Japan's period as the world's leading exporter of capital could last as long as fifteen years, from its commencement in 1983. Part 2 of this book dwelled on the effects that this period has had, and will have, on Japan itself. The period is also, however, having profound effects on the rest of the world. These will be the subject of Part 3.

Japan is reaching out from its small group of islands in the Pacific. It is establishing a diaspora of investments, from Kentucky to Tierra del Fuego, from Sunderland to Bangkok. The growth of that diaspora is causing as much concern and hostility as did the arrival of Japan's exports in the 1960s and 1970s. Yet as the diaspora grows, Japan is also becoming a teacher to the world of, among other things, how to organize businesses and manage employees. In Asia, it is very gradually becoming an economic leader and will eventually become a political one, as Japan becomes the centerpiece of an integrated regional market.

These effects on the rest of the world come, however, complete with their own paradox. It would, perhaps, be most un-Japanese for such things to be simple, clear, and straightforward. Japan is reaching out to the rest of the world, yet at home, while it talks about internationalization, it remains rebuffingly parochial and inward-looking.

This gap between appearances at home and abroad is the greatest obstacle to a smooth relationship between Japan and the rest of the world and, indeed, to Japan taking on any political role. Japan's reluctance to lead makes it seem an unattractive candidate for world prominence. But the muddiness of Japan's power structure also makes it appear devious, untrustworthy, and, perhaps, impossible to deal with on the same terms as other developed nations. That this view is a misunderstanding does not make it any less dangerous. This gap between home and abroad promises to make Japan's period of surplus and wealth tense and awkward. Unless the gap closes, Japan will be condemned, as the Chinese say, to live in interesting times.

CHAPTER SEVEN

円

THE JAPANESE DIASPORA

How courteous is the Japanese,
He always says "Excuse it please,"
He climbs into his neighbor's garden,
and smiles and says "I beg your pardon,"
He bows and grins a friendly grin,
and calls his hungry family in.
He grins, and bows a friendly bow,
"So sorry, this my garden now."

—OGDEN NASH

THE RISE OF the yen, domestic affluence, and the capital surplus have all had profound effects on Japan, changing the way things are done, the way people live, and the opportunities they have, as well, in some cases, as producing new risks and uncertainties. These trends have not, however, merely changed the lives of that strange group of people living on those islands at the edge of the Earth. In the 1980s, Japan's wealth has flowed abroad to affect the lives of more and more non-Japanese. It may not yet have vaulted the Japanese into world leadership, but it has suddenly made it much more likely that an American, a European, a Hong Kong Chinese, or a Mexican will be working for a Japanese employer or living or working in a Japanese-owned building. Alternatively, he may be trying to get hold of Japanese money for his country, region, company, charity, or museum. He is also likely to have a Japanese neighbor or to live near a Japanese school. There is now a Japanese diaspora.

It is not that it is new for Japanese firms to invest abroad or to employ foreigners. A few firms have had overseas operations since early this century, many since the 1950s. The wave of the 1980s is different, however, above all in its size. In 1982, Japan's new direct foreign investment was just $4.5 billion; in 1985, it was $6.4 billion; by 1987 it had jumped to nearly $20 billion, of which more than half was in the United States. Those totals remained much smaller than Japan's portfolio investments overseas in foreign securities, such as Treasury bonds, which amounted to a net $88 billion in 1987, four times the direct investment. But direct investment made up a rising proportion of capital outflows, and its effects will be felt for far longer than will portfolio flows.

The 1980s' wave also differs in its character. Until this decade, Japan had few genuinely multinational firms producing and selling their goods in several countries. Japanese manufacturers preferred to export from their homeland, partly because, all things considered, this was cheaper than producing abroad but also because it gave them more control. Manufacturers' overseas investments consisted largely of sales and distribution networks. The largest investors overseas were firms seeking such raw materials as timber, oil, coal, and iron ore; occasionally, small factories were set up in poor Asian countries to supply local markets from inside a high tariff wall.

Matsushita Electric Industrial, Japan's and the world's largest producer of consumer electronics, is the prime example of the old, stay-at-home spirit: in 1985, although 45 percent of its sales were abroad, only 12 percent of its production was. Until 1984, Toyota, Japan's largest car maker, had no overseas factories. A survey in November 1986 by the IFO (Institute for Economic Research) in West Germany showed that overseas production accounted for about 20 percent of total production by German manufacturers. The corresponding figure for Japan, according to the Japan Machinery Exporters Association, was 4 percent.

When Japanese money began to flow abroad in the early 1980s, little of it was in direct investment because the capital outflow was occurring at a time when the yen was depreciating against the dollar.

That made production in Japan more and more competitive. Japanese businessmen are shrewd calculators of their competitiveness, so it took the doubling in the value of the yen against the dollar after February 1985 to change their attitude to overseas production. This not only made Japan a relatively less competitive place in which to produce, but it also made foreign assets—buildings, factories, companies, land, people—look very inexpensive. Sure enough, firms have poured abroad, creating the beginnings of true Japanese multinationals and making themselves landlords of large parts of foreign cities, especially in America.

By October 1987, the Japan Machinery Exporters Association found that 9 percent of production was now abroad, which is still small but is more than double the 4 percent cited a year earlier. Matsushita, for example, began to shift the manufacture of relatively low-tech electronic goods to other Asian countries and drew up a plan to produce 25 percent of its goods overseas by 1990. Toyota announced plans for its first two independent overseas factories, in Kentucky and Canada. By 1990, Japanese manufacturers will be making nearly 2 million cars a year in the United States.

So what? Plenty of countries have invested abroad before. Japan is not even the largest foreign direct investor in the country that in the 1980s has been its main target for investment, the United States. In terms of annual flow of spending as well as outstanding stock, it still trails far behind Britain and even Holland as owners of America.

Japan may overtake the Europeans in the 1990s as America's biggest foreign investor. But even if it does not, Japanese investment has a special flavor that distinguishes it from that of other countries. Japan's surge of direct investment is that of a supercompetitive power that is seen by some almost as a conqueror. First exports, now our own backyard; proof of the country's success and strength, and proof of America's weakness and decline. To the recipients, its investments are more comparable to American investment in Europe in the 1960s than to the current diversifications abroad of the British and Dutch. The jacket blurb to Daniel Burstein's somewhat overblown 1988 book, *Yen! Japan's New Financial Empire and Its Threat to America,* even describes direct Japanese investments as a "more malignant" problem than trade.

Moreover, a tinge of racism does exist in some attitudes toward Japanese investment in America, Australia, and, to a lesser extent, Europe. During 1988, there were protests in Hawaii and Australia against Japanese purchases of land and property, and calls for legal or constitutional restrictions. Comments have been made that, having failed to beat America by bombing Pearl Harbor, the Japanese have now decided to buy it: first the harbor, then the whole of America. Such things have been said both in serious texts and, in a more lighthearted but still poignant vein, in newspaper cartoons and comedy acts. By contrast, there has been a placid reaction to much larger European investments in America, such as that in 1987 by West Germany's Hoechst Chemical Company in Celanese Corporation for $2.8 billion (larger, then, than any single Japanese investment). Nobody claims that the U.S. dollar has surrendered to the Deutsche mark, despite wartime memories and the fact that since early 1985 the dollar has halved in value against the mark, too.

The most celebrated (or bemoaned) case of double standards came in 1987 and involved the U.S. Department of Defense. Opposition from the Pentagon forced Fujitsu, Japan's top computer maker, to pull out of a deal to buy 80 percent of a Silicon Valley firm, Fairchild Semiconductor, from Schlumberger, a French-owned oil-services and equipment firm. The Pentagon opposed the deal on grounds of national security because Fairchild is, among other things, a defense contractor which supplies the department with some of its semiconductor memories. It is not the sole supplier. Nevertheless, such "strategic" technology, the reasoning ran, should not fall into foreign hands.

Yet the fact that Schlumberger, Fairchild's owner, is a French firm and hence just as foreign as Fujitsu was presumably deemed irrelevant. This ought to be more of an insult to the French than to Fujitsu, since it implies that the Pentagon either thought France unimportant or thought Japan more capable of exploiting Fairchild's technology than the French. It is even odd to worry about that. While France has long had an ambivalent attitude to NATO and the Western alliance, Japan is supposed to be America's closest ally, at least according to a succession of speeches by the U.S. ambassador in Tokyo.

Might wartime memories be the reason? Perhaps but, again, would the Pentagon have opposed a sale to a West German firm such as Siemens? Probably not.

In practice, it seems that Japan is not really America's closest ally (or "most important bilateral relationship," as America's veteran ambassador to Japan, former Senator Mike Mansfield, used to say before he retired at the end of 1988). It is seen as much as a rival as a partner. The sense here is that of Ogden Nash's poem that opened this chapter: not only are Japanese formidable competitors but also Japanese activity is often slightly devious or sinister or may disguise its real motives. Be careful. They are out to get us.

This special reaction to Japan has coincided with a general unease in the United States about foreign investment flooding the country. In 1988, there were times when even British takeover bids for American firms provoked hostility. For example, when C. H. Beazer, a British building materials firm, bid for Koppers, an American competitor, an outcry rose up in Pittsburgh, Koppers' hometown. Local politicians asked civic employees to tear up their American Express cards because Beazer had been advised by Shearson Lehman, a subsidiary of American Express. There was also a worry about dependence on foreign money in general to finance the American economy, or, more particularly, its trade and budget deficits. Was America selling its birthright?

Early in 1988, a Washington, D.C., consultant, Smick-Medley & Associates, surveyed a thousand Americans about foreign investment, and asked the same questions of roughly a hundred opinion leaders—that is, congressmen, mayors, top businessmen, and prominent journalists. It found that attitudes differed widely between the general population and the special group. The general results were far more protectionist than were those for the special group. For instance, 40 percent of Americans supported a law to ban further investment, 89 percent wanted a law to subject foreign investors to special registration procedures, and 78 percent wanted a law to limit foreign investment in some unspecified way. Asked what they would do if foreigners bought the firm they worked for, 25 percent said they would organize resistance, 26 percent would write to Congress, and 6 percent would resign. Among the special group, only 9 percent would organize resistance, and none would either write to Congress or resign (they clearly realize both steps would be futile). Only 1 percent wanted to ban further investment, 48 percent wanted registration, and only 13 percent wanted to limit it.

On the other hand, the general results could be used to suggest a more optimistic conclusion. For instance, 54 percent of Americans oppose the foreign investment ban and more than half think foreign money creates new jobs, introduces the best of foreign techniques, creates more competition, and lowers prices. At least on this evidence, Americans are divided fairly evenly on the issue.

The general concern about foreign investment has been given its most eloquent voice by Martin and Susan Tolchin's *Buying Into America,* a surprise best-seller in early 1988 whose subtitle is *How Foreign Money Is Changing the Face of Our Nation.* This book is not only or even mainly about Japanese investment. Nevertheless, it illustrates the special attitude to America's Pacific ally by reserving some of its sharpest comments for Japan and the Japanese. Among other things, it says that

> There is persuasive evidence that some foreign investors, notably the Japanese, have purchased U.S. companies to acquire their technology and ultimately to eliminate U.S. competition in key industries.

I could not find any evidence in the Tolchins' book for this sort of grand conspiracy; nevertheless, the statement does echo an apparently common American view. The Japanese are widely believed to treat business competition as a form of war, and they fight dirty. *Buying into America* reported a prejudice that Japanese investment may sometimes be "unfair." For example:

> Critics of foreign investment credit Japan's methods of financing selected industries for tipping the scales in that country's favor. The Toshiba company, for example, does all of its long-term borrowing back in Japan . . . since the Japanese long-term prime interest rate was lower than that of the United States. The Japanese government works hard at keeping down the cost of capital.

It's hard to put your finger on it, and we love the jobs the Japanese create or protect in America, but something tells us that the Japanese might be cheating.

ATTITUDES TO FOREIGN INVESTMENT

So is Japanese investment a threat or a benefit? Should it be fought or encouraged? This is an increasingly important issue both in America and in Europe as the Japanese diaspora expands. A negative answer could mean in the United States legislation to control investment and in Europe strict controls to ensure the use of local parts in products manufactured by Japanese firms.

The Tolchins are not all that clear about the answer. They include a chapter extolling the benefits, in terms of efficiency and job security, that ensued from the 1983 takeover of a Firestone tire factory in Tennessee by Bridgestone, a Japanese firm. Bridgestone is a reversed translation of the name of the Japanese firm's founding family, Ishibashi, probably originally adopted because of its similarity to Firestone. Yet in the book's concluding section, the Tolchins question whether, in the long run, it is to the advantage of the United States for Bridgestone or Firestone to dominate the truck radial market. That passage was written well before Bridgestone purchased the whole of Firestone in 1988. Yet in the end, the Tolchins favor ownership by Firestone; they say that Bridgestone is 100 percent Japanese-owned, its top management will remain totally Japanese, and an increasing percentage of its profits will return home. All these are cited as bad things.

It is not entirely fair to single out one book as typical of attitudes to foreign investment. But *Buying Into America* is a useful model that appears to have been read widely in the United States, especially in Washington, and it reports faithfully the skeptical views of many senators, representatives, governors, bankers, industrialists, and others. Moreover, in its conclusion, it advocates a more aggressive approach by the United States to foreign investors. In particular, it makes a strong case for a policy of reciprocity—if we let your firms in, you must give ours similar rights and opportunities—when dealing with investment as well as trade. That principle has taken hold in Europe as well as in America, and the power to enforce it was written into Britain's Financial Services Act of 1986 as well as into America's controversial trade bill in mid-1988.

With this in mind, let us use the Tolchins' book as a sparring partner in trying to determine the best approach to the Japanese diaspora. One difficulty, however, is that *Buying Into America* confuses matters throughout by mixing together two quite separate questions. First: Is it a good idea for America's economy to borrow a lot of money from foreigners? And second: Is it good to allow foreigners to invest freely in the United States?

IT'S ALL MONEY

This is a confusion because the answer to the first question, about borrowing from abroad, has nothing to do with the form in which the money arrives or its source, whether it comes through the sale of Treasury bonds or the sale of Firestone, or whether it comes from Japan or Kuwait. In principle, moreover, nothing is wrong with countries running large current-account deficits and therefore borrowing (i.e., importing foreign capital) to finance them. Countries do not have to have exactly balanced trade accounts. The question that must be addressed is whether or not the deficit can be financed in the longer term without payments of interest, profits and dividends on that money taking up an increasing portion of GNP.

The answer to that, as the Tolchins say, must be no, but not because there is anything sinister about foreign money. America has become a borrower because in the 1980s it has tried to spend and invest more than it has available in domestic savings, generating huge budget and trade deficits. Although nothing is wrong with that per se, it is unlikely in America's case to be sustainable for very long. Foreign borrowing has to be serviced, whether by interest payments or by the repatriation of profits and dividends. The economy has to run faster to stand still. More critically, foreigners may not always be willing to provide fresh funds, in which case they will have to be offered higher and higher rates of interest, which risks causing a severe recession in America.

Ergo, move to the second question and restrict foreign investment? Well, no. To close one channel for foreign money would merely raise the cost of finance through others—which may bring on the recession worried about in the first place. Indeed, when looking at foreign money from this angle, it is arguable that direct investment is a better (i.e., cheaper) way in which to receive the cash than merely by selling Treasury bonds or other debt: Foreign investors in factories do not expect to repatriate profits for the first few years and may well continue to reinvest part or all of them thereafter. Moreover, the investment is productive: It creates employment, income, and spending, and often it increases exports or reduces imports.

Debt, by contrast, has to be serviced immediately and continually, come rain or shine. Ever since the developing-country debt crisis first hit the headlines in August 1982, American and other officials have been trying to persuade Mexico, Brazil, and other debtors to import foreign money in the form of equity capital rather than in bank loans. The argument applies just as well to the United States. If America is going to have to import foreign capital, it should be seeking more, not less of it in the form of foreign direct investment.

Whatever its form, the net import of capital is a symptom, not a disease; an effect, not a cause. The Tolchins make this point, but they neither give it sufficient weight nor carry it through to a full conclusion. If "dependence" on foreign money is a problem, the solution is not to attack the money or to change the way in which it is channeled; the solution is to change the policies that cause the dependence. The government must reduce borrowing by cutting its spending or by raising taxes, and it must find ways to encourage U.S. citizens to save more. It must also allow (or encourage) the dollar to fall sufficiently to restore the competitiveness of American producers. The second of these policies was implemented in 1988; the first has not been, to any serious extent. Until it is, America will remain "dependent" on foreign money regardless of whether it employs such weapons as reciprocity or imposes extra disclosure rules for foreign investors.

US AND THEM

The second, and main, question posed by the Tolchins' book—Is it good to allow foreigners to invest freely in the United States?—differs from the general question of foreign money for another important reason. America's reliance on foreign money is a problem in *net* terms, that is, because it imports more foreign money than it sends abroad, and in terms of whether the borrowing can be serviced. The issue of foreign purchases of factories or buildings is different. It is seen chiefly as a problem in *gross* terms, that is, the absolute amount of foreign direct investment. American worries about Japanese investment have not arisen by subtracting the number of Americans in Japan from the number of Japanese abroad. For direct investment, the net position matters only for the question of reciprocity, and then only peripherally.

The question about the merits of foreign investment is also, on the face of it, an extremely odd one. With tongue only slightly in cheek, it could be rephrased as "Do we want to have jobs; do we want to be prosperous?" While opposition to imported goods is understandable (though mistaken), given that their production provides jobs and wealth to other people, it is less easy to understand why anyone should oppose the arrival of those jobs and that wealth to their own backyard: "First they send us their goods; now they send us their dirty stinking money" seems to be the attitude.

In general, investment is surely A Good Thing, so if foreigners want to bring us more of it, then that should be a cause for celebration, not anxiety. In this light, complaints about other countries' alleged barriers to American investment seem just as odd. Why should America be bothered if Japan prevents American firms from investing in, and hence taking jobs and money to, Nagoya or Hokkaido? More fool Japan, more for us. Might it not be more logical, therefore, to encourage other countries to block foreign investment, since that would divert more of it to the United States? Reciprocity, in this area at least, is like pleading for the right to give away money.

Many Americans clearly do agree with at least part of this argument, as evidenced by scores of states with investment promotion offices in Tokyo and London. They crave money, jobs, and, later, votes. The Tolchins raise a sensible point about this enthusiasm in that sometimes states compete with one another, offering grants or privileges to lure foreign money. Toyota's plant in Kentucky, for instance, benefited from $112 million worth of new roads, low-cost loans, and employee training, as well as 1,500 acres of free land. This sort of thing may often be wasteful, since such grants are rarely the prime motive for plant location. Toyota almost certainly decided to invest in America, then shopped around for the best deal.

If investment in general is a good thing, then why should it matter whether it comes from foreign or American wallets? Beyond the general worry about "dependence" on foreign capital, the Tolchins raise several plausible reasons why it might be thought to matter. One is that "control" may be lost when an American factory is sold to a Japanese or other foreign firm. But control over what? The operation is subject to state and federal laws regardless of who owns it. A domestic owner is just as able, or unable, as a foreign one to hire or fire employees, increase or decrease wages, or change the product.

Perhaps the foreigners' "goals" might be different from those of American managers, the Tolchins ask. This, too, is implausible. American firms want to make profits for their shareholders. This is not a national goal but an individual goal for the firm, in competition with other firms. There is nothing "strategic" about it. Foreign owners would surely work toward a similar goal. They are not investing just for fun. There could be antitrust implications if a foreign firm bought a competitor and thus limited competition, which is, after all, a frequent motive for mergers, domestic or international. But this is not a problem merely because of the buyer's nationality. It can and should be dealt with by antitrust authorities on the same basis as a domestic takeover.

On the local level, it could be felt that a foreign firm would not have the same community spirit as would an American firm. It might take a one-dimensional, profit-oriented view, rather than a wider, long-term view that acknowledged the firm's civic responsibilities. Possibly. But that could as easily be true of a New York firm investing in Tennessee (or, indeed, a London firm investing in Newcastle-upon-Tyne) as of a foreign one; both are outsiders serving outside interests. It is also often the case that newcomers are even more concerned about establishing themselves in the local community than are old hands. They have something to prove.

Might foreign ownership be less stable? A foreign owner could suddenly pull out, leaving hundreds out of work. Yes, it might, but again, why is this more likely with a foreign than a domestic owner? Both are equally subject to laws about firings or the environment. The type of owner matters more than the nationality. For a local electronics firm, ownership by, say, General Electric might be deemed preferable to being bought by an American financier such as Carl Icahn or Saul Steinberg who might be more willing to close poorly performing factories. In any case, it is hard to see why either of these gentlemen is any more or less desirable an owner than would be Sir James Goldsmith, an Anglo-French corporate raider, or why GE would be preferable to Holland's Philips or Japan's Hitachi. Fear of the foreigner is especially strange since it is American firms that are stereotyped as hirers and firers; foreign firms are more often praised for favoring a longer-term approach.

BANKING ON FOREIGNERS

When applied to banks, the notion of losing control sounds more significant. Banks transmit money payments in an economy rather as the blood system does in the body. They are vital. They are also an important channel for monetary policy, since their decisions about deposit and loan interest rates in response to moves by the Federal Reserve chiefly determine the price and availability of money to end-users. Therefore, as is often said, it is safer and better for banks to be under national control than in foreign hands. The Tolchins cite worries about the fact that by 1986 nearly 17 percent of America's total banking assets were foreign-owned. This worry is not confined to America. In supposedly free-market Britain, the governor of the Bank of England, Robin Leigh-Pemberton, said in 1987 that foreigners would not be permitted to buy into "the core" of Britain's financial system.

What to make of this? Certainly, the case for close regulation of banks is a strong one; unstable and unreliable banks could cripple any economy. But it does not follow that banks must therefore be in domestic hands for such hands may be just as unstable or unreliable as those of foreigners—in some cases, more so. It is legitimate for a banking regulator to want to approve who owns banks and how they run them, but again, competence and motive are more pertinent here than nationality. Have any of America's bank failures of the 1980s been foreign-owned? Crocker National Bank in California was the closest to a failure, although the problem there was that its parent, Britain's Midland Bank, gave its American managers too much freedom, not too little. In 1986, it was sold, for a song, to Wells Fargo of San Francisco, which has reaped huge benefits.

Nationality matters for monetary policy only if policy is implemented through financial markets that are directly controlled, in other words, where administrative fiat matters more than price, or supply and demand. In such cases, the supply of money may plausibly be influenced by decree or over a cocktail with bank chairmen. But that is no longer the case in either America or Britain and is ceasing to be in France and Japan. The U.S. Federal Reserve influences interest rates by its own lending and by sales and purchases of Treasury bills. Banks, American or otherwise, respond as they see fit. In free markets, ownership matters only insofar as the authorities might one day seek to restore direct controls. In that case, it could always nationalize or sequester foreign-owned banks.

The Tolchins ask, "Is it good for the United States to have foreign banks control loan policies in New York and California," although they admit there is no clear-cut answer. This question makes sense, however, only if there might plausibly be an effort by someone, locally, nationally, or abroad, to "control loan policies." Until the 1970s, Japan used to channel loans to selected industries, so it would then have had a legitimate worry about who owned its channels. But in recent memory, neither the U.S. federal government nor state governments have attempted such a thing. Loan policies in New York and California are controlled by individual banks and are supervised by federal or state rules governing the capital backing of those loans and the level of risk, insofar as it is measurable. No attempt is made to direct loans toward particular ends, except level of risk. A bank is free to lend to whomsoever it chooses. Federal regulators have every right to ensure that foreign-owned banks adhere to the same rules about ownership and behavior as do American banks—for instance, that industrial firms cannot own banks or vice versa—but they have no obvious reason to discriminate against foreigners.

Might a Japanese bank be biased in favor of Japanese firms? That is a slightly more plausible worry, although one that conflicts with the more usual complaint of American banks—namely, that the Japanese are stealing all their American clients. Nevertheless, it might happen, but it would not if the lending was clearly uneconomic. Market pressures are brought to bear equally on foreign and domestic banks. It might bring in some Japanese cultural characteristics, such as a desire for long-term, stable banking relationships. But that is not a very powerful reason for restricting foreign ownership, which is a symptom not a cause.

THE ALL-AMERICAN TIRE

Let's return to the question of Firestone and Bridgestone. The main a priori grounds that the Tolchins found for preferring American owners to the Japanese were that the latter would repatriate an increasing part of the tire firm's profits to Japan and would select only Japanese for all its top management. Do these points matter? Repatriation of profits certainly matters for America's balance of payments; if it has a net drain of profits and dividends, then it will have to export more goods and services in order to cover the shortfall. That is part of the overall question of "dependence" on foreign money and the overall management of the economy. In an individual case, however, the fact that a sum equivalent, say, to 10–20 percent of the initial investment might in a few years be repatriated must be balanced against the fact that the investment took place at all. Is it a "problem" when IBM repatriates profits from its Japanese subsidiary or when Ford repatriates profits from Europe?

It is inconsistent, in any case, to worry about both foreign direct investment (an inflow of capital) and repatriation of profits (an outflow). They cannot both be "bad." If the Japanese firm were to leave its profits in the economy by building up its investment, then presumably that would be compounding the original "crime." In other words, if the Tolchins want the profits to stay, what can have been wrong with the investment in the first place? It would be more consistent to say that "The only good thing about inward foreign investment is that the so-and-sos take their filthy profits home with them."

A general point that is often forgotten is that foreign investors do not steal domestically owned firms. They purchase them from willing sellers. A ban (or even controls) on inward investment would therefore be a ban on domestic stockholders selling their property as and when they see fit. When they sell their stock, they receive cash they can use for other investments. Nothing is "disappearing."

Moreover, it is not fair to wonder, all things being equal, whether Firestone's ownership would be better than Bridgestone's. All things were not equal; Firestone's management had failed to run the firm profitably and efficiently, so stockholders chose to sell to Bridgestone in preference to backing the American managers. The extra efficiency, profits, and job security generated by Bridgestone may outweigh substantially the profits repatriated. Or they may not. There is no way of telling in advance.

As for management, it is generally true that Japanese firms prefer to use expatriate Japanese for the top executive positions, although many locals are employed too. Japanese dominance of top management is surely not a particularly bad thing, in any case. If you think Japanese management is superior, then their methods will rub off on their American juniors. If those juniors become frustrated, they will simply leave to join American firms, in which case the best American talent will be channeled to domestic firms. In practice, the issue is exaggerated. As Japanese multinationals evolve, they will become more confident about ceding power to foreign executives. Ultimate control will be in the country of origin, but that is also true for IBM's worldwide operations or for Citicorp's.

If Bridgestone had received any sort of substantial government subsidy to enable it to make the investment, then there might be grounds for concern, since it would amount to unfair competition. This was not the case for Bridgestone in particular or for the Japanese tire industry in general, despite a statement by the Tolchins that it did. They claim that Bridgestone benefited from easy access to low-interest capital, while Firestone faced high interest rates; from an undervalued currency, while the dollar was high; and from favorable antitrust laws in an era of tighter U.S. enforcement.

None of these stands up to scrutiny. Bridgestone had no preferential access to cheap capital, unless you count as an "unfair" advantage the fact that the Japanese economy was being run better than the American. Since Bridgestone's exports from Japan were minimal, it is hard to see what benefit came from an "undervalued" currency; indeed, the dollar's strength made the 1983 factory purchase an expensive one to a firm calculating in yen, and it gave it an asset that may have halved in value since. Now that the yen is strong, the whole of Firestone does look cheap to a Japanese, which is why in 1988 Bridgestone was willing to buy it. And was the Reagan administration really one of tighter U.S. enforcement of antitrust laws? Most would come to the opposite conclusion. It favored big business.

"STRATEGIC" INDUSTRIES

At the heart of American and other worries about foreign investment in general and Japanese in particular lies a concern about the loss of national sovereignty. Americans do not like to think that decisions affecting them are being made in Tokyo, London, or Riyadh. They want them made in Peoria, New York, or San Diego, even, it seems, if that means that the decisions are worse.

That same sort of fear explains why Brazil, Mexico, and the Philippines are loath to permit direct foreign ownership of firms. This is understandable, if unfortunate. Developing countries feel in a weak position when dealing with a mighty multinational such as IBM, whose total sales may exceed the country's GNP. If that is ever true of the United States of America, things will have come to a pretty pass; foreign ownership would then be a symptom that death was near; it would not be a cause. At the present or likely future level, American worries about national sovereignty are chiefly based on emotion rather than reason.

A second reason why developing countries (and sometimes the Japanese, for that matter) keep out foreign investors can be summarized as "jobs for the boys." Bans on outside firms make it easier to be corrupt and to reward local, vested interests. That does not make it a good thing to do. For America to want to retain sovereignty over that sort of opportunity would be an astonishing acceptance of inefficiency.

The final argument against foreign investment is that of national security. This is entirely legitimate, although it can be taken too far and can be used to disguise other motives. Mainly, it means maintaining control over important military technologies and confidence in the secrecy of defense projects. The important thing is to keep the definition of "military technologies" as narrow as possible to avoid giving unnecessary protection to domestic defense contractors, who then become fat and inefficient.

National security also justifies a generally careful political eye over foreign money. It might not be very convenient, for instance, to have Colonel Gadhaffi as the largest shareholder in Citicorp, or General Noriega of Panama as the ultimate employer of thousands of auto workers, or a member of OPEC as owner of much of the U.S. oil industry. But these are extreme cases that justify an emergency veto power rather than a general control.

RECIPROCITY?

This discussion has been lengthy because the issue of whether foreign investment should be welcomed or discouraged promises to be crucial during the next five years or more, in Europe as well as in America. It will form a growing part of the international response to Japan, its firms, and its prosperity. The U.S. attitude should be that foreign investors are welcome unless they can be proved unfit, as defined for all American businessmen. America must gradually import less net foreign capital, yet should remain permissive toward direct foreign investment. The former is a problem for macroeconomic policy; the latter is a question of preserving efficiency and growth. As Rudiger Dornbusch, an economics professor at the Massachusetts Institute of Technology, has written, the one problem with Japanese direct investment in the United States is that there isn't enough of it.

Buying Into America did not make a convincing case for re-
straints. The authors' clearest and strongest argument, however, was
rather that America must "demand a level playing field" abroad, talking tough in order to gain a "degree of reciprocity" in exchange for
American hospitality to foreign investors. The United States must
insist that others be as open as it tries to be.

This goal is hard to refute; it would clearly be desirable if every
country were as open to foreign investment as is America. America's
openness is not, however, a source of weakness as advocates of reciprocity imply; it is an advantage, since it brings efficiency, capital, better
productivity, and growth. In any case, others are not so closed as
Americans now tend to think they are (fewer complaints were heard
in the 1960s and 1970s when American firms were flooding abroad to
the same "closed" countries). Of course, barriers do exist. Removing
them would satisfy the free-market-economy theorist, since it would
enable resources to flow to their most efficient uses and further promote
the international division of labor. The earlier joke that America could
rationally try to persuade other countries to discourage foreign investment founders on this theoretical sandbank.

The question, though, is what is the best means to achieve this
ideal state of affairs. Tough, reciprocal threats from America to those
shifty, double-dealing Japanese? Or more considered and gentlemanly
negotiations in a multilateral forum, such as the General Agreement
on Tariffs and Trade (GATT)?

The gut reaction is to go for toughness. Real men don't bother
with GATT, which is all words and no action. The Japanese listen to
force and respect those who use it. The argument is attractive; it seems
to promise results, and fast. But it suffers from two fatal flaws. The
first is that if threats are to be effective, the user must be willing to carry
them out. That means that America must be willing to forgo the
benefits of such foreign investments as are banned, something that will
be more painful the bigger the threat. And for what? The right for
Ford to build a plant in Japan or South Korea rather than in Michigan
or for the remote benefits of the efficient allocation of resources? Tell
that to a trade unionist in Detroit.

Flaw number two is that reciprocity is dangerous and uncontrollable. Not only does it challenge the bilateral target to retaliate; it also

forces other countries to respond. A deal with Japan, for instance, implies the exclusion of Europe and possibly the diversion of pressure to the European market or the loss of markets in Japan for European firms. This retaliation may be avoidable during periods of prosperity, when all can see benefits from openness and growth. But once established as a technique, reciprocity would be disastrous in a recession. Eyes turn inward, tempers fray, doors close. Retaliation would be hard to avoid.

Reciprocity's emotional force is even stronger in trade matters than in investment. America's current-account deficit would be smaller, it is argued, if only those Japanese would play fair by lowering barriers to American goods. That is true, but it does not mean that the deficit has been "caused" by these barriers, nor does it mean that the deficit is proof that barriers must exist. There is no reason to expect trade to balance exactly; many other factors are at work besides barriers. Nor does it follow that reciprocity would be the best approach to secure trading advantages, for the same reasons as in investment. It is dangerous and more likely than not to be self-defeating. Most of the barriers only have a marginal effect and should certainly go, but the question that must be asked is whether it is really worth risking disaster merely for a minor, if emotionally satisfying, gain?

Furthermore, it is tempting to link trade and investment, but misleading. Investment is not a part of "trade strategy" as the Tolchins assert, for it generally substitutes local production for exports. That local production (and the jobs, wealth, and ideas it creates) is not possessed by the investor's home country. Are Ford's assets and locally manufactured sales in Britain somehow un-British? Some corner of a foreign field, in other words, is not forever England (or Japan). Investment is certainly a part of a company's commercial strategy—the effort to increase or maintain market share, to remain competitive, to earn profits—but that is different. The only case when it may be effectively an extension of trade is when an investment is bogus, a way to disguise exports as local goods in order to get around trade barriers. If a country insists on keeping the barriers, it must ban that sort of "screwdriver plant" investment whereby firms import components and merely assemble them locally. Better still, the barriers should not be there in the first place.

CHALLENGE, NOT THREAT

In their introduction, the Tolchins refer to an earlier book on foreign investment that in 1967 "sent waves of alarm through the European community." This was *Le Défi Americain (The American Challenge)* by Jean-Jacques Servan-Schreiber, a French journalist, publisher, and radical politician. This scaremongering best-seller warned that Europe was being invaded by American multinationals and that, if it did not wake up to what was going on, European civilization would fade away, superseded on its own soil by the United States.

Yet although these two books are similar in their subject matter, the difference between them is more interesting. Michael Dukakis, the governor of Massachusetts and the defeated Democratic candidate in the 1988 presidential election, ought to have read *Le Défi* before he turned into an economic nationalist toward the end of his campaign. (This was an even greater mistake than making a speech attacking foreign investment at a car-parts factory that turned out to be owned by Fiat. Not surprisingly, his speech drew a somewhat cool response.)

Contrary to modern nationalists, Servan-Schreiber, a liberal free-market theorist, did not argue or imply that American investment should be halted or restricted or even that anyone should consider this option. However, recently he has often been maligned and misquoted as a xenophobe. He did not favor reciprocity, registration, or closer control. Indeed, the book welcomed American investment while loathing what it implied about Europe's weakness and the state of its industry and its civilization. The American invasion was an effect, not a cause. The best response to it, Servan-Schreiber believed, was to remain open, to learn from the invader, and to build a truly common market in the EEC in order to permit European firms to achieve economies of scale; in other words, Project 1992 and the single market that is now planned, but twenty-five years earlier. If only Europe had listened to Jean-Jacques.

He can be listened to still. It is worth quoting his views at length, for they are as relevant to America and the Japanese diaspora as they were to Europe and the American diaspora:

The problem of American investments is not an isolated case. It is only one special aspect of the problem of power, of the growing displacement of power between Europe and America.

Nothing would be more absurd than to treat the American investor as "guilty," and to respond by some form of repression. No matter how determined we are that Europe be mistress of her destiny, we ought not to forget what Alexander Hamilton said in 1791 about foreign investment in the United States: "Rather than treating the foreign investor as a rival, we should consider him a valuable helper, for he increases our production and the efficiency of our businesses."

What seems like an enormous "rummage sale" of our industry to the Americans could, paradoxically, lead to our salvation. Nothing is spurring Europe more strongly toward the means of her own rescue than the U.S. economic challenge.

The important word is *challenge*. This, not threat nor danger, is the fairest translation of *défi*. Surely, it is also the best word for the Japanese diaspora arriving in America, Europe, and elsewhere. To try to stop it would be self-defeating, for it would deprive the recipient of capital, which would only thus be diverted to some other competitor. To call the diaspora unfair is not only wrong 95 percent of the time; it is also not constructive. It is rather like losing a football game and arguing that the victors had better get worse in order to make things fairer. To insist on reciprocity is absurd, since it is often interpreted as a demand, not only that the playing field must be level, but also that the same number of touchdowns must be scored at both ends.

To argue that the Japanese diaspora should be treated as a challenge is not the same as asking for complacency or placid acceptance. The argument is that it is better to learn from the invaders, to use them as the stimulus for regeneration. If the Japanese really are better at making things than the rest of us, then getting Japanese management, organization, and technology is the fastest route to raising productivity to Japanese levels. What seems like an enormous "rummage sale" of America's industry to the Japanese could, paradoxically, lead to America's salvation.

CHAPTER EIGHT

円

A JAPANESE TEACHER

*Bring me your yen, your pounds, your smuggled pesos
yearning to breathe free.*
—*The Economist* (SEPTEMBER 22, 1984)

BEFORE IT BRINGS salvation to Europe and the United States,
the Japanese diaspora will grow much larger than it is now. Forecasts
of future flows of capital are especially risky, but nevertheless, it is
worth noting as a guide Nomura Research Institute's projection that
Japanese manufacturers' outstanding stock of direct investment will
reach $66.4 billion by 1990 and $114.7 billion by 1995. That compares
with $24.4 billion in 1985. Measured by production the figures are
double those for capital: From overseas production worth $48.8 billion
in 1985, Nomura estimates that Japanese manufacturing abroad will
grow to $132.8 billion by 1990 and $240.9 billion by 1995. Employment by local subsidiaries of Japanese manufacturers is forecast to grow
from 800,000 in 1985 to 1.7 million ten years later.

Even then, the Japanese presence abroad will be small compared
with the total output and employment of the economies in which
Japanese firms are investing. There is a danger of exaggerating the
impact, just as Servan-Schreiber did in Europe. It is also dangerous
merely to extrapolate recent trends in order to assume growth will go
on forever. Nevertheless, the diaspora is likely to have a strong influence, partly for emotional reasons but chiefly because, like Japanese
exports, it is concentrated in a few sectors. In manufacturing, this

chiefly involves automobiles, consumer electronics, semiconductors, and computers. In services, it involves commercial and investment banking and property development. To any non-Japanese firm in these sectors, the Japanese challenge is impossible to ignore and, it must be hoped, impossible not to learn from.

As it grows, the diaspora will also mature. In the mid-1980s, Japanese multinationals were still, at best, adolescents, whether in manufacturing or finance. Plants were only just being built, banks only just being bought or set up, and Japanese executives, by and large, only just getting used to the idea of working closely with foreigners. To evaluate the Japanese starting point, in 1985 Professor Noritake Kohbayashi of Keio University Business School was asked by the Ministry of International Trade and Industry to survey Japanese multinationals to see how they compared with Western equivalents on various sorts of management issues. In 1978, he had made a similar study of 110 firms, while his 1985 study included 170 firms that had sales of ¥1 billion (then about $4.5 million) and operations in at least five countries. He did not cover banking and finance.

In a questionnaire, Professor Kohbayashi asked the firms how international was their handling of eight aspects of operations and ranked the answers on a fairly subjective scale of one to five for how international they were then and how they expected this to change in the next decade or so. He compared the answers with those from a small group of Western multinationals.

When Professor Kohbayashi asked, for instance, whether overseas management is incorporated in domestic management and whether a board director was responsible for international business, the average answer was a parochial 2.6, unchanged from 1978. Overseas management was treated as separate and junior. Western multinationals scored 4.2; in future, Japanese firms expected to integrate more fully and raise the status of overseas subsidiaries, but still not to the Western level. Planning, by contrast, appeared to be handled in a pretty international way, included fully in the annual and midterm plans of the whole company. The score was 4.0, compared with 3.7 in 1978, and not too far behind Western firms' 4.6.

Among the least international scores were those for the promotion of locals and the operation of research and development. Although there were already signs of better prospects for locally hired managers (2.3 versus 1.6 in 1978), there seemed to be little intention of bringing foreign executives to the head office. Western firms scored 4.2, and also gave their own expatriates better promotion prospects than did the Japanese. Research and development is not terribly international for the Japanese firms, but then it rarely seemed to be in Western firms either. IBM, with its Swiss Nobel prize-winners, is an exception.

Some Japanese companies are already talking boldly about how multinational they are going to become, much more than a dominant national headquarters overseeing a lot of foreign subsidiaries. *The Economist,* for instance, has cited two. Honda North America apparently talks of being an American company that will be an equal partner with Honda Japan. And Nomura Securities has talked of having three equal head offices in London, New York, and Tokyo. Both of these claims should be taken with a grain of salt, for both are likely to be rallying cries, designed to convince headquarters to cede more power rather than all of it. But the talk is at least indicative of how things are changing.

The target is more credible in Honda's case since the firm already sells more cars in America than in Japan (738,000 in 1987 compared with 620,000 in Japan) and may soon be making more there as well. In 1988, it began, in a small way, to export cars from the United States back to Japan. Nomura has much further to go before its true overseas business (as opposed to offshore Japanese business) rivals its domestic operations. The trend for both is likely to be toward more independence for subsidiaries if and when they grow large relative to the parent. But the instinct for central control will remain strong. Even Philips, the Dutch electronics multinational, maintains a dominant national headquarters even though its sales in Holland are tiny compared with its worldwide business.

The Japanese multinationals will quickly evolve into organizations similar to such Western firms as Ford, General Motors, Philips, or IBM. Gradually, they will seem less foreign. Just as British children grow up assuming that Nestlé, Ford, and Kelloggs are British firms, so Japanese brands such as Nissan, Sony, Toshiba, and Panasonic are gradually becoming established as local names. It may seem farfetched now, but in time they will become part of the local landscape. Ford is thought of as a British firm; after all, it has made cars there since the 1920s. Japanese names are stranger, but their foreignness will one day be forgotten or, more likely, considered irrelevant.

As that happens, the lesson or challenge that they bring will not be in their overall organization as international firms. That was one of the things that Servan-Schreiber most admired about American companies in Europe, that as multinationals they were organized to treat Europe as a single market rather than as a group of separate countries. The Japanese have no particular scope to innovate in this way. It has been done before.

A BETTER MOUSETRAP

The principal challenge of the Japanese manufacturing diaspora will lie in the management and organization of factories. As that happens, it will have the general effect of shaking locals out of hidebound ways. The automobile industry is the clearest example, although the point is true of other industries, too.

In cars, the challenge begins with a curious fact. Car makers in Detroit are worried about new Japanese plants in the South and West even though, at least until the mid-1990s, the new factories will generally be smaller than the existing American ones. Nissan's factory in Smyrna, Tennessee, which began making trucks in 1983 and cars in 1985, could produce a total of only 240,000 trucks and cars by 1987. That compares with the 2 million cars that Ford produces each year in America and the nearly 4 million made by General Motors, admittedly at several factories. High volume production ought, in theory, to give the Americans an unassailable advantage in delivery costs as well as in covering research and development, and design overheads. But it does not. Smaller Japanese factories produce cheaper cars than large American ones. Similarly, in Britain, Ford's plants manage to make only seventeen cars per man per year compared to the forty-plus that Nissan expects to achieve at its factory near Newcastle by 1992.

This is the most important challenge for American car makers: to become, by whatever means, as good as the Japanese at designing and making cars. Two decades ago, that statement would have been unthinkable. By 1988, however, the unfavorable contrast had been clear for at least five years. Yet not surprisingly, American managers and workers had seized every opportunity to avoid facing up to it.

As long as the competitive contrast almost entirely concerned imports from Japan, the recipients could tell themselves that it must be caused by some strange unfair practice in Japan, or merely by the exchange rate. The 1982 "voluntary restraint" deal that limited Japanese car imports into America was a prime example of a cop-out; it merely allowed Ford, Chrysler, and General Motors to raise prices and thus to rebuild profits without regaining market share, and to pay huge bonuses to their bosses. The Japanese, meanwhile, made bumper profits from their now-scarce imports to America and used them to become even more efficient at home. Protection was self-defeating. Until 1988, that fact was disguised by the strength of car sales in the United States, which gave good profits to all and permitted prices to be increased. It is during a recession that the disguise will disappear.

Moreover, now that Japanese competition has arrived in the backyard of Ford, General Motors, and Chrysler, and that the currency markets have in theory made it cheaper to manufacture cars in America than in Japan, it is going to be much harder for the American firms and unionists to avoid facing facts. Until now, the response to Japanese manufacturing superiority has been a fairly passive one: a mixture of "gosh, golly, aren't they good" with an assumption that it would only succeed with Japanese workers. From now on, that cop-out will not be possible. If the American managers and unions do not match or better Japanese techniques during the next five years, they will simply go out of business. British car firms suffered a similar challenge from American and European rivals in the 1950s and 1960s, and they failed. In effect, they went out of business, kept alive only by the taxpayer. Ford, General Motors, and Chrysler face the same fate if they do not adjust. There will be no hiding place.

Surprisingly, the car makers managed to keep clear of the boom in hostile takeovers and leveraged buyouts that swept American industry in 1986–1988. One reason was their size; another was that protectionism was giving their profits—and hence dividends—a temporary lift. In the battle for market share that will take place in 1990–1993, once the Japanese factories are up and running, there will be no guarantee of survival.

One reason that the Japanese plants in America offer a competitive threat at lower volumes of production is that they are located in parts of the country where some costs, but not all, are cheaper than in Detroit. This is not unfair; domestic car makers could do the same thing if they chose to. Grants and land concessions do help a little. A second and more important reason is that most of their factories are in states beyond the reach of the United Autoworkers Union (UAW). This does not necessarily mean that wages are lower than for UAW plants, for the Japanese have to pay the going rate. But it means that they can be more flexible about working practices and can begin to establish a relationship between bosses and workers that is relatively free of historic tussles. In his admirable book, *The Reckoning,* about Ford and Nissan, David Halberstam relates how much the UAW wanted a Japanese plant in America as early as 1978 and tried to persuade Nissan to open one. When it finally did, however, Nissan made sure it was well out of the UAW's grasp. To run the manufacturing firm in Tennessee, it hired Marvin Runyon, a fifty-five-year-old top executive at Ford who was as eager to get rid of the UAW as the Japanese were.

Some people have criticized the use by Japanese car makers of too many Japanese suppliers of parts. This is somewhat unfair. They have encouraged Japanese parts makers to build factories in America, which have brought jobs and investment with them. Although the Japanese client may occasionally have discriminated unfairly against an American firm, generally they have sought those suppliers most likely to produce to their quality specifications, which have been higher than those for American car firms, and at the best price. Nissan claims to have 123 American suppliers of production parts, providing $521 million worth in 1987.

In Britain, a book published by the Policy Studies Institute, *Manufacturers & Suppliers in Britain & Japan* by Malcolm Trevor and Ian Christie, has argued that Japanese firms have had an extremely beneficial effect on British suppliers, in the car industry as well as in other sectors. Trevor and Christie argue that British firms need to learn more from their Japanese clients, particularly prompt delivery and risk-taking by suppliers, as well as designing and improving products. As they point out, a close, supportive, but demanding relationship between supplier and client is not uniquely Japanese: Marks & Spencer, the British retailer, acts in a very Japanese manner with its clothing and food suppliers. The problem is that too few British firms are used to working in this way.

The *Financial Times* of December 19, 1988, carried an encouraging article about a small Welsh firm called Race Electronics that supplies electronics parts to Japanese manufacturers. In 1985, Race's parent, the Gooding Group, was losing money because of the collapse of the home computer market. The firm recovered after pushing aggressively for supply contracts with Japanese factories in Wales and the west of England. According to the article's quotes from Al Gooding, the firm's boss, quality and consistency are crucial: "If you say you will deliver at 10 o'clock on Friday, then the Japanese want to see the truck rolling through the gates at 10 o'clock, not at quarter past or half past, but on time." Further, he says that with a Japanese client winning a contract is only the beginning. The client's executives expect to be in their suppliers' factories every week, checking on progress down to minute details. "This is where they differ from so many British companies."

KEEPING CONTROL

The greatest reason for the Japanese manufacturers' edge appears to be their techniques for the organization of work and the control of quality. One way or another, they manage to have fewer rejects than their American equivalents and fewer faults once a car is on the road. The techniques themselves are familiar: quality circles to involve employees, statistical approaches to quality standards, just-in-time inventory control, and so on. Japanese firms often send a few Japanese foremen to foreign plants in order to train local supervisors.

What may be more important, however, is the spirit behind these sorts of techniques: working through employees rather than against them and drawing no firm line between managers and workers. It is that spirit and the ultimate goal that must be learned rather than the particular gimmicks employed by particular Japanese firms. The personnel director at Nissan's British car plant, Peter Wickens, has confirmed this judgment in a book called *The Road to Nissan: Flexibility, Quality, Teamwork.* In his view, Nissan's achievement in Britain has not been to brainwash its local workers with Japanese working practices, nor to dominate the firm with heavy-handed intervention by headquarters. The achievement has been that workers have been convinced that it is their factory and their responsibility for quality and for continuous improvement in productivity.

One key technique there has been to eliminate artificial barriers between first-class (i.e., salaried) workers and second-class (paid hourly) by having a single integrated salary structure. Another is to eliminate inspectors who, in other factories, would be responsible for checking other people's work and maintaining quality standards. At Nissan, the production team checks its own work and is responsible for its own quality control. Whatever the particular technique, the aim is the same: motivation and productivity.

There is nothing unique about this. Plenty of American and European firms practice Japanese ways and follow Japanese goals. The difference is in degree, not kind. How, then, do you make an American worker as enthusiastic, loyal, and hard-working as a Japanese? A few years ago, the fashionable answer was to borrow such Japanese techniques as quality circles (teams of workers to improve quality) and suggestion boxes. Such gimmicks proved not to be the magic wand that users imagined they might be. But this does not mean that the problem is insoluble. For example, Monsanto, the large American chemicals company based in St. Louis, Missouri, thinks it has found a better way. A visit to its agricultural chemicals plant in Luling, on the Mississippi delta just outside New Orleans, suggested that it might well be right. I wrote about the visit in *The Economist* in January 1989, but it is worth repeating here.

The trick that Monsanto is attempting to pull off is something many firms are talking about: making employees feel that the company is theirs. How? Mainly, it seems, by asking them to use their brains as well as their hands. At the Luling factory the change in atmosphere is remarkable. The talk even among the lowliest workers is of "total quality" and "making it happen" and "our plant."

Monsanto's main organizational change in its factories has been similar to policy at Nissan in Britain: to do away with most of its foremen, supervisors, and quality inspectors and instead to invite plant workers to oversee themselves. To that end, it has given ordinary workers access to financial information about their part of the operation. Workers are being trusted with information previously treated as secret. The operator of a production line now knows, for example, what his section's profit or loss is at the end of each month.

Sometimes, this information is available on the interactive computers used to control plants; otherwise by more old-fashioned ways. What it means is that workers can now tell what difference it makes whether something is done well or poorly, quickly or slowly. The next step has been to encourage them to form teams, on an ad hoc basis, to make improvements, whether large or small. At Luling, for instance, Monsanto has a plant producing analgesics for use in headache pills. It is thirty years old and the equipment leaks. Instead of just watching it leak or calling in outside contractors, plant workers decided last year to form a small team and make the repairs themselves. They figure they have already saved $155,000 a year. Previously, they didn't even think it mattered.

A further step has been to encourage teams to compete. In November 1988, the entire agricultural division of Monsanto's American operations had a conference in St. Louis called the "Big" meeting, at which sixty teams vied to prove that their scheme, whether for production, quality, or safety, was the smartest, safest, or most valuable. According to Ed Jurevic, the Luling plant manager, the atmosphere on the bus going to St. Louis was like a team on the way to a football game: excited and determined to win. Monsanto's chemicals division has launched a similar annual meeting called the "Tournament of Champions."

Cynical? Well, I met enough workers at Luling to be convinced that they, at least, are not. Two employees, one from a textile fibers plant in Pensacola, Florida, and another from a chemicals factory at Chocolate Bayou, Texas, were summoned to talk to the parent firm's board about changes in their plants—a new idea in itself. One said, according to an evidently awed Richard Mahoney, the chief executive, that it was "so exciting when somebody asks me to use my head. I have so much to offer." Mahoney thinks it is no coincidence that in the past three years the textile plant has increased productivity by 50 percent.

Another important change has been to put workers in contact with their customers so that they know where the product goes and how it is used. A Luling team redesigned the packaging for their product once they had visited a customer, had seen what was really needed, and had been able to ask questions. Previously, the team would have had to make inquiries through the sales staff. Now they can go direct.

Similarly, quality control in the filling of bottles of herbicide improved markedly once workers were allowed to try several different ways of measuring quality and could get feedback from vendors and customers. Complaints per 100,000 halved in 1988. Ceasing to overfill bottles saved perhaps $200,000 last year. Why didn't quality circles work as well? According to Luling staff, they were too artificial, fixed on single projects with little feel for why you were doing it. "It felt as if you were doing it for somebody else."

This sort of change has not happened overnight. It took time to convince workers that management really meant it, that it genuinely wanted to attack the barrier between "us and them." Success meant that the same approach of using self-directed teams could also be applied to other tasks, such as safety. These new methods were introduced first in nonunion plants, where workers were more flexible, but have now spread to some previously tough union plants, too. What has not yet been solved is how to link improvements to pay for ordinary workers, beyond a general system of bonuses. That is what Mahoney wants to tackle next.

On its own, Monsanto's apparent breakthrough in employee motivation will not be enough to make the firm prosper. But as long as it lasts, it will be a big help. One lesson is that in trying to match the Japanese ability to get the best out of workers, it is wrong merely to copy Japanese methods or gimmicks. The question to be asked is not what they are doing, but why. Having answered that, firms can then seek their own means to achieve the same end. That is perhaps the most basic lesson of all from Japanese competition.

A JAPANESE TEACHER

MADE IN EUROPE

More gradually, European car makers will face the same sort of threat as are their American equivalents (and sometimes parents), although they will do their best to avoid it. The largest Japanese car plant in Europe was built since 1983 by Nissan (and mentioned above) at Washington, near Newcastle in the Northeast of England. By 1989, it was producing 50,000 Bluebird cars each year and had begun exporting a few of them to other European countries. That is where the trouble began. In their efforts to avoid learning from the Japanese challenge, European car makers and their governments have tried to prevent those cars from being exported from Britain.

The excuse, used principally by France, has been that these cars are not "made in Europe" because more than 20 percent of the value-added (i.e., parts and labor) comes from Japan. This claim is necessary because France has a protectionist policy against imports of Japanese cars (it wants to protect the French from cars that are too good and too cheap), restricting Japanese imports to 3 percent of its new-car market. By claiming that Nissan's Bluebirds are not sufficiently European, France can count them as part of that 3 percent, rather than as extra cars. Why, then, doesn't Britain protest loudly? The awkward answer is that Britain also has a limit on Japanese imports, a "voluntary" one of 11 percent of its market. That also makes it reluctant to have too many Japanese assembly plants exporting to Britain from other European countries (Spain or Portugal, for instance).

In time, this local content excuse will disappear, as Japanese cars will become almost entirely made in Europe. By 1990, Nissan expects to be producing annually at least 200,000 cars at its British plant, with local content of well over 80 percent. At that level, French protectionists will not have a leg to stand on, since the EEC authorities have long since ruled that a 60 percent local content (which Nissan's Bluebirds had exceeded by 1988) was sufficient to make a product genuinely European. Beyond 80 percent, the French will not even be able to filibuster.

This argument over cars and local content is important because it confirmed Japanese fears that Europe's goal of a single, frontier-free market by the end of 1992 would actually presage the establishment of a "Fortress Europe." Europe will most likely not raise its barriers to trade any higher than they are now, but barriers will most certainly be maintained at their present level. In the car market, this will mean that quotas and "voluntary" restrictions at the national level will be replaced by an EEC-wide voluntary restraint agreement (VRA), probably allowing Japanese imports to take about 11–12 percent of the total EEC market.

Japanese car makers, while officially worried about this, are in practice rather pleased. European ministers think this means that a restraint agreement is a good idea. Just the opposite: It means that, as with America's VRA, Japanese firms know that they will be the beneficiaries. They will charge higher prices, reaping extra profits to plow back into investment. European competitors, cushioned by the import barrier, will have little incentive to match Japanese improvements to productivity and to facilities. That will leave the market wide open for Japanese firms to build their own plants and produce cars in Europe more cheaply and efficiently, and with more enthusiastic and loyal workers, than European makers can. It is curious that Japanese firms (such as Toyota) have tried to lobby for a more open approach under 1992 by threatening not to invest in European factories. In fact, the result of a Fortress 1992 will be a bigger incentive for investment in Europe, not a smaller one.

BANKERS TO THE WORLD

It may be something of a surprise to anyone who thinks of the Japanese as chiefly makers of things that in the year to March 31, 1987, services accounted for more than 75 percent of Japan's new foreign direct investment. Part of that was by trading companies (8.3 percent) and transporters (8.6 percent). But the bulk was in finance and insurance (32.4 percent) and in property (17.9 percent). Banks, brokers, insurers, and real estate firms have been much faster at setting up a diaspora than have their manufacturing clients.

Of these, the most important challenges are from the banks and brokers, which have become the low-cost producers in commercial and investment banking. Their growth shows up in their business turnover as well as in their investment. By 1987, Japanese banks held 35 percent of all cross-border banking assets against 26 percent in 1983, while seven of the world's ten largest banks measured by assets were from Japan. Measured in yen, their assets had risen by 80 percent since 1983, in depreciating dollars by 200 percent. Japanese-owned banks held about 15 percent of the deposits in the state of California, where most have their American headquarters. In London, Japanese banks accounted for 36 percent of all nonsterling lending in what is one of the world's main international banking centers. Securities houses are no less powerful.

By 1988, Nomura and Daiwa Securities had grabbed the top two places in the league table for Eurobond underwriters, and Nikko and Yamaichi were not far behind. Nomura, Daiwa, and Nikko all had primary dealerships for U.S. Treasury bonds, which enables them to deal directly with the Federal Reserve Bank of New York (the government's agent) and hence at the finest prices. They were also causing a stir in London's stock and government bond (gilts) markets, were opening brokerages across Europe, and were playing a powerful role in the large Swiss bond market.

This rapid expansion abroad has caused even more cries of foul than has the growth of industry. Surely Japanese firms must be "dumping" financial services or exploiting their "unfair" domestic advantages? But there is nothing surprising or even sinister about the strength of Japanese banks. It is the most direct by-product of Japan's successful economy and the fact that, since 1982, Japan has become the world's largest exporter of capital. For all sorts and nationalities of banks, their business can crudely be summarized as "have money, will travel." The rise of the yen since February 1985 has reinforced that, ensuring that overseas growth looks cheap and stretching Japanese banks' resources in dollar terms.

There are three other points about the Japanese banks that make their low-cost competition painful for foreign rivals. One is that, as with much of Japanese industry, the banks' shareholders are less concerned about profits than are their American or British counterparts. Japanese banks' returns on assets are low (around 0.2–0.3 percent), lower even than French banks' returns. Contrary to protectionist myth, this does not mean that they will readily bear losses or "dump" financial services;

it does mean they will tolerate lower margins and thus lower prices than will their banking rivals.

The second point is that the two main international credit-rating agencies, Moody's and Standard & Poor's, rate Japanese commercial banks as very creditworthy, especially compared with American banks, because the Japanese have large hidden reserves, few nonperforming loans, and a strong yen to make their Third World loans less worrying. This not only gives the Japanese banks access to cheaper money-market funds than rivals, but also gives them an edge in businesses that involve a bank guarantee. A borrower that uses a Japanese bank for a standby letter of credit, for example, will be able to borrow more cheaply in the market because of the guarantor's AAA or AA rating. That is why about half of America's market in standby letters of credit has gone to Japanese banks. Nothing unfair about that.

Advantage number three gives more reason for grievance. Until now, Japanese banks have operated under easier capital requirements than have American, British, German, or Swiss banks, although not French banks. Even after a recent stiffening of the rules, Japan's Ministry of Finance has only asked banks to have capital backing of 4 percent of assets by 1990 compared with 6 percent or more in America. That helps reduce capital costs and means that more assets have been perched on a smaller amount of capital. This has not meant that Japanese banks are weak, however. The Ministry of Finance has had such low capital requirements because all its charges have vast hidden reserves of shareholdings valued at the original purchase cost. Every rise in the Tokyo stock market, on the back of Japan's economy, directly increases the banks' effective capital, enabling them to lend more and more. The banks are not perceived to be at risk. Not all Japan's commercial banks yet meet the Ministry's 4 percent rate, but all meet a second rate of 6 percent for which, under the Ministry's rules, 70 percent of unrealized securities gains is added.

This is not sensible in the long term. If, in a crisis, the capital was actually needed, it is very likely that the crisis would in turn depress the stock market, lowering the value of reserves. If several banks needed to sell their securities at the same time, that too would push down equity prices. The cushion could disappear from under the banks. That is one reason why a new international deal on capital adequacy, agreed to in 1987 under the auspices of the Bank for International Settlements, has removed that right and hence, very soon, this competitive edge. Now Japanese banks will only be able to count 45 percent of their unrealized securities gains when seeking to meet the deal's capital requirement of 8 percent of risk-adjusted assets, which they have to do by 1992. Even that compromise annoys American banks, which is presumably why they have in return been allowed a dubious privilege, the right to include part of Third World reserves in capital.

KNOW YOUR BANKING CHALLENGER

Japanese penetration of international banking has followed the pattern of earlier "invasions" of manufacturing industries by exporters. Japanese banks appear to target specific sectors and, like car makers, start with bulk, standardized products. That is not surprising; it shows that Japanese banks are good at spotting where their strengths lie. The question is how and whether those strengths will develop, pushing the Japanese into new segments of banking.

A 1987 study by the Bank of England showed how, so far, Japanese banks have concentrated abroad on large-volume sovereign lending and, until the market collapsed in late 1986, on investments in floating-rate notes. More than 90 percent of their assets in London at the end of June 1987 were international, and their share of all London banks' international assets was 36 percent. The Japanese have hardly penetrated domestic banking in Britain, with, in August 1987, only 8 percent of the market in sterling and foreign currency loans to British residents. That is about the same as in America, where in the year to March 31, 1987, Japanese banks took an 8.4 percent share of total corporate loans. In the domestic British market, Japanese banking business was heavily concentrated, however. It accounted for about a third of all loans to five sorts of borrower: wholesale distributors, building societies (savings and loan associations), water boards (municipal water utilities), central and local governments, and securities dealers.

These can be put into two groups. Most of their clients among wholesale distributors and securities dealers are Japanese firms: big trading houses, car importers, and consumer electronics firms in the former case; stockbrokers and the banks' own merchant-banking subsidiaries in the latter. Japanese banks' first advantage is with clients they know from back home. Building societies, governments, and water boards are a different case: Highly creditworthy clients, they command low interest rates and borrow in large volumes of generally simple instruments. This sort of business is where low costs and low profit expectations count the most.

A similar sort of pattern, adapted to local conditions, can be found in the United States and continental Europe. In America, Japanese banks have, for instance, been enthusiastic lenders to leveraged buyouts and to municipal authorities. The billion-dollar question for aggrieved local competitors is, of course, where will the Japanese penetrate next? There can be no firm answer to that, but some clues can be found. The most important issue is the extent to which the Japanese will be in a position to increase their assets. Second is the issue of how much further and where else will their domestic clients expand abroad. What local businesses might be built on the foundation of Japanese multinational borrowers? And finally, where else might low costs and standardized products be brought to bear?

CRUMBS OF COMFORT

The Japanese banks' ability to increase their assets further depends chiefly on the future of Japan's savings surplus. Chapter 11, summing up this book, will argue that over the next decade the surplus will gradually fade away as personal savings and the current-account surplus shrink and domestic demands on savings expand. That is little comfort for rival bankers since they have to compete day by day. A respite in five or ten years is not going to help many of them sleep now. But it is important for the Japanese banks, since it shows that they have a window of opportunity rather than a permanent advantage.

A more immediate comfort, however, is the new international deal on capital ratios. This has already had a dampening effect on Japanese banks abroad. In the first nine months of 1986, Japanese banks' international assets grew by 29 percent. In the same months of

1987, according to the Bank of England, they grew by just 9 percent. That slowdown was a direct result of Japan's own tighter rules on capital. The Bank for International Settlements' rules will keep future growth slow. According to calculations by S. G. Warburg, none of Japan's ten largest banks stands far below the international target of capital worth 8 percent of assets by 1992. But all do have to raise their ratios somewhat, in one of two ways: by reducing their volume of assets or by raising more capital. Shrinking balance sheets goes against the Japanese grain, so most will seek to raise more capital either by placing fresh equity or by retaining earnings.

This puts Japanese banks in a similar position to their American rivals. They are going to have to worry more than before about profitability and so will be less inclined to make just any old loan, regardless of the margin. They will be better able than the Americans to raise new capital because they have tame, wealthy shareholders and solid balance sheets. But again, the need to raise capital will be a discipline. From now on, Japanese banks will only be able to add new assets in line with their capital. That capital will itself be affected by the vagaries of the Tokyo stock market. Even in Japan, it cannot be certain that the prices of financial assets will rise forever.

This returns to the discussions in chapters 5 and 6 about deregulation and the risks of speculative markets, respectively. The gradual domestic squeeze imposed by the removal of artificial ceilings on deposit rates will affect the Japanese banks' competitiveness abroad. In 1980, only 9 percent of the city banks' funds came from market-rate deposits; by 1987, 28 percent did. By 1990 at the earliest, 1992 at the latest, all deposits will be subject to market rates. Other things being equal, that will raise the city banks' cost of funds and lower their domestic profits.

They are also vulnerable to a domestic tripwire, namely, the risky rise of the stock and real estate markets. Remember that the city banks have been the largest lenders for real estate, increasing their property loans by 36 percent a year. The banks' total exposure in this one area could be as much as 30 percent of their loan portfolio. That is a big risk, especially when the real estate market has been so speculative and price rises so rapid. It is just the sort of reckless, overconcentrated expansion that in the 1980s helped injure Bank of America and Crocker in California. Any sustained fall in property prices would cause some defaults by borrowers, edging up banks' loan losses and eating into reserves or profits or both. The larger the losses, the more likely that securities gains will have to be realized to cover them and the more likely that the Tokyo stock market will fall in value. And then the less capital the banks have and so the less assets they can hold . . . and so on.

CHASING THE CUSTOMERS

If there is doubt that Japanese banks will retain all their funding advantages and asset-hunger in future, it is clear that more and more of their Japanese clients will expand abroad. When a Japanese firm first sets up shop in Kentucky or Northumberland, its bank is the one with local expertise. In Britain, the bank with the most local Japanese business is National Westminster, not Sumitomo. But a Japanese firm will likely go to a Japanese bank for large borrowings. And once the Japanese bank has a local branch, the chances are that head-office links, language, and golf will combine to get it more of the firm's business.

That is just what happened during the expansion of American banks abroad on the coattails of American industry, except that in most places local banks now offer stiffer competition than they did in America's heyday. It takes time and money to build a really large international network. As a result, no Japanese bank is now likely to try to emulate Citicorp's presence in hundreds of countries. Still, Japanese banks will grow, chasing these clients and building up local expertise and local staff. As they do, they will edge upmarket toward more profitable business abroad. A Japanese client in the provinces brings a Japanese banker closer to local middle-market companies, for instance. The Bank of England says that three Japanese banks have already opened branches in Britain's Midlands and North and that many intend to find more business with British customers.

In 1987, Dai-Ichi Kangyo Bank paid U.S. Trust, an American commercial bank, a small premium for its $200 million loan portfolio. U.S. Trust's customers were consulted before the sale, and virtually all said they were happy to bank with Dai-Ichi Kangyo, Japan's and the world's largest. So the bank has bought a package of multinational and middle-market relationships. The same idea lay behind Industrial Bank of Japan's 1985 purchase of J. Henry Schroder Bank and Trust in New York: a small bank, but one that brought relationships. The Japanese are burrowing into the core of domestic corporate banking.

ON MAIN STREET, U.S.A.?

What about retail banking? The wealth and size of Japanese banks certainly put them in a position to buy banks, thrifts, or British building societies abroad, if any are available, in order to build retail networks. They are unlikely to grow retail networks organically, since bricks and mortar are costly, and the Japanese have no special advantage or expertise in this area. Consumer credit in Britain is very profitable, and that could tempt Japanese capital. Sumitomo Bank has entered the business, but only in a small way and as a wholesaler rather than directly to the public. That way, it can treat mortgages as a commodity. Sumitomo's president, Sotoo Tatsumi, rules out overseas retail networks because his bank lacks the manpower to manage them.

For the moment, a big purchase would spark too much political opposition for the Japanese to try it, unless invited. There is another problem: Unless the target were already very successful and well managed, a Japanese buyer would find it very difficult to barge in and start cutting costs and firing people. That is always easier for a local. And to buy a good foreign bank would normally require a hostile takeover, which has not yet been a Japanese tactic.

All these things considered, a large-scale Japanese entry into the retail banking business is the least likely of their future moves. It is too expensive. One statistic that is often quoted by scaremongers about the Japanese is that Japanese-owned banks account for about 13 percent of California's $200 billion in bank deposits. All of the California banks ranking from five to ten inclusive are now in Japanese hands. Many of these were purchased from other foreign owners, chiefly British banks. The latest addition was Union Bank of California, which was bought from Britain's Standard Chartered by Bank of

Tokyo in early 1988 for $750 million. It was merged with Bank of Tokyo's existing local subsidiary, California First, to form the state's fifth largest bank.

That sounds like an alarming invasion. But on closer examination it looks much more docile. Most of the half-dozen largest Japanese banks have their American affiliates in California because the state is closest to Japan, has the most Asian residents, and has the most trade and investment links. For the purpose of America's banking laws, that means that they cannot do retail business in any other state, unless it has a reciprocal arrangement with California. This means, among other things, that these subsidiaries really are not the Japanese beachhead in America that they appear to be. Big corporate loans, standby letters of credit, and other wholesale business are chiefly done by branches of the parent bank, spread coast to coast as is allowed for all banks under the interstate banking laws.

The California subsidiaries are no small fry; Bank of Tokyo's merged subsidiary now checks in at $15 billion in assets and about 170 branches, although that is less than a tenth the size of America's largest, Citicorp, and a quarter the size of California's fourth largest bank, Wells Fargo. It and the other California subsidiaries are also tiny compared with their parents' balance sheets. Moreover, their returns are respectable rather than dramatic: moderate profits, moderate growth. They are run as American banks, with all but the very top jobs filled by Americans. They are a sideshow in comparison with the real battle going on among California's top four banks—Bank of America, Security Pacific, Wells Fargo, and First Interstate—to become the most efficient producers in the state's retail and middle-market corporate businesses. Wells Fargo, in particular, is already far ahead of the Japanese subsidiaries in these areas. Its "challenge" is not from the diaspora but from its own shareholders and from other American banks.

The largest of the Japanese subsidiaries do want to expand. Like all American banks, they want to move into areas that are more profitable than bulk lending, which usually means middle-market corporate banking. That was Union Bank's strongest business among a whole bunch of mediocre ones, which Bank of Tokyo says is why it bought it. Most important, they are all preparing themselves for 1991, which is when California state law will supersede the federal McFadden Act and allow interstate banking on a reciprocal basis. That can be viewed from two sides: it lets the Japanese out, or it lets outsiders in. So far it appears that the Japanese subsidiaries are more concerned about invasions than they are excited about chances for expansion.

This may sound complacent, the sort of "it'll never happen" that has greeted previous waves of Japanese competition. It is not. Simply, ownership in California is not the main challenge from Japanese banks. In retail businesses, it can be gladly said, American banks are fast becoming the world's most efficient, thanks to the collapse of interstate banking laws and the construction of new, dynamic regional banks such as First Union or NCNB in North Carolina, or Bank of New England in Boston. The Japanese challenge lies elsewhere: in international lending, in big-ticket deals for multinational clients, and in investment banking. Those are where the Japanese advantage lies. Unlike the manufacturing industry, the challenge is not managerial, since the Japanese banks are not conspicuously well run. But it is a low-cost, competitive pressure that is forcing American and European banks to shake themselves up.

IN THE MARKETS

The rise of such investment banks as Nomura and Daiwa has already been touched upon. The "big four" brokers have been among the fastest-growing firms on Wall Street since 1985 and have come to dominate London's Euromarkets. Their basic strength, again, is Japan's capital surplus; it will last as long as the surplus lasts.

In the meantime, Nomura, Daiwa, Nikko, and Yamaichi have been trying and so far failing to penetrate domestic securities businesses in America and Europe. They have grabbed pension-fund management business, but only for Japan and other Asian markets. They have helped American multinationals raise money, but only in deals related to Japanese cash via the Euromarkets; they have not penetrated domestic underwriting. In New York, all four lost money during the October 1987 crash.

The transaction that aroused the most interest and concern in 1988 was an investment of $100 million by Nomura in Wasserstein, Perella, one of Wall Street's newest investment banks. Wasserella, as the firm is commonly known, was born in February 1988, when two of America's top takeover stars, Bruce Wasserstein and Joseph Perella, quit First Boston after a dispute over the firm's direction. The pair's fame brought clients with them so that by the time of the Nomura investment in July the firm had already given advice on takeover deals worth a total of $19 billion, a phenomenal amount. But it needed capital in order to take part in Wall Street's most profitable and risky practice, namely, investing and lending money for deals on which you also give advice. Hence what some saw as a deal with the devil.

This is misleading. Nomura's investment is an effect rather than a cause. The surge in Japanese firms' direct investment into America has brought with it a growing market in advising them on who to buy and for how much. Back home the clients are often Nomura's, but in America the firm is poorly placed to advise them since it is unfamiliar turf. Also, mergers and acquisitions advisors are generally highly paid prima donnas, who fit awkwardly in the relatively bureaucratic Japanese atmosphere. So Nomura's solution is neat: Hire an outside firm of prima donnas to do the business for you, avoid the management problems, and (since the $100 million is a 20 percent stake) get 20 percent of the profits. In addition, if Wasserella succeeds, Nomura can take some profits from domestic American M&A business, too. Messrs. Wasserstein and Perella lose nothing. They retain management control and simply receive capital and clients. Theirs is a business in which the assets go home every night, so the Japanese firm is never likely to make a fuss lest the assets walk out—as they did at First Boston.

The challenge for foreign firms from these big Japanese investment banks lies first and foremost in trying to get hold of Japanese clients and money. As long as the fattest part of the worldwide investment business is Japanese, Tokyo is where firms will have to try to succeed. Salomon Brothers proved that it is possible by grabbing the third largest share of business there in bond futures trading after 1986.

Outside Japan, the challenge is to remain nimbler and better managed than are the Japanese firms. Nomura's bulk must stimulate Goldman Sachs or Credit Suisse First Boston to hold on to clients with fresher ideas and faster footwork. At the same time, foreign investment banks should lobby their governments to get their macroeconomic policies right in order to get funds flowing in a more favorable way. Once again, this means the stimulation of more savings and less borrowing in America. Other things being equal, that would mean less dependence on foreign money.

CHAPTER NINE

円

A YEN BLOC IN ASIA

Greater rage hath no man than a Japanese mistaken for a Chinese. Save perhaps a Chinese mistaken for a Japanese. Or maybe a Korean mistaken for either.
—RICHARD HUGHES

IN NORTH AMERICA and Europe, the challenge from Japan and its diaspora will be felt chiefly in the form of inspiration and competition. Closer to home, in the vast and diverse area known as Asia/Pacific, the Pacific rim, or the Pacific basin, Japan's future role and influence could be more direct. As the group of countries that constitutes this area becomes more and more integrated economically, Japan most likely will gradually take on a role as leader, possibly of the sort shared by West Germany, France, and Britain in the European Community. It will provide the region's key currency, be at the heart of trade and capital flows, and, through its currency, exert a stabilizing influence on its neighbors' economies and economic policies. From this economic relationship, a political one will flow. Japan is Asia's natural leader.

This sounds extremely farfetched to anyone familiar with Asia and its past hundred years. Consider the objections. Asia/Pacific is not like the European Community: It is far larger, far more spread out, far more diverse politically and culturally. Defined broadly, it could include Australia as well as Communist China; defined fairly narrowly, it would encompass Islamic Indonesia, Communist China and Vietnam, monarchical Thailand, capitalist and authoritarian Singapore, and, well, Japanese Japan. Such a collection appears incapable of being led or united. Indeed, perhaps it does not need or want a leader, particularly not the country that, just half a century ago, drove out the white colonial powers but then proved itself an even harsher master. Asians are a proud lot who harbor deep rivalries and resentments at one another—or, more particularly, against the Japanese.

Contrast all that with Western Europe. Admittedly, half a century ago half of Europe was at war with the other half. Now that this is no longer the case, however, there are powerful forces for unity. West Germany shares borders with six of the EEC's twelve members, all of whom are run as capitalist, fairly free-market democracies, and about half of West Germany's trade takes place inside the community. Crudely, the founding of the EEC in 1956 was helped by a clear trade-off of interests between what were then the two most powerful members: benefits for West Germany's industry in exchange for help for France's farmers.

Japan lacks these advantages. Its only non-Communist neighbor is South Korea, while Tokyo is 3,300 miles from Singapore and Jakarta, and nearly 5,000 miles from Sydney. There is no common political thread connecting Asian countries, nor even a strong cultural one. Moreover, Japan and the four fastest-growing Asian economies— Singapore, South Korea, Taiwan, and Hong Kong—more often seem to be in competition, producing similar products, than in collaboration.

With or without Japan, the region does not appear sufficiently cohesive to permit a trading or currency bloc. Economically, many of its countries seem too similar to permit much of an international division of labor. Commodity producers (such as Malaysia, Thailand, and Indonesia) export relatively little to each other and much more to industrialized countries in Europe and America. Annual output per capita varies from about $18,000 in Japan to $250 in China. In a smaller and more apparently cohesive area, the Association of Southeast Asian Nations (ASEAN: Thailand, Singapore, Malaysia, Indonesia, Brunei, and the Philippines) has spent several years not getting anywhere in encouraging integration.

A YEN BLOC IN ASIA

Japan has hardly given much encouragement to regional economic integration, either. Although its GNP accounts for nearly a fifth of world output, it has offered only a small market for Asian manufactures compared with the United States. Hostile, closed, or merely too competitive, it has not appeared worth much effort by Asian firms. Apart from big exporters of raw materials, most Asian countries run trade deficits with Japan. Why should Japan promote integration, anyway? Its own main export market is in America.

It has not wanted the yen held outside Japan as a reserve or trading currency since that might reduce the Japanese Ministry of Finance's scope to control its domestic money supply and interest rates. And Japanese leadership in Asia? The idea has seemed remote, indeed. The rest of Asia certainly has not favored a co-prosperity sphere with Japan at the head. Too many people remembered the last one.

THE MIGHTY YEN

Those skeptical, pessimistic paragraphs could have been written in 1975, 1980, or 1985. Yet since then, things have changed so rapidly that the notion of regional economic integration in Asia has ceased to be a pipedream. It has not become a reality, nor even a close prospect, but the direction of movement has been so clear and decisive that an Asian economic bloc, led in some fashion by Japan, has become an idea worth speculating about and exploring.

The spur for change was the rise of the yen after February 1985, mentioned so often throughout this book. It had two highly visible effects: It caused a rapid growth in Japan's imports from Asian countries, especially the four "dragons" of Hong Kong, Taiwan, Singapore, and South Korea, turning Japan into a plausible alternative market to America for these countries; second, it caused a rush of direct investment by Japanese firms in Asia, seeking to find cheaper offshore sites for production. That, in turn, prompted the dragons to invest in other Asian countries, in efforts to keep themselves competitive with the new Japanese arrivals. The dragons' own currencies (except Hong Kong's dollar) appreciated against the American dollar, which helped push some firms to produce in countries whose currencies had stayed weak. This was also encouraged by the United States in 1987, when it removed trade concessions to the dragons under GATT's general system of preferences.

The dragons' exports to Japan rose in 1987 alone by 30 percent in yen terms and 50 percent measured in dollars. This was especially dramatic in some mid-tech electronics products. Japan's imports of color televisions from the four rose from 25,000 in 1986 to 370,000 in 1987; imports of videotape recorders rose from 15,000 in 1986 to 138,000 in 1987; those of electric calculators from 1.62 million in 1984 to 6.2 million in 1986 to 11 million in 1987; those of electric cookers from 200 units in 1987 to 17,000 in 1987. Asian firms have not only found that they could export to Japan; they have also found Japanese firms eager to import from them.

This did not immediately improve the bilateral trade balances between Japan and each of the dragons. Although imports from the four grew faster than exports to them, the dragons' deficit widened because exports were starting from a higher base. It also follows a period during which the share of the dragons' exports to Japan were falling. For instance, in 1978, 12 percent of Taiwan's exports went to Japan; in 1985, 11 percent did. For South Korea, the figures fell from 20 percent in 1978 to 15 percent in 1985. But by 1987, the share of Taiwan's exports to Japan had revived to 13 percent, that for South Korea to 18 percent. Measured as a percentage of Japan's GNP, imports from the dragons grew to 0.8 percent in 1987, from 0.6 percent the previous year. That was lower than the dragons' penetration in the United States (1.3 percent of GNP in 1987), but above that in the four largest European economies (0.6 percent) and in line with the average for the twenty-four members of the Organization for Economic Cooperation and Development (OECD).

Overall, intraregional trade in Asia grew by 29 percent, from $147 billion in 1986 to $187 billion in 1987, according to IMF figures cited by David Hale of Kemper Financial Services in a November 1988 paper called "Will the Yen Displace the Dollar as the Pacific Rim's Reserve Currency?" In 1988, intraregional trade accounted for nearly

40 percent of Hong Kong's total trade, 27 percent of Thailand's, and 11.6 percent of South Korea's. That last figure is low because many of South Korea's imports come from outside the region; 29 percent of the country's exports go to other Asian countries. Hale calculates that at current growth rates intra-Asian trade will overtake trans-Pacific trade during the early 1990s.

Underlying these trade benefits has been a change in what the OECD calls "trade specialization indexes" for Asia. By this it means the advantage of countries in producing different sorts of goods, relative to other countries. In nondurable consumer goods, by which the OECD means labor-intensive items such as textiles, the dragons had already overtaken Japan in competitiveness in the late 1960s and early 1970s. In turn, ASEAN (excluding Singapore) overtook the dragons in the early 1980s. For durable consumer goods, the dragons gradually caught up with Japan in the 1970s and 1980s but then rapidly overtook it in 1985–88. In capital goods, Japan retains a comparative advantage, although the gap is rapidly being narrowed.

As long ago as 1975, Japanese firms had made nearly a quarter of their overseas direct investment in Asia, more than in North America or in any other region. But much of this was in mining and other raw materials projects. Manufacturers' overseas investments can, crudely, be divided into two sorts: first, projects designed to gain access to a protected market by producing inside the trade barriers; second, projects aimed at greater efficiency and lower costs. Until the mid-1980s, Japanese investments in Asia were mostly of the first sort, for instance, producing motorcycles for Indians or Taiwanese.

Since the yen began to soar, however, Japanese direct investments in Asia have been mostly of the second sort, aimed chiefly at efficiency. Some of that has been intended to produce goods to export back to Japan, especially components or low- and mid-tech electronics goods such as electric fans or calculators. In 1986, Matsushita announced a plan to shift production of all goods with a retail price of $100 or below from Japan to Asian factories, mainly to Taiwan and Singapore.

The figures confirm a sudden jump in Japanese investment in Asia. In the fiscal year beginning April 1, 1985, Japanese new direct investment in Hong Kong was worth only $131 million; in the year beginning April 1, 1987, it was $1 billion. Admittedly, that included investment in property (which boomed in the British colony), but manufacturing grew too. In Taiwan, Japanese investment rose in the same years from $114 million to $367 million; in Singapore, it rose from $339 million to $494 million; and in South Korea it rose from $134 million to $647 million. ASEAN benefited, too, with more rapid growth but from generally lower bases. In Thailand, for example, Japanese new investment grew from $48 million in the year beginning April 1, 1985, to $250 million in the year beginning April 1, 1987. The Philippines, beset by instability, corruption, and poor economic performance, was the only large exception.

One of the most active foreign investors among the dragons has been Taiwan. Statistics on the country's overseas activity are poor because government regulations send so much of it into the black market. P&E Risk, a consultant on Asian economies that is based in Hong Kong, calculates that Taiwanese foreign direct investment in 1987 totaled about $400 million, with about half in America and most of the rest in Thailand, Indonesia, and the Philippines. P&E reports that Taiwan was the second largest foreign investor in Thailand in 1987, well behind the Japanese but slightly ahead of the United States. South Korean firms have become big overseas investors, too, with a total of $397 million in 1987, of which $177 million was in North America and $131 million in Southeast Asia. The South Korean total was more than double the previous year, while investment in Southeast Asia rose seventeenfold.

What this jumble of figures means is that, after years of inaction, there has been a spurt of regional economic integration. Suddenly, intraregional trade has grown, and the beginnings of a division of labor among Asian countries can be seen. Japan is the fulcrum for change. There is still a way to go before the countries trade more with one another than with the outside world, but the trend is in that direction. Japan now imports as much from the newly industrializing countries (NICs) as it does from the EEC and 60 percent as much as it does from North America. Imports from the Asian NICs accounted for only 12.5 percent of Japan's total imports in 1987, but that is far greater than five years ago. In another five years, the proportion could be very much larger.

A YEN BLOC IN ASIA

THE YEN AS A RESERVE AND TRADING CURRENCY

This development has immediate implications for the role of Japan's currency, the yen. The Reagan administration had often nagged the Japanese about the low international use of the yen in trade, central bank reserves, borrowing, and investments. But now it is growing fast, encouraged by this regional trade and investment. After all, when Japanese multinationals produce parts and finished products in Asia for import to Japan, it is natural for them to price the trade in yen. Similarly, importers of Asian products to Japan want to price them in yen in order to avoid currency fluctuations that might make their products uncompetitive while on board ship. Countries and companies are borrowing in yen, since the interest costs are low and Japanese banks are eager to lend in their own currency. Moreover, if your debts are in yen, it makes sense to earn yen from exports in order to repay them. The yen now denominates about a third of Malaysia's foreign debts, a third of Indonesia's, and about 40 percent of Thailand's.

Japan's starting point for the international use of the yen was indeed poor. In 1980, just 17.6 percent of its exports were denominated in yen and less than 1 percent of its imports. The mighty dollar dominated world trade, particularly in the commodities and raw materials that then made up three quarters of Japan's imports. Only 2 percent of central banks' reserves were held in yen (compared with more than 70 percent in dollars). Nor did the yen play much of a part in international capital markets. In 1982, just 6 percent of all international bond issues were in the currency.

Compare those figures with 1987. By then about 35 percent of Japan's exports were in yen (double the 1980 level) and 11.6 percent of its imports (ten times 1980). The share of central bank reserves held in yen had risen to 7 to 8 percent. And more than 16 percent of international bond issues were made in yen. Those numbers are still low by international standards, but they are rising rapidly. Economists at Sanwa Bank, for instance, say that by April 1988 nearly 14 percent of imports were in yen.

Moreover, these worldwide, overall figures disguise a more advanced position for the currency in Asia. Asian central banks are thought to be holding a much higher percentage of their reserves in yen than are European or North American banks because of their countries' greater use of the yen in trade and capital flows. Figures are not revealed for each individual central bank, nor by region, but Japanese officials say that some Asian central banks are holding as much as 30 percent of their reserves in yen and that all have more than 10 percent in yen.

Two questions remain: What is implied by the yen being a reserve currency? And does Japan really want the yen to become a reserve currency? With regard to the first question, David Hale's paper on the yen laid out at least six characteristics that would distinguish a proper "reserve currency country" from others. First, its economy is large relative to others, which makes its trade and its competitiveness important to others. Second, it will probably have a large and relatively open capital market, needed to finance trade as well as to provide a range of liquid financial instruments for other countries to invest in. Third, it will have a stable economy with a low inflation rate that prevents the need for frequent confidence-denting devaluations. Fourth, the country will have a small foreign-trade sector relative to others, which means that its economy is less vulnerable to price shocks from elsewhere. Fifth, it will probably be a net creditor and have a surplus on the current account of its balance of payments; such characteristics provide lots of liquidity and exports of capital. Finally, the country must have a strong central bank able and willing to play the role of lender of last resort, both at home and abroad.

On these measures, Japan qualifies as almost there, but not quite. Its economy is certainly large but is by no means the largest; that distinction is still held by America. Its capital market is much more open than it was, but there are still problems of liquidity in important areas such as government bonds. It scores top marks for stability and low inflation, but its foreign trade sector is not terribly small (although it is smaller than West Germany's, for example) so that it is vulnerable to price shocks. It is a large net creditor and has a very large current-account surplus. Finally, its central bank is strong, although whether or not it is willing to act as lender of last resort internationally will be known only after a need has arisen.

There is another criterion, however: that the alternative reserve currencies bow out or lose their desirability. In part, the dollar must give up or forfeit its preeminence before the yen can take over. Is that likely? America will probably not give up the dollar's role willingly since, although it brings responsibilities, it provides power over other people's economic policies. More important in the 1980s, it also enables America to denominate its foreign debt in its own currency; this makes it invulnerable to currency risk and means that, in extremis, in order to reduce its debts it can depreciate its currency (usually by means of price inflation).

Forfeiture is the most likely means, although even that is not probable because investors would have to have lost all confidence in the dollar and in the American economy. This has not occurred during a period (1985–88) in which the dollar has halved in value against the yen. To make it happen in the future, the dollar would have to collapse once again and/or America's financial system would have to face severe problems. Liquidity of dollar instruments would have to decline. In that sort of circumstance, allegiance could switch, but a great deal of inertia has to be overcome. In the past, switches of reserve currency have happened after large crises (e.g., wars) rather than by gentle evolution.

There is one way, however, in which gentle evolution could raise the yen's status. Although one country's currency is generally dominant in foreign-exchange reserves, the dollar's current position is unusually strong. While the dollar now accounts for more than 70 percent of foreign-exchange reserves, before World War I, according to Hale, sterling accounted for only 38 percent of reserves compared to 24 percent for the French franc, 14 percent for the German mark, and 1 percent for the dollar. Sterling was considered dominant even at those levels. Large (and growing) proportions were held in francs and marks partly because those countries were exporting capital but also because they had developed distinct trading zones often related to colonies. Where they dominated trade, use of their currency in trade and reserves made sense. In the same sort of way, the role of the yen is likely to grow insofar as Japan develops dominance of a distinct trading zone, for goods, services, and capital. In short, even without toppling the dollar, the yen could develop as a reserve and trading currency for Asia and the Pacific.

Is Japan willing? Until recently, the answer was no. Ministry of Finance and Bank of Japan officials discouraged a similar role for the yen by pointing to the instability suffered by sterling in the 1950s and 1960s. Similarly, West German central bankers have sought for years to restrain the use of the Deutsche mark abroad, which accounted at the end of 1987 for 15 percent of central bank reserves, double the yen's level. The Bundesbank was unhappy when, in 1978, it was abruptly informed that the West German chancellor and the French president had agreed to establish the European Monetary System; central bankers feared that this would lose them some control over the mark.

In Tokyo, at least, views appear to have changed. Officials now say they are in favor of a larger role for the yen. Groups are said to be studying what sort of role that might be and how the yen's exchange rate might best be managed against the American dollar and against Asian currencies. Such comments and studies partly arise from the fact that Japanese bureaucrats know they are supposed to sound like good international citizens, and a costless way of doing so is to state willingness to raise the status of the yen; real opinions may be different. But mainly the comments and studies are being made because matters are no longer entirely in the officials' control.

Japan's huge capital exports since 1983 and the associated development of a market for yen bonds in the Euromarkets have considerably weakened the bureaucrats' power. All they can do is to refuse to encourage the use of the yen; they cannot easily prevent it. Moreover, greater use of the yen may now even be in the interests of some powerful Japanese institutions. For example, Japan is America's largest creditor, yet America's debts are all denominated in depreciable dollars. That is why, in yen terms, Japanese insurance firms lost billions of dollars on their investments in U.S. Treasury bonds in 1985–1988. Capital gains in the dollar bond market partly compensated for those currency losses, but not entirely. If future loans and bond purchases were in yen, Japanese lenders would no longer face a currency risk.

The same logic applies to loans to Asian countries. If Japanese banks are lending to Indonesia, it is in their interest for the loan to be in yen. If Indonesia has no alternative source for the cash at competitive interest rates, it will have to borrow in yen.

By definition, the international use of the yen largely depends on the desires of international users. Just about the only restraint available to the Japanese authorities, beyond reintroducing exchange controls, is to limit the range of investible assets denominated in yen, so that potential holders see yen as inflexible or illiquid. It is hard to say whether the Ministry of Finance is doing this. On this basis, judging the liberalization of Japan's financial markets and the expansion of the range of yen investments is like judging whether a glass is half full or half empty. From being empty the Japanese glass has swiftly become half full since 1983, but there is still much to do; is that proof of encouragement by the Ministry or discouragement?

One judgment that can safely be made is that the Japanese authorities have been more encouraging to yen financial markets than have their West German equivalents to mark business. Japan sees merits in having an international financial center in Tokyo, partly because it thinks it is unavoidable but also because it thinks financial services are a good business and it thinks a liberal market lowers the cost of capital to industry. West Germany thinks differently and is loath to have much of a financial center in Frankfurt. For the time being, Japan seems likely to become more rather than less liberal in its financial ways, which will facilitate the yen's use. Nevertheless, the yen's future is largely in the hands of other countries, companies, and central bankers. As intraregional trade, borrowing, and investment grow, Asians will want to hold more and more yen.

That still leaves a way to go before the yen could become the centerpiece of anything formal like a currency bloc. Until recently, virtually all Asian currencies were pegged to the dollar. Now, some (e.g., Thailand, Taiwan, and Singapore) have switched formally or informally to using a basket of currencies. But others remain linked to the American dollar. Another obstacle is that capital flows in the region are restricted heavily. Only Hong Kong and Singapore allow anything like free movement of capital. Financial markets in Taiwan and South Korea remain closed to outside investment except through special pooled funds, and residents are restricted in their portfolio investments abroad. Shuttered financial markets provide little incentive to trade assets in a common currency, and they prevent investors from moving funds toward the highest returns or the lowest risk.

WHY A YEN BLOC?

So far, all that has been established is that in Asia there has been sudden and rapid progress in economic integration, that the yen has jumped from nowhere to becoming a moderately international currency, and that it is not at all implausible for the yen to gain further international status. It does not follow logically that Asia will develop a trade or currency bloc, or that one is desirable, or that Japan should lead one.

The most immediate reason for supporting a future Asian bloc is a bad one, certainly viewed from the standpoint of multilateral free trade. It is that since about 1985–1986 trading blocs have become all the rage in other parts of the world. One is emerging in Western Europe, which is all aflutter about the EEC's plan to create by the end of 1992 a single, frontierless market for goods and services. The European Community has been nominally a free trade area since its foundation; the 1992 plan, if it succeeds, will mark the first time that trade within the community has been truly free of all barriers. Europe is intended to be a single market in the same way that the United States is one market. The danger of this for the rest of the world is that this single EEC market could become ringed by a high, protectionist wall against certain imports. Only insiders would benefit; outsiders might lose.

Another trading bloc may be developing in North America, where in 1987 the United States negotiated a free trade pact with Canada. This pact, kept alive by Brian Mulroney's victory in Canada's general election of November 1988, was by far the largest bilateral trade pact that the United States has ever struck and was also the first to be made purely for economic reasons. Others have been at least partly motivated by politics and defense (there is one with Israel, for example). In theory, the United States could later add its southern neighbor, Mexico, forming a huge North American free trade zone.

On the face of it, such moves to liberalize trade sound praiseworthy: Surely more free trade is better than less. The trouble is that with bilateral pacts this is not necessarily the result. Free trade is not that simple. The whole idea of lowering barriers between the United States and Canada, for example, is that it will enable Americans to buy goods produced in Canada that they had been buying elsewhere; and vice versa for Canadians. The source of supply that has thereby been made uncompetitive—which may be a previously protected American or Canadian firm or an outsider in Ghana or Japan—has lost out. At the very least, this raises an empirical question about whether or not the overall gains from the pact outweigh the losses. Politically the answer to that sounds simple: We (i.e., America and Canada) have won, other people have lost. Even that is not necessarily true (although it usually is) because the bias in favor of North American producers may prevent consumers from buying from the cheapest and most competitive source. For this reason multilateral, nondiscriminatory free trade is better than such bilateral pacts.

Nevertheless, a free trade pact ought generally to be an improvement on what came before, even if it is inferior to a multilateral solution. There is a worse danger, however: Domestic lobbies might demand increased protection against nonpact countries as a quid pro quo for accepting free trade within the deal. In that case, the result of a free trade zone would be not only to deprive nonmembers of the benefits but also to raise deliberate barriers against them, thus increasing the losses involved. Such an outcome is certainly in the cards in Europe, where many lobbies, including car makers and electronics firms, want increased protection against Japanese imports. It is not inconceivable that North America could develop in the same way.

Although it is pure speculation, one way in which this could happen in the next five or ten years is as an attempt to disguise protectionism. In the United States in particular, a strong lobby exists against protectionism. Since the 1930s experience with Smoot-Hawley tariffs, protection has become a dirty word. Few would admit they were protectionists; most would prefer to say they were in favor of "fair" trade, "level playing fields," and the like. The emotional force for protection remains strong, whatever word is used for it. In that context, a move toward an exclusive free trade zone with increased protection against outsiders could sound as if it were doing good and following a free-market ideology while actually being a means of ensuring protection. It might be politically more acceptable to a wider coalition of Americans than would any outright efforts to restrict trade.

If—and it is a big if—that were to come about, then Asian countries risk being left stranded. Disadvantaged in the EEC and in the United States, where do they have to turn but to each other and, most notably, to the non-Communist world's second largest economy, Japan? As losers from two other trading blocs, it would be tempting to seek at least some compensating gains from freer trade within their own region. The four dragons are by now sufficiently developed and confident to be willing to lower their own barriers to trade and to the flow of capital in return for easier access to other markets.

That is the strongest case during the next decade for an Asian trading bloc. It is sincerely to be hoped that this case will not come about and that there will instead be a multilateral lowering of trade barriers under the GATT. A move toward regional blocs is certainly not something that Asian countries would want to encourage since Japan as well as the four dragons have prospered by taking a global rather than a regional approach to exporting, seeking out markets wherever they might be found. They will not give that up readily. The growth of intraregional trade and economic integration in Asia is desired as a complement to trade with America and Europe, not as a substitute for it. The best source for hope is that the United States will also feel that way: Japan is its second largest trading partner, after Canada, both for exports and imports.

CURRENCIES FIRST, TRADE LATER

Even if the trading world does not split into three, there is another, weaker way in which a yen bloc might evolve. Ask a businessman about his biggest problem in exporting and overseas operations in general, and he might talk about tariffs, or technical barriers to trade, or language. It is more than likely, however, that his answer will be currency fluctuations.

Other things being equal, a 20 percent shift of his domestic exchange rate against that of his export market makes his products that much less or more competitive. In the short run, he can use various financial tricks to hedge against currency movements; in the long run, all he can do is alter his production costs, either at home or by building a factory where the currency looks more favorable. No sooner has he done that than the currency shifts again. If only exchange rates were stable, life would be much simpler. Just consider the dollar: Against the yen, the real (i.e., inflation-adjusted) value of the dollar fell by a third between 1973 and 1978, then rose 60 percent to a peak in early 1985, from which it then fell by a half in 1985–1988. How can businesses plan with all that going on? And this does not just affect export markets; such swings affect competitiveness at home against importing rivals.

For this reason, the sort of bloc to watch for in Asia is quite likely to begin with currency arrangements rather than with any formal dismantling of trade barriers or development of regional institutions. As intraregional trade grows in importance, and as Japan becomes a more and more important market for regional producers, competitiveness within that market becomes critical. The best way to protect that competitiveness and to permit stable strategic planning is to tie currencies together, which would really mean tying them to the yen. In turn, that implies some harmonization of monetary and economic policies with Japan's in order to keep currencies stable and to prevent inflation from eroding business competitiveness. Trade barriers could wait until later.

This would be opposite to the order of development that occurred in Europe. While the EEC began with lowering barriers to trade and only later made steps toward monetary union, it is plausible that Asia might start with monetary affairs. In the extreme, a common currency with a common monetary policy would probably do more to encourage trade and the free flow of capital than could a regional, exclusive, free trade bloc. But a common currency is clearly out of the question given the divisions and differences among Asian countries. Things could begin with countries' currencies being pegged to the yen. That is not at all farfetched.

At present, nobody pegs their currency to the yen. As stated earlier, Asian countries either manage their currencies in relation to a basket of others or they still peg them loosely or tightly to the American dollar. With the United States their main export market, a peg to the dollar has made economic sense since it produces a stable measure of their products' price competitiveness in America. It has also made emotional and political sense, since the United States has been, to most of these countries, their chief protector and political father figure. Since

1985, the fall of the dollar has made this even more sensible: By retaining a peg to the American currency, the Asian dragons have avoided losing export competitiveness. Under pressure from the Reagan administration and from their own strong trade balances, the dragons in 1985–1988 were generally unable to avoid some appreciation against the dollar. But they managed to ensure that their currencies rose by far less against the dollar than did the yen.

There is no reason to assume that Asian countries will always want to be pegged to the dollar. Several things could, over time, change their exchange-rate policies. As hinted at earlier, one pressure would be if a much larger proportion of their trade was with Japan and denominated in yen. Then their competitive position in the Japanese market would matter as much or more than their position in the American market; their currency's relation to the yen might become a more suitable thing to target.

Another factor could be if the dollar were to continue to fall or indeed if it were to collapse. Then a link to the dollar would risk importing inflation as import prices rise, possibly eroding any cost advantage against Japan. Although South Korean and Taiwanese wages were well below Japanese levels in 1988 (a quarter or a fifth of the average wage in Japanese manufacturing), rapid inflation could close that gap. Alternatively, suppose the dollar moved rapidly in the opposite direction, recovering against the yen? Although that would help prevent inflation in the dragons' economies, it again risks making them less competitive against their Japanese competitors.

All this is rather hypothetical, but it at least shows how things could develop. At some point, it may be in the interests of the more developed Asian countries to ensure that their inflation rates do not exceed Japan's. One way to help achieve that could be to tie their currencies to the yen. In effect, that also links their monetary policies to that of the Bank of Japan because, if capital is free to flow among markets and currencies, the relationship between, say, South Korean and Japanese interest rates will begin substantially to determine the demand for each country's currency. Capital is not now free to flow, but steps are beginning to be taken in South Korea and Taiwan to make it so.

These developments may not look likely now, but if countries see them as in their interests, things could change surprisingly quickly. There is a natural, although not inevitable, evolution from informal pegging against the yen, to formal pegs, to some sort of regional monetary system akin to that employed in Europe.

What seems most farfetched about all this is the idea that Asian countries would ever accept leadership from Japan. Wartime and colonial memories live on. Even a peg to the yen sounds like an insulting acceptance of Japanese superiority.

Yet attitudes are changing. Five or ten years ago, the idea seemed too absurd even to consider; now feelings do seem to have become less intense. Some of this may be generational. More likely, it reflects pure self-interest. Everybody wants a share of Japan's money and Japan's market. There is no escaping the fact that Japan is Asia's strongest nation.

Japan still has to tread very carefully in Asia, especially in South Korea, where hatred runs especially deep as a result of Japan's occupation of the Korean Peninsula from 1906 to 1945. An opinion poll published by Japan's Ministry of Foreign Affairs in July 1987 showed that Southeast Asians are also still worried about Japanese militarism. Asked if Japan might again become a threatening military power, the answer "yes" was given by 53 percent of Thais, 47 percent of Filipinos, 34 percent of Malays, 29 percent of Singaporeans, and 21 percent of Indonesians.

Nevertheless, little by little, Japan has been permitted a role in Asia as a sort of elder brother. So far this has been expressed in words rather than actions: Japanese speeches to ASEAN ministerial meetings or a Japanese effort to represent Asian views at the World Economic Summit in Toronto in June 1988. It has not amounted to anything more concrete.

Might that change? Perhaps, if it becomes in the interest of Japan and its Asian neighbors. The most dramatic way in which that could happen would be if the United States ceased to be able or willing to provide regional security. Short of that, however, it is most likely to begin in the economic sphere, for that is Japan's forte. As Japanese aid, trade, and investment grow, so will reasons to consult and confer with the Japanese and other Asian governments.

Monetary links, for instance, might easily stimulate some sort of regular summit meetings of Asian ministers. Those events would quickly evolve into more general summits, nominally economic but in practice political. This is exactly the way that World Economic Summits have developed; political matters have become tacked on to EEC meetings. How long, in any case, before a confident Japan begins to hold meetings with Asian leaders in advance of its attendance at world summits?

Asian leaders are more receptive to this development than is often imagined—in public, if not necessarily in private. For example, Lee Kwan Yew, the prime minister of Singapore and long thought to be a Japan hater, made some encouraging comments in an interview in June 1988 with *Nikkei Business,* a Japanese magazine. He noted that the American political and military presence in Asia was changing and that the United States had become relatively weaker in the region. From that, he concluded that there ought to be a burden-sharing arrangement between America and Japan, covering not merely the costs of American troops in Japan but also the burden of "maintaining stability, security and economic development in the whole Asia/Pacific region." In the same interview, Lee said that an economic bloc along the lines of the EEC would be difficult to achieve because of a lack of common interests in Asia. But he nevertheless was reported as having hinted that a free trade zone could increase bargaining power, giving the countries involved a greater voice in opening up other markets. That is a bit worrying for multilateralists, but encouraging for those favoring Asian integration.

In time, it seems plausible to expect Japan to become something akin to Asia's leader. Other Asians will remain suspicious of the Japanese and eager to avoid its dominance. Japan will have to act more as a first among equals than as a regional boss, and its neighbors will be quick to use wartime sensitivities as a weapon against it. But this need not be a bar to progress. Japan's own reluctance to take charge may be more of an obstacle.

CHAPTER TEN

田

RELUCTANT LEADERS

*The new Japan has a great opportunity to exert an influence
in Asia by what the founders of the United States called
conduct and example. . . . A great liberating influence.*
— JOHN FOSTER DULLES

THIS STATEMENT, made in 1951 before Dulles became President Eisenhower's secretary of state, is hard to disagree with in the late 1980s, even if you substitute "the world" for "Asia." Say it, or something like it, to virtually any Japanese official, politician, or businessman and the response will be a thoughtful but determined nod of approval. Turn it, even, into a concrete prediction that Japan will take on leadership in Asia or into a demand that it must "take responsibilities commensurate with its economic strength," and it would still be hard to find any Japanese, or indeed any American dealing with Japan, who would disagree. And yet, as logical and inevitable as it seems, and despite this book having made just these sorts of prognostications, something still makes the idea seem absurd.

That curious something starts with the fact that for much of the past four decades Japan seems to have done everything in its power to avoid being a leader, to avoid taking any initiative in international affairs. Even in the 1980s, its foreign policy, whether political or economic, has been a timorous creature, indecisive about what it should say or think, reluctant in case it might annoy someone. That is what you would expect, it might be said, from the loser in a world war. Yet West

Germany has not been quite so meek as this; although it too is haunted by its history and is reluctant to throw its weight around, it usually behaves like the medium-to-large power that it has become: It makes its views apparent, it spends a great deal on its own defense, and it plays a full part in international organizations. Japan has done none of these. For it, discretion has seemed the best policy.

In recent years, Japanese ministers have occasionally tried to play the international, pro-American role that has been expected of them. This has mainly involved words rather than actions, although words are not unimportant. Yet often an almost comical gap has existed between what such Japanese big shots have said abroad and what they have said back home. For example, Zenko Suzuki, admittedly the country's most unimpressive prime minister since at least 1960, visited the United States in 1980 and spoke publicly of the "alliance" between Japan and America. That may sound unremarkable, but the comment caused such a furor at home that he had to pretend it was a misinterpretation. Japan, you see, is supposed only to enter into military matters for its "self-defense," and has a "national security" treaty with the United States to that effect. "Alliance" sounded a little too aggressive.

The same sort of thing happened in 1983, when Yasuhiro Nakasone, Suzuki's bolder and more charismatic successor, also went to Washington, D.C., and described Japan's military role as being an "unsinkable aircraft carrier" for the West in the Pacific. Fair enough: the Japanese islands are right against the coast of the Soviet Union, rather as Cuba is to the United States, and they are home to America's Fifth Air Force. But again, there must have been an error in the translation, Nakasone had to claim when he arrived home to a big stink about his "militarist" tendencies.

So what is genuine, the "frank" statement made abroad or the disclaimer at home? It is impossible to tell from words alone. Unfortunately Japanese have a well-known tendency to tell a listener what they think he wants to hear, even if it is untrue. They mouth the *tatemae,* or appearance, while keeping quiet about the *honne,* or reality. Japanese practice this art of lying to each other as well as to unwary foreign barbarians.

Military matters are, perhaps, especially sensitive to the atom-bombed and defeated Japanese, but this double-talk has extended to other, less touchy areas too. In economic matters in the 1980s, Japan has made an art out of producing "packages" of measures to open its markets, boost overseas aid, or stimulate its economy, all in response to foreign pressure. More often than not, however, these have amounted to little more than summaries of steps already taken or planned. In trade and "market-opening measures," there have been so many empty packages since 1980 that the whole exercise has lost credibility. Beware Japanese bearing gifts, is the conclusion all too often left behind.

Another more recent example was Japan's proud boast in 1986–1987 that it was doubling its overseas aid and becoming the world's largest donor, exactly as its foreign allies were demanding. True in dollar terms, this conveniently ignored the fact that the real cause of growth was the rise of the yen against the dollar. In yen terms, aid was rising only by 5 percent a year. For all the hype, policy had not changed.

This loss of credibility has been aggravated, unfortunately, by the Japanese government's conscious effort to turn a handful of elder statesmen into full-time international problem-soothers. One is Saburo Okita, an economist who was once foreign minister; another is Naohiro Amaya, a former top bureaucrat from the Ministry of International Trade and Industry; a third is Yasuke Kashiwagi, formerly a top Ministry of Finance official and now chairman of the Bank of Tokyo. These and other globetrotting diplomats are chosen because of their fluency in English and their experience in dealing with foreigners. They are sent on missions to foreign capitals, they meet visiting dignitaries, they speak at conferences, they appear on satellite television debates, they produce "reports" about how Japan is going to do this or that. They sound convincing, fair-minded, and international. Alas, while this practice is designed to increase Japan's credibility as a member of the community of nations, it has tended to diminish it.

It is sad but not too cynical to say that in reality Messrs. Okita and Co. are merely pacifiers, designed to keep the rude and insistent foreigner at bay. They are supposed to create an apparently acceptable image for Japan as being no different from other pro-Western, free-market countries and fully responsive to Western demands. The trouble is that what these elder statesmen may say bears no necessary relation to what is really going on in Japan. They are powerless, and rarely do they even have much influence. Occasionally, the tactic works, probably because some foreign negotiators are so convinced by the idea of Japan Inc. and its supposedly monolithic character that they can be led to believe that they have been talking with the "real" powerbrokers. More often, however, the result is frustration and mistrust when the pacifiers turn out, whether in good or bad faith, to have been economical with the truth.

A STRANGE WORLD OUTSIDE

Why is Japan so awkward? In part, it reflects an unease in dealing with foreigners that contrasts oddly with its export success. The Japanese language perpetuates a powerful sense of us and them, which can be linked to the country's centuries of isolation, and to more recent political attempts to create a sense of common identity. Those attempts sat uneasily in a nation that is, in reality, a cocktail of foreign influences. The word for international, for example, is *kokusai,* which translated directly means "outside the country." Unlike the English word, it contains no connotation of "between." It is really an equivalent of foreign rather than international. A foreigner is a *gaikokujin,* abbreviated to *gaijin,* meaning "outside country person" and is mildly derogatory. Perhaps such semantic points should not be taken too far, but they do coincide with an attitude to the outside world that is a mixture of fear, mistrust, and contempt.

This can readily be seen in popular culture. For instance, there is a prime-time television quiz show called *"Naruhodo za worudo,"* or, roughly, "Really the World." In it, a narrator travels to foreign countries and films people doing strange things, usually traditional arts, crafts, or habits. Amid great hilarity, the panel back home has to guess what on earth these peculiar foreigners are doing and why. Usually, the show is just silly, but sometimes it goes too far. In mid-1988, the program caused a row with Malaysia because the cameramen had bribed some tribesmen to move around on their hands and knees and bark like dogs, which was not in fact part of their everyday behavior. The outside world was evidently not strange enough for their purposes.

The Japanese are clannish and xenophobic. So are the British. When in 1988 Britain's largest-selling daily newspaper, the *Sun*, printed an editorial attacking the ailing Emperor Hirohito for Japan's wartime atrocities, Japan's Foreign Ministry protested (quite justifiably) at such racist bad taste. The irony is that some Japanese publications are just as capable of such bad behavior and similarly racist attitudes.

One example of Japanese clannishness is the country's attitude to immigrant labor: Despite labor shortages and an increasing unwillingness of rich Japanese to accept dirty jobs, the instinct has long been that to bring in foreigners would be dangerous. They would not fit in. The Japanese already feel uneasy about the presence of domestic outsiders: the 650,000 Korean-Japanese brought to Japan to work during World War II and the 2 million *burakumin*, or Japanese untouchables, who were originally tanners and butchers in pre-Meiji times (1850) and who remain outcasts. In the past few years, Japan has not been able entirely to ban foreign workers since the country is a natural magnet for poorer Asians wishing to support their families back home. They can enter the country as tourists and stay on illegally. Nobody knows how many do this, but guesses range between 50,000 and 300,000 in the country at any one time. Some work in the construction industry, many in the restaurant trade, and in the case of Filipino women, as maids and in "entertainment," which really means prostitution.

A lobby is beginning to press for the organized and regular import of guestworkers into the construction industry, which is suffering a severe shortage of labor. Lots of committees are anguishing about the idea, and about how to implement it if it is allowed. This sort of resistance appears at the other end of the employment scale, too. Japanese firms want to employ a few foreign executives to help with international work, but they are horrified at the possibility that such people might get into positions of real power. A British investment banker in Hong Kong relates how he has had several offers to work for Japanese banks. But when he asks, just as he would an American or British firm, whether he will get a seat on the bank's board, he is greeted with astonishment. In all things, the idea of blending *kokusai*—outside the country—with *kokunai*—inside it—is simply unthinkable.

A JAPAN PROBLEM

What does all this amount to? Briefly, there have been four components in this apparent criticism of Japan: Japan displays a reluctance to lead in international affairs, or even to follow decisively; there is a wide communication gap between Japan and its allies; the Japanese do not feel comfortable with foreigners; and they prefer to keep international and domestic affairs separate. In all, perhaps no country is an island, as John Donne might have written, but Japan does its best to be as isolated as possible.

The first answer to these criticisms can be an optimistic one: that this does not amount to very much at all. As was discussed in chapter 1, many similar points were made about the United States in the first forty years of this century: how it was selfish, reluctant to involve itself in foreign affairs except where its economic interest was involved, and how its political position was not commensurate with its economic strength. It only came out of its shell when it felt it had to in order to guarantee its security and prosperity. If and when it feels a similar need, Japan will develop in the same way. Sadly, there is nothing unusual about a country giving priority to its domestic interests. It is quite possible that the critical comments about Japan's lack of international presence indicate more about the worries and frailties of the critics than about the Japanese.

Japan is capable, on this theory, of looking and sounding more like an international leader. Some may be born to greatness, but others have greatness thrust upon them. For the time being, the thrust has not arrived. It may never, but if it does, the Japanese will respond. This theory accounts for the country's shy and awkward character, as well as the parochialism of its people. Are they really, it could be asked, that much more parochial than are Americans? Middle Americans have a horizon that extends no farther than middle America; they have no need to, since America is such a big place and such a big economy. Unlike Europe, much of America is unaware that the country borders on anything except the next state. Frustrating though it can be, this parochialism has not noticeably held America back. The same applies to the Japanese, especially now that their economy is so big and successful. Why bother with the rest of the world? Answer: Don't, until it bothers you.

Such a benign theory does, however, overlook some significant difficulties. First, it overlooks the communication gap, which provides problems and tensions that are at least important in the short term. More crucially, though, it overlooks the most curious fact of all about Japan and its politics: that the country appears to have no leaders. America from 1900 to 1941 may have been reluctant to interfere in foreign affairs, but it certainly had leaders: the Roosevelts, Woodrow Wilson, and so on. Such leaders fought against parochialism at federal and state levels. The same is not true of Japan.

There, the prime minister has the least amount of power or influence of any head of government in an industrialized country. Whenever in 1982–1987 Yasuhiro Nakasone promised Ronald Reagan that Japan would do a particular thing, he was really expressing a hope rather than making a pledge. To an extent, the same would be true in reverse; an American president has to work through a recalcitrant Congress, not to mention belligerent states and judges determined to uphold the Constitution. But in Japan, power is spread much more diffusely than in the United States. The difference is of degree, not kind, but the difference remains.

An eminent Dutch journalist, Karel van Wolferen, who has lived in Japan since 1962, has described this lack of a power center in "The Japan Problem," an article in *Foreign Affairs* in mid-1987. His view, also developed at length in his 1989 book *The Enigma of Japanese Power*, was very controversial in Japan, and not only because he blames the power structure for the country's trade surplus and the poor performance of imports; mainly, people were upset because he concluded that the only way for the United States to deal with a center-less Japan was to forget about free trade and free-market economic theory. Instead, it must fire a protectionist broadside at its rival and then negotiate direct quotas to manage trade and the international division of labor. In his view, a country that has no leaders requires special treatment.

Van Wolferen's analysis is worth examining, since the nature of the country's power center affects both how it faces up to the outside world and also how it reacts to unpleasant circumstances or to the need for change. In particular, the way in which power is distributed and exerted in Japan matters to outsiders for two reasons. Reason number one is that anyone involved with, for example, business or politics needs to be aware of how the country works in order to know how to get things done. On its own, that is not a cause for much concern; Japan can run itself in whatever way it chooses as long as it is honest about it and foreigners do their homework.

The second reason is more important, however: The way power operates in Japan tends to make it inward-looking, ensuring that international affairs are neglected in favor of purely domestic interests. It instills and preserves a protectionist instinct. The lack of a power center matters because it means that there is nothing to challenge that instinct, no leadership to ensure that the country does what is right on international grounds rather than what is in its narrow interest. This is the nub of the collection of worries aired so far in this chapter.

POWERS THAT BE

To understand why leadership is diffuse, begin with the well-known point that, in Japan, bureaucrats matter more than politicians. Since the end of the American occupation in 1952, ministries rather than parties have run the country, initiating as well as executing policy. This has been possible because the Liberal Democratic party (LDP) has been in power throughout the period, under different names until 1958, and then under the present one. Governments have not changed after general elections and neither have policies. The Liberal Democrats have been divided into various factions, but not on ideological grounds. By and large, politicians have left bureaucrats to get on with the business of government. That neat picture has changed somewhat in the past decade but in ways that reinforce rather than counter the effect of bureaucratic power.

The idea that bureaucrats run the country conjures up a picture of a unified squad of administrators who study a policy problem, achieve consensus on how to solve it, and then do so efficiently and ruthlessly. Such unity of purpose and freedom from petty political interference have commonly been given credit for much of Japan's postwar success. The truth, however, is muddier than that. Japanese bureaucrats are divided among themselves; ministries compete with one another, as do sections within ministries. Consensus building, it must be remembered, is only possible through argument.

What is more, bureaucrats are not separable from the industries and sectors that they administer. In effect, they represent their charges. They use the institutions under their control both to gather and to disseminate information. Regulated and regulator discuss problems together as well as possible solutions. The regulator is in a superior position to his charge and considers himself so especially since he has the power to make law. The power of his section or ministry, however, depends to a considerable extent on the health and financial strength of those he regulates. As a result, that is often his prime goal. Where there is a conflict between institutions, the respective sets of regulators will battle it out.

Some bureaucrats are more powerful than others, either because of a revenue-raising strength (for the government, not as individuals) or because they can show that the health of their sector is important to the health of the economy as a whole. In the 1950s and 1960s, that gave the Ministry of International Trade and Industry a preeminent position. More recently, power has shifted toward the Ministry of Finance and, to a lesser extent, the Ministry of Posts and Telecommunications. At times when the economy's overall health is in danger, such as during the oil shocks of the 1970s, competition among ministries is likely to cease in favor of cooperation. At other times, battle will resume.

There is nothing unique about this. Similar sorts of things do happen in the United States or Britain, but not to the same extent. In the Anglo-American systems, more of a separation exists between civil servants and their subjects, and activities by lobbies are more open. Politicians, elections, and the courts act as a check on collusion and provide a nudge in the direction of a particular ideology or the rule of law. In Japan, there is barely any check.

A STRANGE SORT OF POLITICS

One recent change in the role of politicians is that members of the Liberal Democratic party have begun to make a more substantial habit of selling favors to outside interest groups. This is a very good way to raise money, which is essential for electoral campaigns, but it is also a prime motive for getting into politics in the first place. So LDP parliamentarians bone up on legislation about, say, transport, farming, or the construction industry and can raise money by pushing through minor amendments to laws under discussion. While bureaucrats change jobs every two or three years, LDP members may hold their seats for a decade or more and can thus become even more expert on technicalities of law than can the officials. This development is, however, not really what is meant by a check or balance. It makes the legislative process even more beholden to interest groups than before.

A second related change is that, in certain areas, the LDP has at last become an important generator of policy. Although most people expect this sort of thing from political parties, it has not generally occurred in Japan. Yet battles in 1986–88 over policy toward agriculture and tax reform have been fought in the party, not in the bureaucracy. One reason is that the money-raising activities of ordinary parliamentarians make them unusually concerned about the fate of farmers; around two hundred of the party's four hundred–plus parliamentary members depend on farm votes for their election. As a result, those LDP leaders that favor a reduction in farm support have to convince those who oppose it. Even bureaucrats cannot ride roughshod over politicians. In the case of tax reform, a similar line within the party divides those who have strong ties with retailers, who expect to be hurt by a proposed sales tax, and those who feel reform will serve the economy's general interests.

This increased party role in the resolution of conflicts over policy could, if it is sustained and extended, gradually bring policymaking more into the open. If that happens, senior party members will begin to act and sound more like political leaders in America or Britain, building coalitions of interest to achieve their goals. But a long way remains before that becomes a realistic description of the LDP. For the time being, even intra-party policymaking is closely linked to lobbies and other pressure groups. Moreover, it is still unusual for Japanese politicians to hold views about policy issues, let alone to make them known. Yasuhiro Nakasone, prime minister from 1982 until 1987, is a very unusual character.

In Western democracies, an individual could not become prime minister unless his views and approach echoed sentiments popular in the electorate and among his political allies. That is not so in Japan because, with the LDP an apparently permanent government, prime ministers rise from the shifting sands of factional politics, not from any popular vote or mandate. Ministerial posts have principally been sought as sources of patronage and prestige, not as the means to achieve political goals. The post of prime minister is, in effect, rotated among the larger of the party's five factions, the occupant of the job never needing to be more than a figurehead.

The picture changes only when, by coincidence really, the post happens to be occupied by somebody with genuine political goals. One such was Kakuei Tanaka, who became prime minister in 1972 but had to resign in 1974 after a financial scandal. No other strongly motivated prime minister emerged until Yasuhiro Nakasone. He did manage to demonstrate that, once occupied by somebody with ideas and real aims, the job is not totally without power. Nakasone was able to use familiar political techniques to get his way over some things, although he failed over others.

Nakasone's strongest weapon came after he proved his ability to handle foreign affairs by speedily settling a dispute with South Korea and then establishing a good personal relationship with Ronald Reagan. At a time when foreign pressure over trade and defense was becoming more and more uncomfortable, Nakasone showed himself adept at keeping foreigners at bay. Fairly quickly, he also proved to be popular with the electorate. While previous governments' poll ratings tended to begin high and then sag, his began fairly low and then went up and up. Evidently, his charismatic style and his tall, upstanding, statesman-like behavior abroad brought him favor with ordinary Japanese.

Even the LDP worries about how well it will do in elections, so being an electoral asset helped Nakasone in the party; being a foreign asset helped him in the bureaucracy. As a result, he was better able than his predecessors to control and direct the bureaucrats and was able to stay in office beyond his initial two-year term. He managed to increase spending on defense even while the rest of the government budget was being squeezed. Under his leadership, the LDP won a landslide victory in the lower-house elections of July 1986, gaining 300 of the house's 512 seats for the first time ever. Despite that, and despite the fact that he was very different from the typical Japanese politician, Nakasone was unable to achieve all that much. Outside the mainstream, he lacked the power to defeat bureaucratic resistance and vested interests.

Nakasone's one enduring legacy may have been to change the style of the post of prime minister, if not the substance. His successor in 1987, Noboru Takeshita, is a dull, colorless fellow who had never admitted to any political views until he reached the top office. Takeshita's rival and most likely successor, Shintaro Abe, is a similar type. Yet in 1988 Prime Minister Takeshita took a surprisingly prominent role in international affairs, producing initiatives at the Toronto summit and seeking lots of coverage in the media. It seems that he wants foreign prominence in order to court popularity. Bureaucrats also seem eager to use the prime minister as an international spokesman. But all this is skin deep.

The practice of politics and politicians is unlikely to change radically as long as the LDP remains secure in its power. That was shown most clearly by the Recruit scandal, which dominated politics for a year before fizzling out in May 1989. An up-and-coming firm had bribed scores of LDP politicians, including Nakasone and Prime Minister Takeshita, who had to resign. But the LDP stayed in power and replaced Takeshita with a crony of Nakasone's, Sosuke Uno. Real reform of the corrupt political system appeared unnecessary, for the party seemed impregnable. For the moment, no other party offers a credible alternative; none even puts up enough candidates at lower-house elections to form a government. The largest opposition group, the Japan Socialist party, is divided and remains hamstrung by its Marxist origins. In the 1986 election, it was routed, falling from 109 seats to 85. There are four center parties—the New Liberal Club, Komeito, the Democratic Socialists, and the Social Democratic League—but all seem more willing to join a coalition with the LDP than to form one against it. At least an LDP coalition might force a more open and genuine debate about policy than is the case with a solid one-party majority. That would, at least, be a start.

WHY THIS MATTERS

So what? The system seems to work, even if it is a bit corrupt and prone to encourage cartels. Bureaucrats have run Japan remarkably well, certainly from the point of view of prosperity and economic development. The problem is that this way of doing things tends to encourage Japan to remain parochial and inward-looking.

Within the structure of interest groups and their agents, nobody really represents overseas interests or has the power to reconcile contradictions between domestic and foreign policy. The Ministry of Foreign Affairs has no financial clout and no domestic power base. The Ministry of International Trade and Industry only worries when protectionism abroad seriously threatens domestic interests. While there is bureaucratic pressure for, as the Japanese would call it, "harmony" between competing domestic interests, little pressure is exerted for harmony with foreign interests. Or put another way, when domestic and overseas interests conflict, then, other things being equal, the domestic issue will prevail. This is so even when, in the long term, the overseas interest is more important to Japan. The domestic interest feels more immediately pressing.

Until the 1980s, this way of doing things was occasionally irksome to foreign governments (insofar as they noticed it), but it did not appear to be very important. Although some Western industries felt aggrieved at competition from Japanese exports, the country's overall surpluses remained moderate. By the end of the 1970s, Japan had lowered formal barriers to trade and investment roughly to the level maintained by other industrialized countries. Its tariffs were the lowest in the industrialized world, and it used relatively few import quotas or subsidies to protect domestic firms. Japan's foreign policy was quietly pro-Western. Even if Americans occasionally grumbled that it ought to pull more of its weight, Japan's meekness was not a pressing issue.

In this decade, however, the conflict between domestic and foreign policy has become more and more apparent, as has the reluctance to resolve it. In macroeconomic policy during this period, the bureaucracy had in effect two goals: to maintain growth in the GNP and to reduce drastically the government's need to borrow in order to prepare the nation's finances for the period between 1995 and 2020, when the population will age rapidly. These aims are, other things being equal, contradictory, since a cut in government borrowing is likely to result in a contraction in economic growth. Unless something else stimulates the domestic economy, it will slow. That something was provided by growth in exports, chiefly to the United States, and by a fall in imports caused by a drop in the price of oil and other raw materials. As long as the current-account surplus could keep on growing, the policy of fiscal austerity could be maintained without domestic injury.

It is not at all surprising that these contradictory policies were pursued. What is, perhaps, remarkable is that Japan managed for so long to put off the day when the contradiction would have to be resolved—that is, when Japan would have to cease austerity and begin to boost domestic demand. Before action was taken, the current-account surplus was allowed to grow to more than $100 billion, the largest in absolute terms that the world has ever seen. No leader or center of power was able or willing to prevent this.

Supposedly, Japan had been worrying about protectionism abroad ever since 1980 or even earlier. Yet it made no serious steps to alleviate the cause of the protectionist pressure—its current-account surplus—until 1985–1986. Makoto Kuroda, who became the Ministry of International Trade and Industry's top trade official in 1986, summed up the real Japanese attitude in an interview when he told me that congressmen and other Americans were always claiming that a trade crisis was looming and that time was running out. Yet, as Kuroda said, "The earth still turns." Foreign moans were not taken seriously because they were not a serious threat.

DEALING WITH JAPAN

At this overall, macroeconomic level, how should foreign governments respond to "The Japan Problem," as Karel van Wolferen calls it? The problem, in the sense of how Japan works and how that affects its external policy, certainly exists. Japan is inward-looking and has no power center capable of forcing it to look outward. The problem matters principally because of Japan's huge trade surplus but also because Japan has become more and more intertwined with the rest of the industrialized world, especially the United States. Not only is it a reluctant leader; it is also an awkward member of the team.

Agreeing with van Wolferen's diagnosis does not, however, necessitate agreeing with his cure. It is by no means clear that the best response to Japan is that recommended by van Wolferen in his article in *Foreign Affairs:* force, followed by attempts to administer trade flows. Japan does not need to be treated as an island unto itself, either in this issue of trade or in foreign policy.

To understand why, it is important first to recognize that a failure to reconcile domestic and foreign interests is not unique to Japan, even if the particular structure and set of attitudes that cause Japan's failure are unique to that country. The United States also failed, in the 1980s, to accept either the external consequences of its domestic policies or the economic consequences of its foreign and defense policies. America's current-account deficits of more than $150 billion were not caused by the way Japan runs itself, although they may have been aggravated by it. Almost certainly, this coincidence of failures helped both sides to postpone necessary changes of policy. Japan could (and did) blame its surplus on the inability of other countries to export and to work hard at penetrating the Japanese market; America could (and did) blame its deficit on the failure of other countries to grow fast enough and to open their markets. It could always be somebody else whose policy had to change.

Nor is Japan, therefore, the sole cause of its trade surplus. For every surplus, there is a multilateral deficit, and in Japan's case, one particular deficit corresponds largely to its surplus: America's. There is no necessary reason to blame a surplus country for such an imbalance or to blame a deficit country. The problem and the need to solve it are both shared.

Changes in macroeconomic policies in Japan and the United States, if they are carried out (a big if), will remedy the general trade imbalance. Japan, as chapter 11 will argue, is moving toward a more balanced set of international payments, having been passing through an unusual period (a period lengthened and aggravated, admittedly, by its inward-looking nature). Its apparently low propensity to import is changing. Historians will see this as having merely been equivalent to America's low propensity to import in the 1950s: a product of economic circumstances, not conspiracy.

Van Wolferen doubts that this will be so, for two reasons. One is that, in his view, Japan is not a free-market capitalist economy in the Western sense. It is what Chalmers Johnson of the University of California at Berkeley has called a "capitalist developmental state," not quite a Soviet-style command economy but closer to it than to a free-market economy. It will not therefore respond to the free play of market forces, such as the rise of the yen, shifts in demand, and the lowering of import barriers. Reason number two, van Wolferen thinks, is that the Japanese system is unwilling to permit imports because they undermine its aim of prosperity through industrial expansion. Some token rises in imports will be allowed in order to deflect foreign pressure, perhaps, but not enough to solve anything from the Western point of view.

The first of van Wolferen's reasons is based on a misunderstanding. It is true that Japan does not practice pure laissez-faire, free-market economic policies. Close relationships between bureaucrats and industrialists do guide the economy and seek to distort market forces. Freedom of the market is not desired as an end in itself, but merely as one of several instruments available to promote expansion. But this lack of a free-market ideology does not mean that the Japanese economy is immune to market forces. Economies are not either "free market" or "non–free market"; they are on a spectrum somewhere between these two extremes.

Signals about prices and quantities, about demand and supply affect Japanese producers and consumers just as in other countries. Indeed, Japanese bureaucrats and industrialists have proved themselves masters of the art of spotting those market forces and fully exploiting them. Japan, like other East Asian developing economies, was expressly opened to trade and free competition, at least in key sectors, in the 1950s and 1960s in order that firms and individuals could be exposed to market forces. It may not seem so open as America, but compared with genuinely protected economies (such as India and much of Africa and Latin America), it has been open to the winds.

Controls, cartels, conspiracies, a labyrinthine distribution system, and all the other distortions in Japan do act as a powerful drag, but they do not render market forces inoperable. Movements in prices and changes in policies have to be grander in scale and more radical to overcome the drag, but Japan has not repealed the laws of economics. All this simply means that those dealing with Japan have to understand that these drags exist and must take them into account. The most common mistake lies in assuming that they do not.

The second obstacle to a solution is a tougher one to overcome. Rephrased to acknowledge that market forces do operate in Japan, the argument is, in essence, that threatened with imports stimulated by market forces the Japanese system, the drags mentioned above, will do all it can to block them because they undermine its basic aim: The protectionist instinct will win out.

There is some evidence for this. Those injured by imports or expecting to be injured do anything they can to prevent the pain. Japanese makers of skiing equipment resorted to absurd claims that Japanese snow is different in order to justify protectionist rules, and the bureaucrats regulating their industry carried out their wishes. Textiles manufacturers complained about unfair Chinese competition and demanded protection (temporary, of course) barely years after they themselves were the targets of similar complaints in Europe and America. In 1985, even as Prime Minister Nakasone was boasting to the world about how open Japan's market was becoming, officials at the Postal Ministry were drafting for the telecommunications market a new set of regulations that was deliberately designed to keep out foreign firms. That is what their counterparts in industry had asked them to do, so they did it. In the end, after fierce American lobbying and anguished pressure from the prime minister, the scheme was changed to a very open one. But the first instinct was to keep it closed.

Plenty of other anecdotes confirm this. Yasuhiro Nakasone is just as vulnerable to lobbies as are other politicians. When in mid-1985 he trumpeted an "action program" to open Japan's markets, one thing he did not trumpet was that a particular foodstuff—*konnyaku,* a Japanese delicacy derived from a root crop—had been expressly exempted from tariff cuts and other measures. The main Japanese producers of *kon-nyaku* just happen to be in Nakasone's constituency, in Gunma prefecture. Power center or no power center, dirty tricks will be played.

Nevertheless, the fact that on particular and far too numerous occasions Japan exhibits a protectionist instinct is not sufficient to establish that it is basically or generally protectionist, or "closed." This too is based on a misunderstanding, namely, the notion that Japanese industry has a "goal" of increasing domestic output plus exports, so that imports are therefore a bad thing. The economy is no longer as simple as that, if it ever was. Japanese firms are importers as well as exporters and recognize the benefits of trade. They may not shift sources of supply overseas after a 5 percent movement in prices, but they will after 40 percent. There is nothing "bad" about imports, even in Japan; imports are only bad if they exceed exports for longer than your country's ability to finance a trade deficit. The trade surplus is perhaps a poor symptom of the problem. After all, it could be "solved" without increasing imports at all if a sufficient quantity of Japanese factories were to be shifted offshore.

Is Japan really unwilling to accept a fairly balanced current account? If so, not only would there have to be a protectionist instinct but Japan would also always have to export far more than it imports. A current-account surplus would have to be a policy goal.

When Japan's domestic demand was providing no stimulus to growth, this instinct certainly existed. Japan depended on exports for its economic well-being. That is no longer the case. Since 1986, the trade account has hindered growth. It has become accepted that net exports can no longer be depended on. That does not mean that everyone accepts that the trade surplus should disappear overnight or that its fall should be so rapid as to cause a domestic recession. There is a clear interest in an orderly, gradual decline, and "the system" is directing policy toward that end. There is nothing surprising or especially sinister about the desire for slow change. It is what you would expect, through different political forms, in West Germany or Britain or, indeed, the United States.

The gist of this argument is that, despite its oddities, its awkwardness, and its international reluctance, the Japanese system will act to resolve contradictions between domestic and foreign policy if a sufficiently broad interest develops for it to do so. Perhaps this process takes longer than in a more conventional, centrally directed power structure, but still it happens. Reluctance, even here, can be overcome. The difficulty for outsiders dealing with Japan is to know how to secure this interest, how to convince the country that a contradiction requires attention.

SELFISHNESS AND POWER

This, rather than the existence or otherwise of a power center, is the nub of the question. A clear power center would make it possible for a systemic instinct to be overcome, perhaps. But all that really amounts to is that it would enable Japan's wider interests—in peace, international harmony, open markets, free trade, and so forth—to take precedence over narrow, parochial, or sectoral interests. A "leader" or set of leaders would make the country see sense. In fact, the role of such "leaders" in other countries is exaggerated by those bemoaning the lack of it in Japan; everywhere except, possibly, in totalitarian regimes, leadership derives from the country's society and system itself. There is always some blend of reflection of trends, popular opinion, and the distribution of power, with an attempt to superimpose ideas and aims.

The question in Japan is whether or not international policy and, particularly, an open attitude to foreign competition can develop a sufficient strength in order to defeat parochial, protectionist instincts. Imports and foreign competition have penetrated in many areas, to an extent far beyond what van Wolferen dismisses as tokenism. Even in the free-market United States, imports have only recently penetrated far into the economy. This is a question of development and transition. When the overseas interest becomes stronger and shared by a wider cross section of Japan, then the country will assume its proper international role. As van Wolferen writes, it is not a country that is capable of selfless gestures. Yet international politics is not usually a selfless affair, and it is naive to expect Japan to behave otherwise. It is not going to be nice to imports, or to spend more on defense, or to give more overseas aid merely on moral grounds. Nobody else would, either.

Van Wolferen's prescription of using retaliatory force would be one way to shorten the transition to a selfishly harmonious Japan. It would force the Japanese system to adjust, in its own interest. The trouble is that it is not clear that such a radical departure from free trade would bring benefits to the United States, or to anybody else. It could eliminate or in some way manage the trade imbalance, but that should not be an end in itself, for there is no reason to think that this would restore health to the American economy, or to anybody else's economy. Healthy economies, prosperity, and jobs are surely the aim of policy, not balanced trade.

In any case, Japan's imbalance is not only bilateral, it is also multilateral, so that any negotiated deal between America and Japan would force other trading partners to seek similar deals in order to avoid exports being diverted toward them. Then, they would probably require deals with one another, if only to control Japanese exports from offshore bases. The whole trading system would then collapse, hurting not just the division of labor with Japan but also that between other countries. Closed trade means shrinking trade. Even if the policy were justified, it would be likely to explode in the user's face, all for the sake of dealing with one admittedly large country. Fighting general protectionism with general protectionism is a recipe for disaster—even if the grievance that it attempts to address is genuine. I happen to believe it is not. But even if it were, managed trade would be a bad solution.

This is an awkward conclusion because it seems to provide for a policy of impotence. Nothing can be "done" about Japan. The argument seems to suggest that we have to just sit and wait, and everything will be all right. It is not quite that. Macroeconomic policymakers should not expect exchange-rate movements alone to shift trade flows; fiscal policies (that too-large budget deficit, America; that too-small budget deficit, Japan) must also be employed, along with other means. Moreover, firms and officials should negotiate with Japan with their eyes wide open to the way the place works, without being spooked. It is tiresome, but if dirty tricks are exposed and shouted about, then in most cases the overseas interest in Japan reacts to and squashes the protectionist instinct. A tough, well-informed attitude is not the same as a violent one.

RELUCTANT LEADERS

DEFENSIVE ABOUT DEFENSE

Japan will develop a better balance between foreign and domestic policies, and it will take on more leadership if and when it is required. Nevertheless, its present position is reminiscent of the old story about a young man asking a wise old soul about how to get to a particular place. "If I were you, I wouldn't start from here," comes the reply. That is especially apt for Japan's defense policy.

The weakness of Japanese defense is not simply a matter of numbers. Japan has, by any standards, a large military force, the non-Communist world's sixth largest, with more than 270,000 men in uniform, more than 1,000 tanks, 14 submarines, 60 ships, and close to 400 combat aircraft. Its spending on defense broke through 1 percent of its GNP in 1986–1987, an artificial ceiling imposed in 1976. That is well below levels of spending in America, Britain, France, or West Germany (all of whom spend a proportion of their GNPs at least triple Japan's), but it has been rising more rapidly than elsewhere and, in pure cash terms, is the largest sum spent on defense outside the two superpowers. Defense spending in Japan has risen by 5–7 percent a year in nominal terms, which means 3–5 percent in real, inflation-adjusted terms, faster than in any other Western country. Moreover, Japan plays a vital role for America's defense efforts; the U.S. bases closest to the Soviet Union are in Japan. In addition, Japan houses important listening posts, nearly 50,000 American servicemen, and the Fifth Air Force.

The main problems with Japan's defense policy are of attitude and organization. The country pretends it does not have a policy because its postwar constitution renounced the use of military force. It calls its sailors, soldiers, and airmen a "self-defense force" and holds them in pretty low esteem. The army, quite apart from being too small to resist a conventional invasion for more than a day or two, is top-heavy with officers (the average age is a little over thirty) and is short of ammunition and other supplies. The chain of command is cumbersome, speed of reaction poor.

In August 1985, when a Japan Air Lines jumbo jet crashed in the mountains between Tokyo and Osaka, it took the army twenty-four hours to mount a rescue effort. By the time they got there, newspapermen had already flown over the crash site by helicopter and had taken pictures. The army found four survivors; it was clear that others had lived through the crash only to die before rescuers arrived.

Another blow to the forces' morale and reputation came in July 1988, when a submarine collided with a pleasure boat in Tokyo Bay, killing thirty civilians. Not only did the Maritime Self-Defense Force come under criticism for the fact of the collision, but the submarine's sailors were also accused of failing to rescue drowning people. The *Asahi Shimbun,* an influential daily, said that

> We do not know the reasons for the accident, but we wonder why an organization supposedly dedicated to the defense of citizens could become involved in something like this.

One of the nineteen survivors was quoted as accusing the submarine's crew of "wandering about aimlessly on deck while we were frantically waving our arms for help."

What remains to be straightened out is the status of the armed forces and what they can be used for. This, really, is more important than calculating the amount spent on them, at least until and unless Japan seeks to become a nuclear power. That development would be the only truly important jump in Japanese defense spending. Short of that, what are the Japanese army, navy, and air force for? Why can they not defend Japanese oil passing through the Persian Gulf, as American or British navies do? Why can they not participate in international peace-keeping forces, as even the Fijian army has? Why can they not send small task forces to sort out little local difficulties in Asia, as India sends troops to Sri Lanka or the Maldive Islands?

If answers ever come to these questions, and if Japanese policy changes, it will likely be by necessity rather than by desire. Japan will need to be convinced that it has no alternative but to change policy, not that one policy is better than another. What all this really amounts to is that Japan, like the United States before it, will eventually have to take a broader view of what constitutes self-defense. This view, adopted in a baptism of necessity, might coincide with involvement in some future local crisis, in which the United States failed to act as regional policeman. Such involvement need not, however, change the Japanese view, since overseas military entanglements can just as readily turn into disaster. Ask Americans about Lebanon.

Short of taking a robust and supportive attitude to having a military force, Japan will be left with its current policy for the foreseeable future. This, essentially, is that of filling in some gaps in America's Pacific forces and of paying most of the direct cost of the American bases in Japan. The gaps that Japan covers are for things like over-the-horizon radar or fleets of antisubmarine aircraft. Although the trend is for spending to continue to grow and for many of these costly items to be purchased, there is no sign yet of a solution to the problems of attitude and organization. For the moment, Japan would rather sign checks than worry about what they are for. This is unlikely to change quickly.

AN AID MYTH

The same is true for the country's overseas aid policy. Since Japan has become awash in cash, it has felt that aid is one way in which it can be seen to fulfill its international responsibilities without having to make awkward choices about foreign policy or military spending. To a small extent, it has begun to channel aid toward places that matter for America's foreign policy, such as the Philippines and Turkey. But mainly, it has just sprayed money around.

Unfortunately it has also partly just talked about spraying money around and, as mentioned earlier, has made false boasts about it. In 1988, it seemed poised to overtake America as the world's largest aid donor in absolute terms, having increased its aid by 40 percent in dollar terms between 1986's $5.6 billion and 1988's $7.8 billion. But that was almost entirely due to the rise of the yen against the dollar, which does make Japanese aid go further but is hardly something for Japan to take credit for. In yen terms, Japan's overseas aid fell in 1983 and 1984 and has risen by just 5–8 percent a year since 1985. That leaves it equivalent to only 0.29 percent of Japan's GNP, about as low as in the United States and Britain but well below the 0.4 percent typical in Western Europe. It is also too low for Japan to claim that it is using aid to make up for its deficiencies in defense spending.

The difficulty lies in the Ministry of Finance's continued insistence on fiscal austerity. Defense and aid have been the only parts of the budget to grow in recent years, but they too have been restrained. If Japan's overseas role is to begin with money rather than force, then the money has to be made available. Hopes were raised when in May 1987 Prime Minister Nakasone announced a plan to "recycle" $30 billion worth of Japanese money to developing countries over the next five years. But they were dashed when it became clear that a third of this had in fact already been pledged as contributions to the World Bank's soft-loan agency, to the International Development Agency, and to the Asian Development Bank, and was thus not new money at all. Most of the rest is to come from the private sector in the form of bond issues in Japan by international institutions, which they might have made anyway. Little extra money was being put up. Foreign policy does not come free, or cheap.

ACCEPTING THE CONSEQUENCES

Japan is coming from a poor starting point in the leadership game. There is also another problem. Those who want Japan to play more of an international role and to put up more money for international causes also have to accept the consequences: Japan will want power to match its contributions, and its actions and desires will not always perfectly match those of the United States. In most cases, more power for Japan will mean less for America.

In incidents where America has called for Japan's assistance and little has been forthcoming, generally American leadership has not been at risk. An example was in late 1987, when America asked Japan (along with other allies) to share the costs and the trouble of protecting oil tankers in the Persian Gulf. Since 55 percent of Japan's oil comes from the Gulf and since its boats had been attacked, Japan's interest in taking part seemed clear. It refused, however, because of its nonmilitary constitution. The Gulf would have been the first place to which Japanese military men or weapons had been sent since 1945, and virtually nobody (except, it seems, the then outgoing prime minister, Yasuhiro Nakasone, but he was overruled) wanted to set a precedent. If Japan had agreed, it would have been an unblemished gain to the United States; no power was lost in asking.

On two occasions, however, the United States has balked at giving up power to the Japanese. Both involved increased Japanese contributions to international development banks—the World Bank in 1984–1986 and the Asian Development Bank in 1987. In both cases, Japan asked, quite reasonably, that its voting power be increased in line with its greater share of the costs. It was not asking for America to cede its veto power or its dominance. But in both cases, the United States blocked the proposal. It was not willing to relax its grip on these two important development institutions. It was not prepared, in other words, to accept the consequences of its own relative decline. It may ask for "burden-sharing," but in return it is unwilling to offer "power-sharing."

国

A TALE OF TWO COUNTRIES

クニ

CHAPTER ELEVEN

円

THE SUN ALSO SETS

They blossom, and then
we gaze, and then the blossoms
scatter, and then. . . .
 —Onitsura (1660–1738)

The winds that blow—
ask them, which leaf of the tree
will be next to go!
 —Soseki (1867–1916)

THE DEATH OF Emperor Hirohito at 6:33 A.M. on January 7, 1989, just a few days into the sixty-fourth year of the *Showa* period, brought to an end both an era in the imperial sense and an age in the real sense. The nation, the government, the priests of shinto, the domestic and international media, the stock market, the nationalist groups, and, sadly, a handful of suicidal octogenarians had all endured nearly four months of waiting for the ailing eighty-seven-year-old emperor to die. As soon as Hirohito had fallen seriously ill, on September 19, 1988, suffering from cancer of the duodenum, talk in Japan as elsewhere had turned to the end of one era and the beginning of a new one. Unfortunately, a few newspapers jumped the gun and mistakenly ran obituaries before the emperor had actually died.

When, after having received transfusions of more than eight gallons of blood, the emperor at last passed away, there was almost a sigh of relief across Tokyo. The waiting, and the joking about the condition of the poor old man, had become rather macabre. Despite that, on the day of Hirohito's death hundreds of thousands of Japanese turned up at the gates of the somewhat austere imperial palace in Tokyo to pay their respects: some to prostrate themselves; a few to demonstrate their nationalist sentiments; but most simply to mourn, sign books of condolence, and see what was going on. They wore casual dress rather than the formal clothes requested by government officials, but still they came.

Hirohito's death meant that January 8 began a new imperial era, known as *Heisei*. While *Showa* meant "enlightened peace" and had seemed like a bad joke for the first turbulent and warlike quarter century of Hirohito's long reign, *Heisei* means something like "achievement of peace," which is suitably both optimistic and true, at least for the time being. The new Emperor Akihito, the fifty-five-year-old son of Hirohito, was not exactly a celebrity in the sense of Britain's Charles and Diana, but he was certainly well known in Japan as being more modern than his father, having in 1959 married a commoner, Michiko Shoda, the daughter of a flour miller whom he had met on the tennis courts.

What is more, in recent years the normally discreet Akihito has done a bit of mingling with foreign journalists, beginning in 1985 when the Foreign Correspondents Club of Japan celebrated its fortieth anniversary with a grand ball at a posh Tokyo hotel. Merely for form's sake, the club sent an invitation to the Crown Prince and Princess, confidently expecting that they would be politely unable to attend. To everybody's surprise, a message suddenly came from the imperial chamberlain's office summoning the club's president, Jurek Martin of the *Financial Times,* to a meeting, from which it emerged that their imperial highnesses did indeed intend to come.

And so they did, looking very quietly grand, with Princess Michiko speaking in very fluent English and Akihito in less confident but still more than passable English. They danced with the club president and his wife, Kathleen Newland, and left discreetly early, permitting the journalists to resume their normal dubious behavior. Subsequently, it emerged that the couple were members of the same tennis club as both Jurek and William Horsley, the BBC's resident correspondent in

Tokyo, and each of these was occasionally invited to play against Akihito and Michiko.

However, it would be incorrect to conclude from this that Akihito plans his era to be an altogether more modern and active form of constitutional monarchy than that of his father. The new emperor, it seems, has been schooled in the same way as his father was, to remain discreet and restrained. Throughout the 124 reigns known to history, Japanese imperial families have never really sought the public eye, nor usually have they been allowed to. Emperors have always been symbols or, occasionally, puppets, which is why it is wholly irrelevant for the West to debate endlessly Hirohito's role in World War II or in Japan's invasion of China in the 1930s. Even if Hirohito had been in favor of war, conquest, torture, and experimenting on prisoners, it would have made little difference. The decisions were not his to make, so his view was beside the point. That is also why it is futile to speculate about whether he opposed wartime atrocities, since even if he did he had no power to prevent them. A Japanese emperor simply could not be a driving force in the style of Adolf Hitler. He is in the background, not the foreground.

The *Heisei* era will be no exception. Although the various rites of transition following Hirohito's death inevitably attracted fresh interest in the imperial throne and fresh debate about the role of religion and even about Japan's position in the world, the imperial accession was not a decisive or even terribly significant event. Most Japanese will soon conclude that nothing has really changed except that the television reports on the emperor's New Year's Day speech and on his annual planting of rice will no longer feature a frail old man with small round glasses but instead a handsome, fit man with a fairly aquiline nose who looks at least half a dozen years younger than he is.

ALREADY A NEW ERA

In fact, Japan had already entered a new era months if not years before Hirohito died. Since 1945, Japanese eras have principally been driven by economics, and this one was no exception. Throughout 1988, it became steadily clearer that something fundamental was changing in the Japanese economy and indeed in Japanese society and politics. Like most changes in Japan, however, it emerged only gradually rather than in one big bang, and it reflected trends that had begun several years before and that would continue for several more years before they reached fruition.

Those changes, of the recent past and for the future, have been the subject of this book. The inexorable rise of Japan's trade and current-account surpluses, through the 1960s and 1970s but especially in the early 1980s, had been driven by the fact that Japanese were, compared to most Europeans and Americans, inclined to save more, to consume less of their incomes, to buy fewer imports, to take fewer vacations, and to travel at home rather than abroad. Exports were a priority for industry and government alike, while the Ministry of Finance strained in the early 1980s to cut its budget deficit back almost to zero. The population was younger than that in America or Europe and had far less freedom to invest money where it chose.

Life is never as simple as this oversimplification suggests. Nevertheless, this is broadly how Japan was seen and how it saw itself, and by 1983, it was clear that Japan had arrived as an economic superpower, not only in its own right (it was that by 1970 or so) but, more important, relative to the United States. Helped by the yen's weakness against the dollar, Japan's trade surpluses soared on past 1983, reaching nearly $100 billion a year by 1987, five times the 1981 surplus. The current-account surplus of nearly $87 billion in 1987 was five times the peak in the 1970s and nearly nineteen times the 1981 current surplus of $4.8 billion.

With the arrival of surpluses of this size, Japan became an exporter of capital, chiefly to the United States, which had established deficits even larger than Japan's surpluses. Wealth began to ooze out of every Japanese pore, as firms and individuals began, it seemed, to buy up the world. The sun had indeed risen, but more than that, it seemed destined to continue rising, leaving America in the shadows. From money would come more money, from which eventually would come power.

Yet the metaphor in the previous paragraph, that of the ever-rising sun, does not really work. Suns do not just rise. They also set. That is the new era in Japan, the era of the setting sun. It was already under way in the mid-1980s, even as Japan's exports of capital were prompting speculation and concern about the emergence of Japanese power. The factors that characterized Japan's rise have changed, under the influence of the rise itself: that is, of affluence, international exposure, the capital surplus, and the now-strong yen. Japan is becoming a nation of consumers, of pleasure seekers, of importers, of investors and of speculators. Abundant money and free financial markets risk turning this new nation of speculators into one of boom and bust. More certainly, time and the maturing of the baby-boom generation will make Japan a nation of pensioners.

THE SUN AND ECONOMICS

What this means economically is that Japan's trade and current-account surpluses will disappear, not forever necessarily, but for a significant period. With them will go Japan's role as an exporter of capital. This is very hard to accept, for it is hard to imagine Japan without trade and current-account surpluses, harder still to imagine Japanese exports not battering one Western industry or another. Moreover, if the capital surplus does continue only for these few years, then Japan's candidacy as a top power would have to be consigned to the dustbin of history, along with that of the oil producers of OPEC, whose 1970 surpluses lasted for less than a decade.

The dustbin is not a popular place in which to put Japan. Most analysts have concluded that Japan's surplus must be a long-term phenomenon. Japan's strength, after all, is based on more than merely a rise in the price of a single commodity, as OPEC's was. Many of its industries have built a technological and managerial lead over their rivals that should provide a lasting competitive edge. In semiconductors, cars, consumer electronics, optoelectronics, factory automation, and even financial services, Japanese firms are incontrovertibly ahead of their American and European competitors. Helped by the current-account surplus that has ensued, Japan's net overseas assets have risen from $25 billion at the end of 1982 to $180 billion at the end of 1986 and further to $240 billion by the end of 1987. On current trends, the figure will reach $900 billion by the mid-1990s. This would mean that

Japan would own net overseas assets equivalent to the entire 1986 gross national product of West Germany. That would be quite an empire.

Nevertheless, usually without realizing it, those who see this prospect as inevitable are making an economic forecast based on a simple extrapolation of the past three years. They are assuming that it is more likely than not that recent trends will continue uninterrupted. Simple extrapolation is always a poor method of forecasting, and it becomes poorer the longer the period over which it is used. Surprises may turn up, but in any event, trends often contain the seeds of their own destruction.

It is worth remembering that in the 1960s many Europeans thought that the rise of American multinationals was unstoppable; Jean-Jacques Servan-Schreiber, a French journalist and politician, warned in his best-selling *Le Défi Americain* (*The American Challenge,* discussed in chapter 7) that

> Fifteen years from now it is quite possible that the world's third greatest industrial power, just after the United States and Russia, will not be Europe but American industry in Europe.

He too was extrapolating, and he was wrong. It was Japan. Also, the flow of American multinationals to Europe was stemmed by shifts in exchange rates, by the sharp rise in oil prices after 1973, and by the revival of some European businesses. Nobody in Europe worries about, or even notices, American multinationals any longer. Europe has plenty of problems, but that is not among them.

In the 1970s, the best example of erroneous simple extrapolation was provided by the environmentalists of the Club of Rome. This group looked at the world's finite resources and worked out how quickly, at then-current rates of exploitation, the resources would be exhausted. The answer was: scarily soon. Yet as with American industry in Europe the market had an answer. Prices moved, forcing a reduction in exploitation and an increase in innovation. To take just one example, less oil is used when the price rises, and the incentive increases both to discover new reserves of oil and to invent new ways to tap other sources of energy. Almost as fast as the Arab countries became super-rich, their surpluses had gone. A shortage of oil turned into a glut.

These examples should be born in mind when thinking about Japan's surpluses, whether of trade, of the current account, or of capital. Why should they continue to grow in a straight line? Why, in particular, should Japan's capital surplus continue to grow so much that the country's overseas assets become as large as West Germany's GNP? Such an idea assumes that, unlike American industry in Europe or the finite resources of the Club of Rome, the forces that have produced Japan's capital surplus will not respond to changes in prices or to other market pressures. This has to be wrong. Eventually, the surplus is bound to adjust and disappear. On its own, this truth is not terribly helpful, however. As Lord Keynes said, "In the long run we are all dead." In principle, Japan's surplus could last fifty years, even if it is eventually doomed. The important question about the surplus is: How soon will it disappear?

THROW AWAY THE RULER

The answer is likely to be: sooner than most people realize. To understand why requires a switch into strictly economic analysis and language. The first and most important point is that the question is more complicated than is popularly imagined. Japan's capital surplus has not risen from nowhere. It is not simply there because Japan makes better cars than other people or, indeed, because the Japanese are richer than others. Japan could make the best cars in the world and still not have a surplus. That it does have one is the product of a particular combination of circumstances: abundant savings, low and falling government borrowing, low and falling domestic corporate investment, a strong dollar in 1982–85, and, last but not least, a rapid growth in productivity. These more technical descriptions correspond to the more social and commonsense descriptions used earlier in this chapter when discussing Japan's previous economic era. Whatever you call them, however, the surplus's prospects depend on how long these circumstances are likely to persist or whether they might be replaced by other circumstances with the same effect.

A surplus of capital, then, is not merely the outcome of success. One way of explaining how it arises is to use a bit of very simple economic analysis. A basic accounting truism is that, broadly defined, exports minus imports must equal output minus expenditure. If a country spends less than it produces, it must be exporting more than it is importing. Similarly, exports minus imports must also equal savings minus investment, broadly defined. If you save more than you invest, or produce more than you consume, the difference must go somewhere: abroad. In turn, this brings in the net flow of capital overseas. Consume more than you produce, and the result must be foreign borrowing. Produce more than you consume, and the result must be an outflow of capital.

This is no more, and no less, than a set of accounting equations or principles; it says nothing about causes or about human or corporate behavior. But it helps to show the variety of variables and relationships involved when examining a country's external surpluses and deficits. The four factors mentioned—the output-spending gap, the export-import gap, the savings-investment gap, the capital inflow-outflow gap—are always equal by definition. What the gap is and how it is affected by such other factors as exchange rates, government policy, prices, wages, and so on is harder to determine.

Come back to real life and to Japan's case. Japan saves much more than it invests domestically. Its households are hefty net savers, stashing away 16 percent of their disposable incomes in 1986, for example, compared with 3–5 percent in the United States and 5–10 percent in Britain. The government and companies are, overall, net borrowers or, in other words, net investors. They spend more than they consume. But their borrowing is not enough to utilize all of the household savings surplus. Savings exceed investment. As stated earlier, that means that, one way or another, capital must flow out of Japan. Put through a different equation, exports must also exceed imports. No surprise: Japan has an enormously large current-account surplus.

This has not always been so. From 1945 until the mid-1960s, Japan usually ran a deficit on its current account. It was an importer of capital. Since then it has enjoyed a surplus in all but five years. But the surplus has varied greatly in size. Only after 1982 did the current-account surplus grow really large, from $6.8 billion in that year to $49 billion in 1985 and $86.6 billion in 1987. Only in 1984 did Japan begin to export large sums in long-term capital: $49.7 billion in that year, rising to $137 billion in 1987.

The savings-investment gap helps to show why. Japan's personal savings rate was high throughout the period 1982–1988, varying only between 16 and 18 percent of disposable income. But during this time, domestic investment, or the use of savings, altered substantially. A high savings rate would not have turned into a large current-account surplus if, say, the government had been running a large budget deficit; in Italy, where the personal savings rate is even higher than in Japan, the public sector deficit is huge, and the country has a current-account deficit. Japan's general government deficit rose very fast in the late 1970s, reaching 5.5 percent of GNP in 1978 and mopping up lots of savings. During the 1980s, however, Japan's Ministry of Finance has been determined to cut that deficit, preferably to zero. It gradually did so, by 1987 reducing the deficit to just 0.2 percent of GNP. Put another way, the Japanese government was borrowing and investing less and less of the country's savings every year. The same was true of companies during this period. After 1982, their capital investments declined while profits remained strong. The result was that their demand for funds declined.

This widening gap between domestic savings and investment is crucial to understanding how and why Japan's current-account surplus grew so enormous after 1982 and why it came to export so much capital. The process can be described in another, more dynamic, way. If, as was the case, the surplus of household savings exceeds the deficits of government and companies then, other things being equal, domestic interest rates will be pushed down. As the gap expands over time, rates will be pushed further down. There is lots of money, and relatively weak domestic demand for it. That in turn may push down the exchange rate against other currencies, for example, if the returns to investors in yen become lower than the returns on investments in dollars. This, in turn, affects trade by making exports more competitive. The trade surplus generates flows of money into corporate accounts, reducing their borrowing needs and increasing the domestic savings surplus. One way or another, such a domestic savings surplus will flow abroad as capital.

The above is a description of what appears to have happened in Japan in the 1980s. It did not happen in isolation, however. Just as Japanese savings started to generate large capital flows, the U.S. federal budget began to run large deficits that were beyond the capacity of American savings to finance. Encouraged by America's policy of benign neglect in the exchange market, the dollar climbed as foreign capital, much of it Japanese, chased the high interest rates available on dollar assets and thus financed the budget and trade deficits.

This was made easier by coincidental increases in the mobility of capital, enabled, among other things, by the removal of exchange controls by Britain in 1979 and by Japan in 1980. That allowed British and Japanese institutions to diversify their foreign investment portfolios. Such mobility of capital enabled the United States to run and finance, relative to its budget deficit, a trade deficit larger than economists would normally have thought possible. In theory, America's budget deficit ought to have "crowded out" the markets for borrowing, forcing interest rates to rise, choking off domestic demand for goods and services, and holding back imports and the trade deficit. Thanks to free-flowing foreign capital, this did not happen, at least not for a long time.

WHY IT WON'T LAST

Japan's capital surplus has been generated, then, by three forces: high savings, low domestic demand for those savings, and an excess of exports over imports. These three are not independent. If Japanese savings remain high relative to the domestic demand from government, companies, and private individuals, Japan must run a current-account surplus. Conversely, a current-account surplus must be reflected in an imbalance between the supply and demand for savings. That is what is meant by the accounting principles discussed earlier. Nevertheless, in trying to determine the durability of the Japanese surplus, it is useful to look at the prospects for all three of its components to see whether they tell the same story.

Start with the current account of the balance of payments, the most familiar part of Japan's surplus and the part most often thought to be invincible. Here, movement has begun. The trade component of the current-account surplus was already on its way down by 1988, thanks to the doubling of the yen's value against the dollar since early 1985. Japan's trade surplus fell to $92.2 billion in the year to August 1988, compared for instance with a surplus of $101.8 billion in the year to July 1987.

Import volumes rose strongly in 1986, 1987, and 1988, thanks to the risen yen and to a boom in consumer spending, while exports weakened. This took time to show through in the dollar trade figures because of the familiar J-curve effect: in this, a falling dollar continuously lowers the dollar value of Japan's imports and raises the dollar value of exports, until the currency stabilizes and changes in volume outweigh those in value. But trade flows are, nonetheless, responding to exchange-rate changes. Japan's import volume rose by 21 percent in the year to end March 1988 after increases of 9.5 percent in 1986 and 9.3 percent in 1987. Export volumes fell slightly in 1986 and 1987. Imports from the four Asian dragons (Taiwan, Hong Kong, Singapore, and South Korea) benefited especially, rising by 30 percent in yen terms during 1987, 50 percent in dollar terms.

Another contribution to this adjustment has been the shifting of production offshore. A large and growing part of the capital outflow has been in the form of direct investments overseas. As such overseas projects come on stream, particularly of Japanese car makers in the United States, exports could fall very sharply. New factories take time to build, adding, in a sense, to the J-curve effect; they also initially increase exports of capital goods (machines and other equipment) as they are being set up.

Japan's mighty trade surplus will not disappear overnight, even if the severity of currency movements suggests that it might. One reason is that trade patterns take time to shift; Japanese car makers have built up wide networks of dealers in America, establishing a solid market share, while American exporters have often wound up their dealerships. New networks, in response to more favorable exchange rates, will take time to establish.

Another reason is that the yen has not risen as much against all currencies as it has against the dollar. Although it had doubled against the dollar between February 1985 and early 1989, it had appreciated by only 60 percent on a trade-weighted basis. Moreover, both rises were from an abnormal position. Although the dollar was briefly worth ¥260 in early 1985, Japanese exporters were generally budgeting on the basis of an exchange rate closer to ¥200 so that the removal of the first ¥60 made little difference to them. It merely changed them from making extraordinarily high profits on their exports to ordinary profits. In any case, it was only when the dollar fell past ¥175 that the yen exceeded its previous peak, set in 1978. The result is that the currency swing has been gentler than would seem at first sight, which suggests that the trade adjustment will not be instantaneous. Nevertheless, adjustment is happening at a speed that, with the benefit of hindsight, will appear quite rapid.

TRAVELERS VERSUS INVESTORS

Trade in services may prove just as important a component of Japan's current-account adjustment as movements in merchandise trade. Given Japan's ubiquitous exports, this may seem hard to believe. Nevertheless, the services account—principally travel, transport, royalties on patents, and interest payments—is what is likely to determine whether Japan's current-account surplus lasts for five years or fifty. This is the part of the balance of payments that registers the income from Japan's overseas investments. In theory, as the trade surplus gradually shrinks, this growing overseas income could make Japan's surplus self-sustaining. Or will it?

Since 1945, Japan has generally had a deficit on services, tempering its surpluses on visible trade. It had to pay for patents and transport as well as coughing up the interest, profits, and dividends on its capital imports. Beginning in 1983, however, the services account has been changing in three important but different ways. First and most prominently, Japan's vast portfolio and direct investments abroad generated net income in the form of interest, profits, and dividends. These reduce the deficit on services, inflating the overall current-account surplus. In 1987, net investment income rose to $16.6 billion from $9.5 billion in 1986. That net income will grow as long as Japan's overseas net investments grow.

Change number two, however, is a move in the opposite direction. Domestic affluence and the rise of the yen have enabled more and more Japanese to travel abroad on vacation. In 1986, the Japanese spent $5.6 billion more in traveling abroad than foreigners spent in Japan. In the year to end March 1988, that deficit on tourism and travel rose to $9.7 billion. The Japanese government forecasts that by 1991 this deficit will rise to $13 billion. This could well prove too conservative, given the current 20 percent annual rate of increase in the number of trips abroad taken by Japanese.

The third change has also added to the services deficit. The use of foreign ships and other forms of transport by Japanese residents moved into an expanded deficit of $6.1 billion in 1987, up from $2.5 billion in 1986. Japanese shipping lines have become less competitive compared with, for instance, Taiwanese lines.

In 1987, the outcome of these three changes was the opposite of that assumed by forecasters of a self-sustaining surplus. Japan's services deficit rose because the growth of net outflows for travel, transport, and others exceeded the growth in net investment income. The net services deficit reached $5.7 billion, compared with $4.9 billion the previous year. That reversed six years during which the services deficit declined, from a peak of $13.6 billion in 1981. In 1988, the deficit widened again, exceeding $8 billion.

This could, of course, change again. Two declines do not make a trend, and income from investments abroad is notoriously hard to measure accurately. Income from overseas investments is one reason why in recent years Britain's current-account figures have had to be revised so often. The same could happen with Japan. Nevertheless, one way to estimate Japan's future overseas income is to apply an average interest rate, or rate of return, to its total of net overseas assets. The net assets of $240 billion at the end of 1987 and income of $16.3 billion suggest an average rate of return of around 7 percent. That sounds reasonable, given yields on such favored investments as U.S. Treasury bonds.

If Japan's overseas assets were to grow at the same rate as in 1987, then by the end of 1989 net assets would have reached $430 billion. At a 7 percent yield, that would imply annual income on the interest, profits, and dividends account of $30.1 billion. This extra $15 billion income could well cancel out all or most of a decline in the trade surplus. But will the assets grow that fast? This depends, in part, on the movement of the trade surplus itself, as well as on domestic savings.

John Greenwood, chief economist at GT Management in Hong Kong, points out that there is a relationship between the trade surplus—more precisely, the difference in the rates of growth of Japan's imports and exports—and the growth of the country's net overseas assets. After all, it is the current-account surplus that provides much of the money for overseas investment. His model suggests that if imports grow only 10 percentage points faster than exports (e.g., import growth of 10 percent a year while export growth is zero), then net assets would rise to $450 billion to $500 billion by 1990. But if the differential were to be 20 percentage points (import growth of 10 percent a year, exports shrink 10 percent), then net assets would prove to have peaked in 1988 and would be falling by 1990.

Sounds unlikely? This last is roughly the differential seen during 1987 and early 1988. If, moreover, the differential were to expand to 30 percentage points, Japan's net assets would fall rapidly. By the early 1990s, they would be back below their end 1985 level. Greenwood may be wrong; no forecast is sacred, nor is any model inviolable. But his projections show, at least, how uncertain is the future course of Japan's investment income. It cannot merely be extrapolated from the income's present status.

What is surely more certain is that the amount of foreign travel undertaken by Japanese tourists will grow and grow. Foreign tourism is starting from a very low base; despite rapid growth, the 120 million Japanese took only 5 million overseas trips in 1986 and 6.8 million in 1987. Although Japanese are only gradually becoming more likely to take vacations, they are switching existing vacations rapidly from domestic to overseas trips. Domestic resorts are crowded and costly; it is often cheaper to fly from Tokyo to Saipan, Manila, or Hong Kong than it is to travel inside Japan. Everything, from golf to meals to souvenirs to sex, is now cheaper outside Japan than in.

Much more was said about Japanese tourism in chapter 3. For the present purpose, it suffices to apply the crude extrapolation approach to tourism as it is so often applied to overseas investment. If net spending on travel grows as it has since 1986, then by 1990 the tourism deficit could pass $20 billion, enough to neutralize a significant part of investment income. That tourism deficit would, on its own, have exceeded Japan's entire 1982 trade surplus. Other parts of the services account, including the use of foreign ships, may expand as well. If all this were true, then the services account would give the overall current-account surplus a useful nudge downward.

Magic? Not necessarily. This downward assistance given by travel and tourism is exactly what happens in West Germany's current account. Relatively few people go to West Germany to vacation (except, these days, the Japanese), while West Germans all go and lie on Mediterranean beaches. West Germany's deficit on services was $16 billion in 1987, making a trade surplus of $70 billion seem far more acceptable internationally once it became a current-account surplus of $54 billion. Japan is moving in a similar direction. After all, who can afford to visit Japan?

SLIDING SAVINGS

Next, take a look at Japan's personal savings rate, the main determinant of the supply of domestic savings. A pervasive myth is that the Japanese are the industrial world's most prolific savers and that these peculiar creatures resist all inducements to spend their hard-earned cash. Yet both Italy and Taiwan, to name but two, boast higher ratios of savings to disposable income than does Japan. And Japan's ratio has fallen steadily, from as much as 23 percent in 1975 to a low of 16 percent in 1985. Pension and social security schemes became more generous in Japan in the 1970s, removing one of the chief reasons for the need to save.

Moreover, as chapter 2 described, a new, less thrifty postwar generation is coming to maturity, entering the twenty-five-to-forty age range, which has in the past been Japan's thriftiest. While not exactly rebellious, this new generation of *shinjinrui,* or new humans, appears keener than its predecessor on consuming, borrowing, and living for the present rather than saving, staying out of debt, and preparing stoically for the future. The change coming over Japan is not radical, but it appears real enough to imply a further gradual fall in the savings rate.

If the savings rate were to continue to fall at the pace it did in 1975–1985, it could be down to 13 percent or below by the early 1990s. Awkwardly, however, it rose in 1986 and 1987, returning to about 18 percent. The most plausible explanation for this is that individuals feared that the rising yen would cause a severe recession in Japan, doubling or trebling the rate of unemployment. This worry was especially acute in 1986, when growth slowed to un-Japanese levels of 1–2 percent. That year a member of the ruling Liberal Democratic party echoed common fears when he said that "Japanese industry would be destroyed if the yen-dollar rate were to fall as low as ¥135." It fell well past that level, and Japanese industry appears to have remained intact. But the worry, at least, was genuine.

Savings rates are notoriously hard to predict and measure, as they are calculated as a residual between the statistics for income and expenditure and as they depend on the fickle behavior of individuals. Nevertheless, now that Japan's economy is again enjoying annual rates of growth in real GNP of 4 to 5 percent and with the new generation feeling rich and spendthrift, the savings rate could well resume its slow slide. Fear, at least, is less of a reason to save than it was in 1986. And as from April 1988, the government removed a tax incentive for savings, the *maruyu* exemption of some forms of saving from tax on interest. The supply of domestic savings is likely gradually to be squeezed.

SUPPLY, MEET DEMAND

For the consideration of Japan's capital surplus, however, it is not just the absolute supply of savings that matters. It is the balance between the supply of savings and the domestic demand for them (i.e., for investment), whether from the government, business, or households.

On this demand side, as has already been seen, a significant contribution to Japan's savings surplus was made in 1983–1985 by the government's efforts to reduce its own borrowing. It became obsessed by eliminating "deficit-financing bonds" by 1990 at the latest. Since net exports were leading the economy during this period, the government could afford such a contractionary fiscal policy. Once export growth was hit by the rising yen, it could not. So in 1987 and 1988, the government acted to use public works spending to stimulate the economy. This boost to domestic demand was also a response to diplomatic pressure from the United States.

The result was that, in 1987 and 1988, for the first time in fifteen years, fiscal and monetary policies were simultaneously expansionary. The government's demand for savings was rising, if only gently. Will that continue? Not if the Ministry of Finance can avoid it. It will grab any available opportunity to return to austerity since it wishes to keep borrowing low in preparation for the aging of Japan's population in the 1990s.

Yet opportunities for austerity are likely to be few and far between unless and until Japan slides into a sizable current-account deficit. Unless that happens, it will be politically difficult to allow exports to provide a strong pull to growth. At any time when the economy looks likely to weaken, the government will be tempted to expand its fiscal deficit in order to boost growth. At worst, the deficit will not again be contractionary. At best, during the next five years, it is likely often to be expansionary.

Similarly, the fall in corporate investment that was seen in Japan in 1982–1986 ceased in 1987–1988. After four years of cutting borrowing and playing the stock and bond markets, Japanese companies sharply increased their domestic fixed investments in response to the high yen. Part of this was investment aimed at cutting costs and rationalizing production, part was aimed at expanding capacity to meet demand from domestic consumers. It is hard to predict the future course of corporate investment, dependent as it is on many economic variables as well as on the "animal spirits" of businesses. At the very least, however, it can be expected to remain buoyant for as long as the domestic economy stays strong.

GRAYER HAIR, SLIMMER SAVINGS

This prediction of future domestic demands for funds is, admittedly, rather a short-term view. In five or ten years, things could look different, in either direction. Against that, however, there is a longer term force. Japan's demographic structure is likely both to reduce the supply of savings and to increase the domestic demands for them. Japan, as we saw in chapter 4, is getting older very fast.

The proportion of those over sixty-five is growing faster in Japan than in any other industrial country and will pass 16 percent by 2000 and 20 to 25 percent by 2020. A falling birthrate and the postwar baby boom have been reinforced by a falling death rate and the longest average lifespan in the world, producing a growing number of old people. In any country, old people typically spend more than they save. They consume savings and receive transfer payments from other people. To an extent, the impact on savings of the rise in the number of elderly will be countered by a fall in the number of school-age children, another group of dissavers. But not by very much.

How large a net impact will this have on the savings rate? No one is sure, but Peter Morgan, chief economist in the Tokyo office of Barclays de Zoete Wedd, an investment bank, recently presented three alternative projections. Respectively, they were based on the following forecasting methods:

1. Simply applying official estimates of the change in the ages of Japanese heads of households to official statistics on present savings data broken down by age groups.

2. Using an equation for savings variables developed by Professor Charles Horioka at Kyoto University. This relied on net private savings rates in twenty-one OECD countries, with data chiefly from the early 1980s.

3. Using Barclays de Zoete Wedd's own equation for the variables that determine savings. This was estimated using data for Japanese
household savings broken down by age.

The table shows Peter Morgan's results:

IMPACT ON SAVINGS RATE OF DEMOGRAPHIC CHANGES

(percentage points change from national private savings rate in 1985)

	1990	1995	2000	2005	2010
Method 1	−0.6	−1.4	−1.9	−2.8	−2.9
Method 2	+0.4	−0.2	−5.4	−11.6	−18.2
Method 3	+1.0	+1.2	−6.3	−17.1	−28.7

SOURCE: Barclays de Zoete Wedd.

There is a tremendous variation in the numbers, as so often occurs
when forecasting; doubtless, none of the figures will turn out to be
exactly right. But there is considerable unanimity about the trend, and
the range of results show how large—given certain assumptions—the
impact could be.

The three methods appear to agree that the aging of Japan's
population will have little impact on the savings rate until 1995.
After that, however, the impact could be very significant. Even the
most modest result would cut the savings rate from 1985's 16 percent
to 13 percent. The other results eliminate Japan's personal savings
altogether. What that would mean, other things being equal, is that
Japan would again become a net debtor, just as the United States is
now.

Other things will not, entirely, be equal. The government will
certainly take measures to ease this burden and stem such a fall in
savings. Even so, the trend is clear. It is quite possible that by 2010
Japan's personal savings ratio could be as low (3–5 percent) as America's is now. By then, as Morgan writes:

Studies of Japan's high savings rate will be of only archaeological significance.

A WINDOW OF OPPORTUNITY

If all this economic analysis is correct, it places grave limitations on Japan's potential as a great power. It confirms that the sun also sets, that Japan's economy, too, moves in cycles. In the medium term, savings are slipping, the current account is moving more rapidly toward balance than anybody realizes, and the government and companies are borrowing more. In the longer term, the country is aging rapidly. Japan's capital surplus has already passed its peak. It is destined to last at best for another decade, to 2000; more likely, it will be gone soon afer 1995. It might even disappear earlier. That means that Japan has a window of opportunity, not a long-term advantage. Another five to ten years of surplus gives Japanese firms and individuals plenty of time to make money and to set themselves up abroad. But it is likely to be too short a time for Japan to become a significant power, still less a dominant one.

To many, this argument will seem impossibly complacent, even naive. In his spring 1986 article in *Foreign Affairs,* for example, Ezra Vogel wrote that

> A careful analysis of Japan's competitive advantages suggests that the problem is far deeper and requires a far more concerted effort than most Americans realise. Public discussion of these issues has unfortunately been dominated by economists who take far too narrow a view of the problems and think chiefly in terms of exchange rates, interest rates and savings rates.

His argument, hinted at here and elaborated later in his article, is that Japan's technology, its education system, and its management methods, *inter alia,* give it such a lead that its trade surplus cannot swiftly be corrected. Exchange-rate changes, in his view, are no more than an adjustment to superior Japanese productivity and do not solve the problem of continuing American economic decline. Japan's current-account surplus is with us for the foreseeable future.

There is a grain of truth in Vogel's argument. The surplus cannot swiftly be corrected, if by "swiftly" is meant in one or two years. Moreover, if Americans and Japanese rely on exchange rates alone to correct current-account imbalances, then the necessary movement has to be far greater than if they also adjust other macro- and microeconomic policies. The argument here is that such adjustments must take place; there is no room for complacency. Moreover, the more complacency there is, the more likely it is that adjustment will be painful. That does not, however, mean that it will not happen. Japan is changing under the weight of its surplus, just as America is under the influence of its deficit and of Japan's growing diaspora. Exchange rates, interest rates, and savings rates are not mythical creatures dreamed up by economists; they are at once causes and effects of more concrete factors such as education standards, productivity, and industrial relations. Nor are competitive advantages written in stone. They depend on price, and they vary over time. Japan's surpluses will not, indeed, disappear easily or overnight. But they will go more quickly than Vogel appears to believe.

Japan's capital surplus may not last forever, nor will it turn Japan into a superpower, but it is still having a profound effect on Japan and on the world. It is turning the Japanese into consumers and financiers. It will affect how Japan survives the first quarter of the twenty-first century as a nation of pensioners. It is establishing a worldwide Japanese diaspora, as Japanese firms and individuals invest abroad, own foreign assets, and employ foreign workers and managers. Moreover, although Japan is unlikely to become a Great Power, the surplus is changing the way its reluctant leaders behave politically. It is giving Japan a political role and responsibilities. Chief among these is likely to be a leadership role in Asia, at first economically as head of a yen bloc in the region, but gradually it will also take on a political flavor.

To say that the Japanese sun also sets is not to argue that Japan's economy is going to collapse, nor is it to argue that the force of Japanese competition throughout industry is suddenly going to vanish. "Made in Japan" will never again be a joke, nor will Tokyo be a place that financial markets can ignore. The argument is that Japan's economy is passing through a phase of imbalance with the world that will soon be righted, removing the main source of Japan's growing political strength. The correction of that imbalance will reveal the limits to Japanese power; it will not remove that power altogether.

Another important point has so far been neglected. Japan's economic and political position cannot be viewed in isolation. For a start,

Japan's economy has become inextricably linked with that of the United States, as trading partners, as investors, as creditors, and as the fiercest of competitors. To a great extent, the economic strength of Japan in the 1980s has been mirrored, if not by economic weakness in America (for that country has been more prosperous than ever), then by an increased frailty in the American economy. America's economy has been living on money and time borrowed from Japan, which have together disguised a decline in the competitiveness of American business. It is as true today, that "the business of America is business," as it was when President Calvin Coolidge coined that expression in 1925, which is why this decline in competitiveness is so worrying.

Most important of all, Japan's political power is not an absolute quantity. It can only be gauged relative to that of America, the clear leader of the non-Communist world since 1945, if not before. This relationship also defines Japan's political role, whether in defense, multilateral organizations, foreign policy, overseas aid, or international economic cooperation. Only if America fails to lead will Japan have to initiate; only if Japan becomes more powerful than America will Japan really begin to set its own international agenda. The story of Japan's sunrise and its eventual sunset is really a tale of two countries, of Japan and of America.

CHAPTER TWELVE

田

AMERICA AS NUMBER ONE

What will may hap
out in the world!—I, turning priest,
go to my noonday nap!
            —Soseki (1867–1916)

Somehow it seems wrong.
to take one's noonday nap and hear
a rice-planting song.
            —Issa (1762–1826)

AT VIRTUALLY the same time that Japan departed from its *Showa* period, the United States was also saying good-bye to an era. The farewells and the soul-searching about what was to come were as emotional and anxious on the American side of the Pacific as on the Japanese. For, during the last years of the Reagan presidency, the United States exhibited an unusually clear division of opinion about where it stood, concerning both its economy and its politics. Some saw America as stronger than ever and on the verge of new greatness. Others were equally convinced that America was an economy and a nation in decline, an already humiliated country that had taken itself to the brink of disaster. By comparison, Japan was on its way to the top; the Soviet Union was shaking itself up through *perestroika* and opening its ways through *glasnost;* even sleepy old Europe had its single-market 1992 project. America was doing nothing. To these gloomy folk, the American century was over.

Some of this, of course, was merely the stuff of presidential election campaigns: George Bush and Dan Quayle, as the Republican ticket in 1988, were bound to claim that Americans had never had it so good and that their country was the envy of the world; Michael Dukakis and Lloyd Bentsen, as the Democratic challengers, were bound to reply that they too could create an illusion of prosperity if they were allowed to write $200 billion in hot checks every year. Yet they were also optimistic about what would happen to America if they were elected. At the close of one of the two televised debates between the presidential candidates, Michael Dukakis echoed an old American sentiment when, looking dewy-eyed into the cameras, he declared that "The best is yet to come."

The opening lines of Dickens's *A Tale of Two Cities,* although now somewhat of a cliché, really are the best summary of opinion in America at the close of the Reagan era:

> It was the best of times, it was the worst of times, it was the age of wisdom, it was the age of foolishness, it was the epoch of belief, it was the epoch of incredulity, it was the season of Light, it was the season of Darkness, it was the spring of hope, it was the winter of despair. . . .

THE SPRING OF HOPE

The division of opinion was not all campaign bluster, nor was it merely between Republicans and Democrats. The indicators of the mid-1980s were genuinely confusing. The signs of strength and prosperity were there for all to see and for many to share. Ronald Reagan had been elected in 1980 to an America bedeviled by inflation, high unemployment, and low economic growth, and demoralized by the failed attempt to rescue hostages from Iran as well as by the more distant specters of Vietnam and Watergate. His election was, in part, a product of fears about America's diminished stature as well as, very directly, of the rise in the United States of a new conservatism.

Arriving in office in 1981, Ronald Reagan promised Americans a "new beginning for the economy." Sure enough, during his eight-year presidency, inflation was squashed and, by the time George Bush took over, the country was in its seventh consecutive year of economic expansion. Unemployment had been halved and was far lower, at 5.3 percent of the labor force, than the levels of 8–12 percent in many Western European countries. Nearly 20 million new jobs had been created. The Kemp-Roth Act in the summer of 1981 had slashed income tax rates, a move that was later reaffirmed when a radical reform of taxes passed through Congress, bringing marginal rates of income tax down to the lowest levels of any industrialized country.

In the area much dearer to President Reagan's heart, international politics, success seemed even more evident. Republican sympathizers could infer a direct connection between Reagan's initially sharp increases in spending on defense, his tough anti-Russian rhetoric (the "evil empire" speeches), and the successful conclusion in 1988 of a pact virtually to eliminate some sorts of nuclear weapons. At the same time, the Soviet Union began to withdraw its troops from Afghanistan after nearly a decade's stay. Elsewhere, there were victories to celebrate in smaller wars: The invasion of Grenada and the bombing of Libya seemed to be followed by a sudden cessation of terrorist attacks on American citizens. Foreigners respect a tall, tough, confident American stance. Once again, America stood supreme. Given Ronald Reagan's unremitting cheerfulness, it was hard to believe otherwise.

THE WINTER OF DESPAIR

Or was it? Even in political affairs, evidence could be found to support a case for America as a still-diminishing, even incompetent giant. Notably, the Iran-Contra scandal (which concerned the sale of arms to Iran in proposed exchange for the release of American hostages, while the proceeds were to be funneled to the Contra rebels in Nicaragua, bypassing congressional controls) did not look like the action of a supreme, confident, and omnipotent power. Nor were fiascos in Lebanon and the accidental shooting down of an Iranian civil airliner, at least in the minds of those ready to associate military mistakes with a national malaise. Along the same lines, the tragic explosion of the space shuttle

Challenger in January 1986 was a severe blow to self-esteem. While the Soviet Union still had men in space, America could no longer do so safely, or even worse, it could no longer afford to at all.

More important, although the arms control agreement with the Soviet Union in 1987–1988 was an undeniable achievement, not all, or even much, of the credit should go to the United States. Historians may well see Mikhail Gorbachev as making the more important contribution. What is more, the charming Mr. Gorbachev won many of the propaganda battles in the later Reagan years, successfully presenting himself in the West as the chief peacemaker, as more flexible than his American counterparts, and at times, as more sincere. His efforts at domestic reform in the Soviet Union even made him appear radical.

Economics, however, provides many more signs that when President Bush stood on the inauguration platform America stood on the brink of disaster. In the space of a very few years, the country had swung from being the world's largest net creditor to being far and away its largest net debtor. The cost of servicing that debt will be a huge burden on American children and grandchildren, taking up annually perhaps 2 percent of the GNP. After decades of telling other countries how to run their finances, America risks the tables being turned as it depends more and more on foreign borrowing to finance its budget and current-account deficits.

All this was at a time of mounting problems in America's financial system. In 1986, 1987, and 1988, the number of bank failures broke all records set since the Great Depression of the 1930s. A third of all savings and loan associations (thrifts) were insolvent by the end of 1988, and another third came pretty close to it. Estimates of the eventual total cost of those insolvencies topped $100 billion, much of it ultimately an obligation to the taxpayer since it dwarfed the resources of insurance funds. Amid such financial wobbles came apparent financial excesses, as corporate America, egged on by Wall Street, increasingly chose to exchange debt for equity through leveraged buy-outs. The battle for RJR-Nabisco, a tobacco-to-foods firm, propelled the firm's then-boss, Ross Johnson, onto the cover of *Time* magazine as a symbol of the greed of American managers. He stood to make $100 million in personal profits if his buy-out plan had been accepted. He lost, and the firm went instead to Kohlberg Kravis Roberts, a Wall Street buy-out specialist, for $25 billion, by far the largest takeover in American (or anybody else's) history.

Already the mighty dollar, symbol of America's prosperity and strength around the world, had collapsed, halving its value in barely two years from 1985 to 1987. Then on October 19, 1987, the New York stock market crashed, falling in a single day by 508 points, or 22.6 percent, twice as great a drop as in the famed crash of Black Tuesday in October 1929. The tumultuous financial event of 1987 lured doomsayers out of the shadows, eager to go on record with their predictions that a slump was now inevitable and that it would be equal to, or even worse than, the Great Depression. Even before the crash took place, a book by Ravi Batra, a professor of economics at Southern Methodist University, had topped the best-seller lists and attained some notoriety. In *The Great Depression of 1990*, Dr. Batra wrote that a disaster of the same, if not greater, severity as that of the 1930s ". . . will occur in 1990 and plague the world through at least 1996." Also, in a phrase not quoted extensively by George Bush during the election campaign, Dr. Batra wrote that "The seeds of a new depression have already been sown by the Reagan administration."

Which brings us to the small matter of a current-account deficit of more than $150 billion and a federal budget deficit that in 1986 topped $200 billion and was still $155 billion in the fiscal year to September 30, 1988. The economic expansion of the Reagan years had been genuine, but it had been financed by borrowing. The original belief of Reaganomics, that tax cuts would produce an increase in revenues that would bring the budget into balance, had not come to pass. When he took over the Oval Office from Jimmy Carter, the federal deficit was $79 billion, which Ronald Reagan described as a budget "out of control." The national debt was then $914 billion. By the time Reagan retired to his new home in Bel-Air, Los Angeles, the national debt had tripled and the budget deficit was double that inherited from Jimmy Carter.

The budget deficit passed on to President Bush, it is well to recall, was there at the end of seven years of economic growth, during which tax revenues were supposed to swell and spending on cyclical things

THE SUN ALSO SETS

such as welfare and unemployment were to have shrunk. Other things being equal, therefore, the deficit ought to have been in decline. In a recession, the deficit could be expected to become much larger, regardless of the Gramm-Rudman-Hollings Balanced Budget and Emergency Deficit-Reduction Reaffirmation Act. Tax revenues fall in slumps, while spending on welfare, unemployment compensation, bank rescues, and industrial subsidies tends to soar. In short, although its time in office had been prosperous, the Reagan administration has left America's finances in the worst possible condition to deal with an economic downturn, however mild or severe: a government in debt, $100 billion worth of insolvent thrifts, a heavily leveraged corporate sector, and deeply nervous financial markets.

The trade deficit remains the single most powerful symbol of America's economic decline. To pessimists and those unwilling to accept the common claims that it is all due to unfair trade practices abroad, the deficit suggests that many American goods and services are no longer the best. The country can no longer compete. American goods are seen as shoddy, American businesses as no match for the nimble Japanese. Virtually every videocassette recorder in American homes is manufactured abroad, as are most of the new color televisions. A third of the new cars sold in the United States in 1988 were made by foreigners, and that in the home of the mass-produced automobile. Behind this loss of markets is an even scarier point: Japan, long sneered at as a mere imitator of technology, as a copier of products, now appears to be taking the technological lead.

Increasingly, moreover, foreign investors are coming to America and buying it cheap. The sale of a large chunk of American manufacturing, finance, and real estate to foreigners does not look like a sign of strength. It looks, rather, like a sign that the Japanese have arrived. American hegemony, on this argument, must surely be at an end.

A SOBER VIEW

Judging from the election of George Bush, can we assume that the American public favored the more optimistic of these two views? Not necessarily. An election result can rarely be taken as a precise indication of ideas or judgments, particularly when the vote is between two people. All that can be concluded is that more Americans favored George Bush than favored Michael Dukakis, which may say as much about Dukakis as about Bush. Another hypothesis, however, might be that support for Bush reflected a refusal to admit to problems, to weakness, or to the need for painful measures. "Read my lips," said Bush frequently during the campaign, "no new taxes," even though it is universally agreed that the federal budget deficit must be cut. Perhaps America has become, as Sir James Goldsmith has described it, "the king of the soft option."

So which is it, the best of times or the worst of times? A sober approach to the state of America's economy has to include many of the points of pessimism—national debt, trade deficit, leveraged buy-outs, bust thrifts, weak competitiveness—but it can do so without concluding that the country is on its way out. The risks created by Reaganomics and the behavior of the 1980s are severe and unacceptable, but they do not presage an inevitable decline—unless, of course, nothing is done about them.

Perhaps a fair clue to the state of America is that, although "the winter of despair" view of the economy seems the more plausible, it is "the spring of hope" view that is more convincing for politics and foreign policy. America's leadership is no weaker or in any more doubt now than it was a decade ago or even two decades ago. The world still looks to it as the leading superpower, the source of political initiative, and, in many cases, a sort of policeman. This view will prevail unless the economy drags America into a decade or more of depression and poverty, and eventually, it is unable to finance its military pretensions.

As things stand, this outcome may loom large: if America's budget deficit were allowed to stay large or to get even larger; if the dollar were maintained at its level of early 1985; if the tax structure were not reformed; if savings and loan associations were allowed to continue getting more and more bust, backed and encouraged by a government guarantee; if education were left untouched; and if, in particular, America closed its borders to trade, investment, and immigration. In other words, disaster could come if present problems were ignored and if future policies were not only no better but were actually worse. The question is whether or not that happens.

TOWARD SOLUTIONS

In order to avoid that outcome, the problems must be properly understood. An important point to realize, for instance, is that America's trade and current-account deficits are not, as is often assumed, conclusive evidence either for the theory that America can no longer compete or for the (often-connected) theory that the rest of the world is "unfair" in trading matters. All that the deficits prove is that, at present prices and exchange rates, America is annually importing about $130 billion to $150 billion more than it is exporting. There is nothing wrong with that per se. Nor on its own would it enfeeble America politically. The problem is that it is unsustainable in the long term because foreigners will not finance the deficit indefinitely. In time, they will require higher interest rates; in time, that probably not only will make American firms even less competitive but also will push the economy into recession or slump.

Similarly, nothing is wrong with America's budget deficit as such; in the 1980s, it has not been so large relative to the GNP as were deficits in some European countries. Its peak this decade was 3.8 percent of GNP in 1983 (on a general government basis, under the OECD's standardized measure), compared with 12.6 percent in Italy in 1985 or 7 percent in Canada in 1985. The only thing that is wrong with the American deficit is that it is too large in relation to the domestic savings available to finance it. America's net household savings rate as a percentage of disposable income fell from 7.7 percent in 1981 to 3.9 percent in 1987. Nothing is wrong with that, either, except that it does not cover domestic investment needs.

To say that the budget deficit must be cut is hardly an original insight, but it is no less necessary for that. It has to be cut not for moral reasons or because deficits are bad for their own sake, but rather because its present level is unsustainable, because it risks damagingly high interest rates in the future, and because this is the easiest way to ease the pressure on savings. If savings would only rise, then the budget deficit could be financed. Unfortunately, the savings rate is a very difficult thing to manipulate because it depends on many different levels of individual perceptions and decisions about savings and consumption. Ceasing to dissave, or borrowing less—which is what cutting a budget deficit amounts to—is easier than seeking to save more.

This is not to say that it is inconceivable that America's savings rate could rise again. It is as wrong to assume that there is something innate about Americans that prevents them from saving and forces them to consume as it is to assume that there is something innate about Japanese that forces them to save. Household savings in the United States, having been fairly steady at 7–9 percent during the 1970s, fell extremely rapidly during the 1980s. Nobody really knows why; indeed, some tax reforms were expressly designed to achieve the opposite. The factors popularly blamed for lower savings—the availability of consumer credit and the maturing of the baby-boom generation—were both under way well before 1980 and should, in theory, have contributed to a gradual slippage in savings, not the abrupt drop that occurred.

If the savings rate can fall so rapidly and mysteriously, then it can rise again, if not to Japanese levels of 16 percent, then to more normal American levels of 7–9 percent. For that reason, it would be beneficial if government policies (i.e., the tax code) promoted rather than discouraged savings. Nevertheless, steps to cut the budget deficit will be more sure to ease the pressure on available savings than will efforts to increase the savings rate. Nor will cutting the deficit be a one-time measure; rather, it must be a long process of raising revenues and trimming back spending.

What needs to be remembered is that the deficit is as large as it is at the end of seven years of growth, a time when it might have been more reasonable to expect a surplus. The future depends critically on whether or not growth continues and at what rate. It would be absurd, therefore, to allow a "rosy scenario" to guide fiscal policy, since, as growth slows and monetary policy tightens, the result would always be worse than planned. Such disappointments would hurt the confidence of financial markets, which do more to determine interest rates than does the government. Far better, then, to assume the worst and therefore to surprise the markets pleasantly when things turn out better than expected.

UNBENIGN NEGLECT

This remedying of macroeconomic errors is the basic task facing the United States. A fiscal policy more in line with the savings available will enable interest rates to be lower and thus to stimulate capital investment. The fall of the dollar since early 1985 will help to eliminate the current-account deficit, by making exports competitive and imports less so, but it cannot do so on its own—at least not without severe disruption.

If, when, and as sensible economic policies are implemented, this should also signify, to an extent, a swing toward pragmatism and away from the extreme of ideology about economic policy that characterized the Reagan era. At the far extreme of free-market thinking, advocates of Reaganomics believe that markets are best left alone to conduct their own affairs, that whenever government intervenes it makes matters worse. This view reached its apotheosis in the policy of benign neglect toward the dollar in 1980–1985, even as it doubled in value and crippled much of American industry.

The view was not wholly wrong, just cruelly blinkered. For government cannot withdraw its involvement in the economy. Insofar as, for instance, it spends money, taxes people, and runs a fiscal policy, it is and must be involved. The dollar in 1980–1985 was not, in fact, being neglected and left to the sway of free market forces. Policy toward the dollar was neither benign nor neglectful. A better title would have been malign interference. The exchange rate of the dollar was being manipulated by the government, if inadvertently, through its fiscal policy, which kept American interest rates higher than those available elsewhere and pulled capital into the dollar, inflating its value. The market was not free. Nor, sadly, was government intervention in that market being directed by an intelligent awareness of America's interests.

Japan's Ministry of Finance would never have operated either its fiscal or its exchange rate policy in the manner of the Reagan administration. This is so not because of any faith in Japan Inc. or in "industrial policy," or in an ability to manipulate markets. The Ministry would have felt that it was irresponsible to act in that way. Government affects the money markets, so it has a duty to try to affect them in a way best suited to the country's interests. Its fiscal and monetary policies inevitably affect the level of the yen, so it seeks to have them affect the yen in the best possible way, insofar as that is compatible with its other policy aims. That is not manipulation; it is realism.

In the same way, American economic policymakers need to come to terms with the role of government in an open market economy. The main tenet of free-market philosophy, that the government is more likely to do harm than good, is indeed a sound basic principle. Around the world, governments have tended to be poor directors of resources. Central planners, even in Japan, have not picked the best industries nor have they allocated scarce resources correctly. But this is only a starting point. Markets should not be interfered with unless there is good reason. The burden of proof must, indeed, be on those proposing interference. But that does not preclude government involvement when it can be justified. When that involvement is unavoidable, as in fiscal and monetary policy, it must be directed with a broad view of its consequences.

What this also means is that American policymakers must accept the fact that they preside over an international economy, not an isolated, self-sufficient American economy that happens also to deal with the rest of the world. In this, America remains astonishingly and damagingly parochial. Japan may be inward-looking but so is America, each with a decreasing right to be so. James Baker, Secretary of the Treasury in President Reagan's later years, protested that his policy had been nothing of the sort, that he had initiated "international policy coordination" first under the Plaza Accord in 1985 and later at the Louvre in Paris in early 1987. But this effort at coordination was a shallow affair. In effect, it treated exchange rates as the only component of policy or of the economy to deserve an international role. Fiscal policy, even monetary policy—these remained domestic, uncoordinated affairs.

OF FREE TRADE AND FAIR

The greatest worry after the Reagan era is that the United States could turn protectionist. That word will not be used, however, for it is taboo;

ever since the Smoot-Hawley tariff proved disastrous in the 1930s, nobody has wanted to be called a protectionist. Instead, such phrases as "fair trade" and "level playing fields" have gradually taken over the language of trade and protection. To demand these sounds terribly reasonable, even worthy. The trouble is that they are always linked to a demand for protection.

In this context, intervention may sound like a welcome and radical departure from the free-market, free-trade dogma of Ronald Reagan and his acolytes. It will not be, however, for in trade the Reagan era had little to do with freedom. Just the opposite: Ronald Reagan was the most protectionist American president since 1945. During his term of office the share of total imports subject to quota or other restraint rose from 12 percent to 23 percent. Protective schemes or agreements were imposed on markets for cars, machine tools, semiconductors, and carbon steel; tariffs were raised on motorbikes and specialty steel. Furthermore, President Reagan signed a trade bill that allows, even obliges, the government to use trade retaliation ("reciprocity" in the fair-trade lingo) in bilateral disputes, rather than settling them through the multilateral framework established by the General Agreement on Tariffs and Trade.

The starting point, then, is an extremely bad one. All this fresh protection was imposed during seven years of economic expansion and prosperity; if the next seven years bring harder times, what protection will then be demanded? The case against protection has often been stated, and this is not the place to repeat it. But the basic principle is that protection prevents an economy from buying the best products at the cheapest price available. That inefficiency works through the economy, making it steadily less competitive in other areas. Protection does not, in other words, "merely" harm consumers, as is often claimed, for there is no such separate class of economic agent. The consumers of semiconductors are businesses; barriers to the import of Japanese chips hurt American computer, telecommunications, and other electronics makers. The same applies to steel, to machine tools, even to cars.

What is most worrisome about the movement toward "fair trade" is that it represents defeat for those who believe that unilateral free trade is good for an economy, regardless of whether or not other countries have open markets. In other words, fair traders think that, if the Japanese are being "unfair" by hindering American exports to Japan, then America should be unfair back; this view does not acknowledge that, by doing so, America is also being unfair to itself, by raising its input prices and sanctioning inefficiency. Evening up the score only hurts oneself.

This criticism applies equally to so-called voluntary restraint agreements, under which for instance Japan has agreed to restrain its exports of cars. Such deals sound acceptable because the other side has agreed to them; in some cases, the other side has even appeared to favor the deals. That ought to be the clue; if Japan favors a voluntary restraint agreement that fact shows that Japanese firms expect to benefit the most; it is a prize for Japan, a punishment for America. What took place after the agreement on cars began in 1981 should discredit this method in perpetuity: The deal led to a scarcity of Japanese cars relative to demand, and Japanese firms simply raised their prices and, helped further by the strengthening dollar, made enormous profits. This windfall could then first be invested at home, which made them even more competitive versus American firms, and later be invested in factories in America.

General Motors, Ford, and Chrysler could have responded by keeping prices low, regaining market share, cutting costs, and driving the importers out. Instead, they followed Japanese price hikes. They did the same when the yen's rise forced Japanese car makers to raise prices again. Did the "breathing space" provided by protection increase the American car industry's competitiveness? No. It simply enabled Chrysler's Lee Iacocca to appear as a business hero by having "turned his firm around" and enabled General Motors and Ford to pay executives huge bonuses. In the 1990s, such protection, if retained for cars and extended to other industries, risks the demise of American corporate competitiveness, not its revival. Companies restructure, reorganize, and become competitive when they are exposed to the chill winds of trade and open competition, not when they are cushioned from it. Free trade will be a key policy for the 1990s—unilaterally, not based on reciprocity.

THE LEVERAGING OF AMERICA

As that process of reorganization gathers speed, there will be more and more concern about whether corporate America is being driven by managerial or industrial imperatives or by the financial excesses of Wall Street. In particular, the leveraged buy-out will come under further attack. Reminders that Kohlberg, Kravis, Roberts, the investment bank specializing in LBOs, is only performing the sort of restructuring role adopted in earlier times by J. Pierpont Morgan will fall on deaf ears. Instead the worry is that corporate America has taken on too much debt and too many investment bankers and that something should be done about it.

This is a legitimate worry, although things are not quite so bad as they seem. A study by Stephen Roach of Morgan Stanley in November 1988 showed that business did, indeed, take on more debt in the 1980s. Since 1982, new debt of nonfinancial firms grew by an average of 12 percent a year, which was roughly a third faster than in the 1970s. But according to Roach, 95 percent of the total growth was taken on by three sectors that together account for only about 30 percent of GNP—public utilities, services, and the manufacturing of nondurable goods—and is the part of the economy that is least vulnerable to a recession. In other words, leveraged buy-outs are taking place in sectors that are best able to cope with the risks: relatively recession-proof areas such as food and tobacco.

That point does not make LBOs safe per se, just not necessarily a recipe for disaster. Threats of takeovers and buy-outs are beneficial because the fear of them is a fine motivator to management to become more efficient; for that reason, they must not be stopped. The best way to think about them may be from the point of view of the providers of finance, not the recipients. In other words, are the banks assessing their risks accurately when they lend billions to an LBO? In a recession or when interest rates rise sharply, heavy borrowers would be hurt, but so too would a bank that had become heavily exposed to LBOs. The collapse of a lender would pose more danger to the American economy than the collapse of a borrower, just as the bankruptcy of Brazil is less critical than the bankruptcy of Citicorp. Third World loans seemed like a good idea during the 1970s; rather a bad one in the 1980s. The same could be true of leveraged buy-outs. For that reason, the most appropriate policy response is one of closer supervision of banks. Let business borrow, but ensure that banks are taking full account of the risks.

THE WRONG INDUSTRIAL POLICY

As America passes through the painful process of cutting budgets, raising taxes, encouraging savings, and so on, it will be increasingly tempted to give the adjustment process a powerful helping hand by setting up some sort of federal industrial policy. After all, the Japanese have one that is steered by the infamous Ministry of International Trade and Industry, and it works for them, so why not for us? Surely we should learn from the Japanese example?

This idea contains two severe dangers. The first is that America will learn from the wrong Japanese example, will emulate something that Japan has in fact abandoned. The heyday of the Ministry was in the 1950s and 1960s, which is when it used its regulatory and licensing muscle to guide industry. Its role in the 1990s will be far smaller. Already, the Ministry's role is as an information broker, not as an initiator. As Jagdish Bhagwati has written in his admirable book, *Protectionism*, there are two sorts of bureaucratic interference: the Indian sort, where bureaucrats tell people and firms what they can and cannot do; and the Japanese sort, where bureaucrats tell people and firms what they ought to be doing. In the 1960s, the Ministry of International Trade and Industry was a little closer to the Indian sort; the danger is that an American industrial policy might use this as its model.

Danger number two is more basic: A great deal of time and money will be wasted, quite possibly dragging industry and investment in the wrong direction. Japanese-style money would be spent with French-style success. Already the Department of Defense has been involved in setting up Sematech, a firm designed to accelerate research and development in semiconductor technology. It has been suggested that the military become involved in, of all things, the development of high-definition television, on the spurious grounds that America needs a consumer-electronics industry if it is to remain competitive in "strategic" technologies.

The question is, what makes either a soldier or a bureaucrat qualified to direct investment or research and development? Historically, Americans have never been good at this sort of thing. Why should they be now? Solutions to problems of competitiveness cannot assume that Americans are really Japanese. They cannot assume that an interventionist government operating with managed trade will run America well.

American solutions have to use American methods: free enterprise, open markets, individual initiative. That is how Americans work best.

ENDURING STRENGTHS

The darkest hour, it has been said, is just before the dawn. There are many reasons to think that things are dark indeed in the United States, what with uncompetitive industries, large deficits, wobbly banks, second-rate education, and first-rate crime. But that is not inconsistent even with Ronald Reagan's early-1980s claim that it is still "morning in America."

Compare America in the late 1980s with declining Britain, even as Britain stood at the turn of the century, let alone by the 1930s. The technological lead that Britain had established during the Industrial Revolution had almost gone. France, Germany, and, even then, Japan had become virtual equals rather than, as during the mid-nineteenth century, distant rivals. The United States was overtaking Britain not only in the absolute size of its economy but also in its industrial base. Britain's relative preeminence was gone. That is not true of late twentieth-century America. Even after the fall of the dollar, America's GNP remains nearly 50 percent larger than Japan's, at around $4.8 trillion compared with $3 trillion. For Japan to overtake the United States would require a sustained further halving of the dollar's value. There is no reason to assume that this is likely.

Britain's other main characteristic as it began its long decline was that it had lost its economic vitality. An American, Martin Wiener, summed this up in the elegant title to his splendid book *English Culture and the Decline of the Industrial Spirit, 1850–1980*. Business had never been thought a terribly respectable pursuit by Britain's elite, and successful entrepreneurs sought to establish their credentials by buying land and evolving into aristocrats rather than by reinvesting their profits. Britain's industrial spirit was in decline as the nineteenth century came to a close; it withered during the twentieth century. That, also, is not true of late twentieth-century America. Enterprise, the creation of wealth, and the ownership of equity remain the country's driving force. There is no shortage of entrepreneurs, nor any sense that involvement in business is not a fit career for a civilized man or woman. Just the opposite.

That continued economic vitality is, furthermore, reinforced by immigration. The continued flow of immigrants into the United States (10 million have arrived in the past decade) is helping to keep the country's population relatively young and thus relatively unburdened by pension transfers to the elderly. It is also supplying low-cost labor as well as budding new entrepreneurs. Asian students are the stars at Harvard and Stanford universities. Small Asian and Hispanic businesses are part of the new fabric of Los Angeles; more a region than a city, its population is expected to rise from 13.5 million in 1988 to around 19 million by 2010. These are not the signs of a dying or even declining economy. They are the signs of one that has both macroeconomic and microeconomic problems—in particular that of providing a better basic education to all those immigrants and to existing Americans—but one that is capable of solving them. They are the signs of a country that, economically, politically, and technologically, is still number one.

JAPAN, AMERICA, AND EUROPE

This is an optimistic view not only for the United States but also for Japan, Europe, and the rest of the world. Also optimistic has been this book's view that the Japanese sun also sets, although many Japanese might not think so. To them, it may sound pessimistic to say that there are limits to Japanese power and to the durability of the country's capital surplus. But just consider the alternative.

If this future were not to come about, if America were indeed to be toppled from its perch, then that would be very dangerous indeed. Instead of having, as after 1945, one clear-minded overseer of global law and order and a stable balance of power, the world would be leaderless. Instead of, as since about 1965, a world of roughly balanced, middling powers led by two powers of which one was dominant, the world would have a number of evenly balanced powers, for which there would be no umpire or guide. Eventually, perhaps Japan could become that guide, although it is extremely doubtful (for it would not merely have to achieve parity, but it would have to pull well ahead). In any case, that "eventually" would cover many evenly balanced, unled years. Such times, generally, have in the past proved the most dangerous.

The enfeeblement of America would, for instance, force the Japanese to rearm and, probably, to seek nuclear capability simply because they would have to provide for their own security. Otherwise another power of similar strength—China, perhaps—might be tempted to use military means to attain preeminence. China might even seek to preempt Japan's arrival as a nuclear power by launching an attack, for the Chinese would fear a nuclear-armed Japan just as much as the Japanese would worry about a mighty China. This is more likely than it might seem to the many who judge that Japan and China somehow make a natural match: both oriental, both Buddhist or Confucian in cultural origin, one technology rich and resource poor, the other technology poor and resource rich. But there is an underlying antagonism between the two countries, for reasons of history, of ideology, and of cultural rivalry. Looking beyond the short term, the greatest danger posed by a balanced world could well be a battle for the dominance of Asia between China and Japan.

Speculation, all of it. Nevertheless, the point stands that the world could become unstable if American leadership were to collapse. Merely to warn of this provides no guarantee that it will not happen. But it does show that a setting Japanese sun would be a more comfortable outcome for all, including the Japanese.

Fortunately, if this book turns out to be correct, it is also a more likely outcome. The economic and social changes that are taking place in Japan are developing an economy that will be more in tune with those of America and Europe, and less apparently confrontational. The economies of Japan and America are so deeply intertwined and interdependent that an adjustment in one will have a corresponding effect in the other. A Japan that imports, consumes, and invests abroad also helps to create an America that exports, saves, and invests at home. While Japan's evolution does not guarantee the solution of America's problems, it does make it more likely.

Europe, too, will benefit from the spread overseas of Japanese investment and technology; that spread helps to raise European and American technology and productivity closer to Japanese levels. As Japanese multinationals expand, so will their influence over local economies and businesses. But that is not malign interference, nor is it correct to argue that it increases Japan's power overseas. It increases the influence of Japanese firms and Japanese technology, not Japan itself.

Europe can, in any case, expect a prominent place in the world of the 1990s and the early twenty-first century. Taking its hesitant steps toward a single market, a currency union, and, to an extent, political integration, Europe has the opportunity to rival Japan's prominence. Taken as a unit, it has a larger economy and a far larger population. Located on the frontiers of the Soviet Union, its political and military actions will remain central to the superpower conflict. It has an even greater task than does America in revitalizing its arthritic economy, but that does not mean it is doomed to fail. Far from it—as long as it retains open borders and a welcoming attitude to ideas, technology, and cash.

That said, if America remains number one, then Japan will be a clear number two. As such, it will have to be consulted and listened to just as much as European countries have been since the 1950s, and it will play at least as large an international role as they do, whether in investment, trade, aid, or politics. That role will be more prominent in Asia than elsewhere but will nevertheless be highly visible on the world stage. Protected by America, it can retain its low military profile as long as it continues to agree broadly with America's foreign policy. Japan will, in other words, be an economic superpower, a strong political voice, and a quiet, defensive soldier. That is not a bad fate.

BIBLIOGRAPHY

BOOKS AND ARTICLES

Batra, Dr. Ravi. *The Great Depression of 1990.* Simon & Schuster, 1987.

Bhagwati, Jagdish. *Protectionism.* MIT Press, 1988.

Bronte, Stephen. *Japanese Finance: Markets and Institutions.* Euromoney Publications, 1982.

Burstein, Daniel. *Yen! Japan's New Financial Empire and Its Threat to America.* Simon & Schuster, 1988.

Chikushi, Tetsuya, editor-in-chief of the *Asahi Journal.* "Young People as a New Human Race." *Japan Quarterly,* July–September 1986.

Dale, Peter N. *The Myth of Japanese Uniqueness.* Croom-Helm, The Nissan Institute of Japanese Stories, 1986.

Dornbusch, Rudiger. "Your Next Landlord May Be Japanese." *The International Economy,* October/November 1987.

Fields, George. "New Rich, New Poor: Are the Japanese Polarising?" *Tokyo Business Today,* June 1988.

Friedman, Benjamin M. *Day of Reckoning.* Random House, 1988.

Fukao, Mitsuhiro, and Inouchi, Masatoshi. "Public Pensions and the Savings Ratio." *Economic Eye,* June 1985, translated from Shukan Toyo Keizai, March 2, 1985.

Fukutake, Tadashi. *Japanese Society Today,* 2nd ed. University of Tokyo Press, 1981.

Halberstam, David. *The Reckoning.* Avon Books, 1986.

Hale, David D. *Britain and Japan as the Financial Bogeymen of U.S. Politics.* Kemper Financial Services, Chicago, 1987.

————. *The Post-Chicago Era in American Economic Policy.* Kemper Financial Services, Chicago, November 1988.

Hayashi, Kenjiro. "Passing the Torch of World Leadership." *Japan Echo,* vol. XII, no. 4, 1985.

Henderson, Harold G. *An Introduction to Haiku: An Anthology of Poems and Poets from Basho to Shiki.* Anchor Books, 1958.

Higuchi, Yoshio, and Shimada, Haruo. "An Analysis of Trends in Female Labor Force Participation in Japan," Keio University, published in *Journal of Labor Economics,* vol. 1, January 1985 supplement, University of Chicago.

Hiraishi, Nagahisa. *Social Security.* Japan Institute of Labor, Japanese Industrial Relations series No. 5, 1987.

Kennedy, Paul. *The Rise and Fall of the Great Powers: Economic Change and Military Conflict from 1500 to 2000.* Unwin Hyman, 1988; Random House, 1988.

Moreton, Antony. "How Race Made the Japanese Grade." *Financial Times,* December 19, 1988.

Ohmae, Kenichi. *Beyond National Borders.* Kodansha International, 1988.

Okasaki, Morio. "Stock Prices: The Land Factor." *Economic Eye,* March 1988.

Prestowitz, Clyde V. *Trading Places: How We Allowed Japan to Take the Lead.* Basic Books, 1988.

Roach, Stephen S. *Living with Corporate Debt.* Morgan Stanley, New York, November 1988.

Servan-Schreiber, Jean-Jacques. *Le Défi Americain.* Editions Denoel, 1967; published by Hamish Hamilton in Britain, 1968.

Soros, George. *The Alchemy of Finance.* Weidenfeld & Nicolson, 1988.

Suzuki, Yoshio, ed. *The Japanese Financial System.* Oxford University Press, 1988.

Tasker, Peter. *Inside Japan: Wealth, Work and Power in the New Japanese Empire.* Sidgwick & Jackson, 1987.

Tolchin, Martin and Susan. *Buying Into America: How Foreign Money Is Changing the Face of Our Nation.* Times Books, 1988.

Tsurumi, Professor Shunsuke. *A Cultural History of Postwar Japan.* KPI Ltd, 1987. Published in Japanese by Iwanami Shoten, 1984.

Van Wolferen, Karel. "The Japan Problem." *Foreign Affairs,* Summer 1987.
———. *The Enigma of Japanese Power.* Alfred A. Knopf, 1989.

Viner, Aron. *Inside Japan's Financial Markets.* Economist Publications Limited, 1987.

Vogel, Ezra F. "Pax Nipponica?" *Foreign Affairs,* Spring 1986.

Wickens, Peter. *The Road to Nissan: Flexibility, Quality, Teamwork.* Macmillan Press, 1987.

Wiener, Martin J. *English Culture and the Decline of the Industrial Spirit, 1850–1980.* Cambridge University Press, 1985.

Wilk, Robert J. "The New Japanese Consumer: Five Major Trends for Marketing." *Journal of the American Chamber of Commerce in Japan,* June 1988.

REPORTS AND REFERENCE BOOKS

"Aging and Social Expenditure in the Major Industrial Countries 1980–2025" by Peter S. Keller, Richard Kenning, Peter W. Kohnest and a staff team. IMF Occasional Paper 47, September 1986.

BIBLIOGRAPHY

Bank of England Quarterly Bulletin, November 1987 article "Japanese Banks in London."

Facts and Figures of Japan, 1987 edition, Foreign Press Center.

"Globalisation of Merchandising, Manufacturing and Marketing," paper by Teruyasu Murakami, associate director of Social and Economic Systems Department, Nomura Research Institute, at NRI Tokyo Forum, June 29, 1988.

Hakuhodo Institute of Life and Living. Report entitled "Young Adults in Japan: New Attitudes Creating New Lifestyles." Tokyo, 1985.

Hakuhodo Institute of Life and Living. Report entitled "Japanese Seniors: Pioneers in the Era of Aging Populations." Tokyo, 1987.

Health and Welfare Statistics of Japan, Health and Welfare Statistics Association, 1987.

Housing Information Service, Jutaku Sangyo Handobukku, 1985 and 1986.

Japanese Working Life Profile, the Japanese Institute of Labor, 1987.

"Japan 1988: An International Comparison." Keizai Koho Center, 1988.

National Land Agency, nationwide official land price survey. *New Social Indicators,* March 1987, EPA Social Policy Bureau.

"Restructuring of the Japanese Economy," MITI report, June 1988.

"Social Security in Japan," Foreign Press Center (*About Japan* series), March 1988.

"The Profile of Overseas Travel," JAL Marketing Report, 1988.

"The Situation of the Aging Society in the Beginning of the 21st Century and the Prospect of Social Security." Report by the Ministry of Health and Welfare/Ministry of Finance, March 10, 1988.

OECD annual report on Japan, August 1988.

Tokyo Stock Exchange fact book, 1988.

INDEX

INDEX

INDEX

Newland, Kathleen, 236
New Liberal Club, 218
newly industrialized countries (NICs), 194
new poor, 73–74
new rich, 71–73
New York Stock Exchange, 92, 113, 129
New York Times, 52
NHK, 30
Nihonjinron, 25
Nikkei Business, 206
Nikkei stock market index, 129
Nikko Securities, 111, 177, 185
Nippon Life, 114
Nippon Telegraph and Telephone (NTT),
  41, 92, 118
Nissan, 132, 167–68, 170, 172, 175
Nixon, Richard, 5
nokyo, 44
Nomura Research Institute, 8, 70, 72,
  82–83, 165
Nomura Securities, 111, 167, 177, 185–87
non-nuclear nations, power and influence
  exerted by, 14
Noriega, Manuel, 159
Norin Chukin, 44, 113
North American free trade zone, 200–201
North Atlantic Treaty Organization
  (NATO), 146–47
nuclear weapons:
  Japan's lack of, 13–15
  stalemate guaranteed by, 14
  U.S.-Soviet agreements on, 260
nursing homes, 89

o-bon festival, 29
Ohmae, Kenichi, 68
Okita, Saburo, 209
Onitsura, 235
Organization for Economic Cooperation and
  Development (OECD), 54–55,
  192–93, 252
Organization of Petroleum Exporting
  Countries (OPEC), 159, 239
Orient Finance, 130
Osawa, Akira, 61–62, 66
Oshin, 30
Other Hundred Years War, The
  (Braddon), 7–8
outplacement agencies, 78
output-spending gap, 242

Pacific basin:
  accepting Japanese leadership in, 205–6
  China vs. Japan in, 274
  countries included in, 189–90
  EEC compared with, 189–90, 206
  exports from, 191–93, 195, 198
  foreign investment in, 191, 193–94
  Japanese diaspora in, 189–206, 255
  power of yen in, 191–203
  progress in economic integration in, 200
  trade in, 192–205
Panasonic, 167
P&E Risk, 194
parks, 36, 55, 58
Pearl Harbor, bombing of, 7, 146
pension system, 81–86, 90
  cost to government of, 84–86
  domestic savings and, 83–84, 86–87
  surpluses in, 86
Perella, Joseph, 186
Perry, Matthew, 12
Persian Gulf crisis, 228, 230–31
Philips, 67, 154, 167
Pink Panthers, 47
Plaza Accord, 131, 267
Policy Studies Institute, 170
politics, 20, 213
  bureaucracies in, 214–16, 218–19
  farmers and, 42–43
  interest groups in, 216–19, 223–24
  in U.S., 259–60
  women in, 47
pop stars, 48
post office savings banks, 92, 105–7
Posts and Telecommunications Ministry,
  Japanese, 105–6, 215, 223
postwar baby boom, 77
potential demand, 126
pound sterling:
  dollar in linkage with, 7
  in world trade, 197–98
Prestowitz, Clyde, 9
price/earnings ratio (p/e), 120–23
price inflation, 58
prime ministers, 217
Procter & Gamble, 67–68
profits, repatriation of, 156–57
Project 1992, 162
protectionism, 201, 219–20, 223–26, 267–
  69

INDEX

INDEX

service trade deficit and, 246–49
tax deductions for, 65
by West Germans, 249
among women, 61–62
Treasury, U.S., 100–101
Treasury bills, 155
Treasury bonds, 19, 94, 112–13, 144,
 150–51, 177, 198, 247
Trevor, Malcolm, 170–71
trust banks, 95
Tsurumi, Shunsuke, 28
Twain, Mark, 3

UBS-Phillips & Drew, 121
unemployment, 5, 34, 259, 262
Union Bank of California, 183–85
Union Bank of Switzerland, 54
United Autoworkers Union (UAW), 170
United States, viii, 257–75
 access to Japanese markets of, 100–103
 banking in, 177–79, 181–87
 borrowing from foreigners by, 150–51
 consumer credit in, 39
 consumption in, 34
 decline of, 9–11, 274
 domestic savings in, 264–66
 domestic vs. foreign affairs of, 221
 emergence as top power of, 12
 enduring strengths of, 272–73
 exports of, 27
 foreign investment in, 146–47, 161, 262
 foreign investment of, 162–63, 240
 free trade pacts negotiated by, 200–201
 historic background and circumstances of,
 15
 immigration to, 273
 industrial policy of, 271–72
 international leadership avoided by,
 212–13
 investments in Pacific basin countries by,
 194
 Japanese bases of, 208, 227
 Japanese car dealer networks in, 245
 Japanese foreign policy and, 12–13,
 230–31
 Japanese investments in, 144–63
 Japanese-owned banks in, 177, 182–186
 Japanese strength linked to weakness of,
 256
 Japanese surrender to, 146

Japan occupied by, 95
Japan's economic influence over, 19–20
LBOs in, 260–61, 270–71
life expectancy in, 56, 77
myths about Japanese in, 25–26
nuclear balance between Soviet Union
 and, 14
optimistic view of, 258–59, 272–75
pension benefits in, 82–83
percentage of elderly in, 76
p/es for stocks in, 120
pessimistic view of, 259–62
political affairs in, 259–60
in power game, 16–17
during Reagan presidency, 257–63,
 266–68, 272
relative strength of Japan compared to, 9
role of women in, 45
sober view of, 262–63
solving problems of, 264–67
Soviet arms control agreements with, 260
Soviet Union as chief rival of, 9
trade and budget deficits of, 7, 10, 19, 21,
 35, 100–101, 150, 221, 244, 260–64
Uno, Sosuke, 218
untouchables, 211
U.S. Trust, 182–83

van Wolferen, Karel, 213–14, 220–22,
 225–26
Veblen, Thorstein, 51
Versailles, Treaty of, 13
Vietnam War, 9, 14, 258
Vogel, Ezra, 8, 254–55
voluntary restraint agreements (VRAs), 169,
 176, 269

Waseda University, 37, 39, 42
Wasserstein, Bruce, 186
Wasserstein, Perella, 186
Watergate scandal, 258
Waterloo, Battle of, 16
wealth, distribution of, 71–72
Webb, Sidney, viii
Wells Fargo, 155, 184
Wickens, Peter, 172
Wiener, Martin, 272–73
"Will the Yen Displace the Dollar as the
 Pacific Rim's Reserve Currency?"
 (Hale), 192–93, 196–97